THE SIMPSONS

BEYOND FOREVER!

**A COMPLETE GUIDE
TO OUR FAVORITE FAMILY
...STILL CONTINUED**

ALSO IN THIS SERIES...

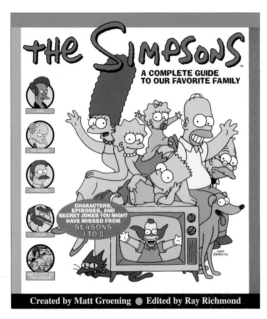

Created by Matt Groening ● Edited by Ray Richmond

Created by Matt Groening ● Edited by Scott M. Gimple

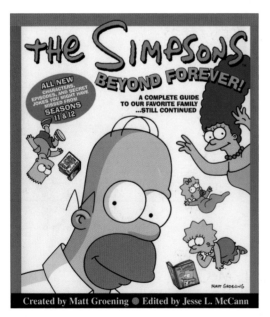

Created by Matt Groening ● Edited by Jesse L. McCann

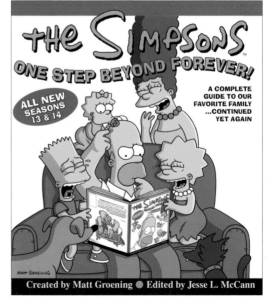

Created by Matt Groening ● Edited by Jesse L. McCann

THE SIMPSONS

BEYOND FOREVER!

A COMPLETE GUIDE
TO OUR FAVORITE FAMILY
...STILL CONTINUED

Created by Matt Groening
Edited by Jesse L. McCann

HarperCollins*Publishers*

TO THE LOVING MEMORY OF SNOWBALL I:
YOU ALWAYS MANAGED TO LAND ON YOUR FEET.

THE SIMPSONS™, created by Matt Groening, is the copyrighted and trademarked
property of Twentieth Century Fox Film Corporation.
Used with permission. All rights reserved.

THE SIMPSONS BEYOND FOREVER! A COMPLETE GUIDE TO OUR FAVORITE FAMILY...STILL CONTINUED.
Copyright © 2002 by Matt Groening Productions, Inc. All rights reserved. No part of this book may be used
or reproduced in any manner whatsoever without written permission except in the case of brief quotations

Concepts and Design
Mili Smythe, Serban Cristescu, Bill Morrison

Art Direction
Bill Morrison and Nathan Kane

Computer Design and Layout
Christopher Ungar and Karen Bates

Contributing Artists
Shaun Cashman, Chia-Hsien Jason Ho, Istvan Majoros, Bill Morrison, Kevin M. Newman, Phil Ortiz, Mike Rote

Production Art and Character Designs
Brad Abelson, Scott Alberts, Mike B. Anderson, Jeanette Bose, Dale Hendrickson, Kevin Moore, Kevin M. Newman,
Raymond Persi, Joe Wack, Paul Wee, Jefferson R. Weekley, Lance Wilder

Production Team
Karen Bates, Serban Cristescu, Terry Delageane, Nathan Hamill, Chia-Hsien Jason Ho, Nathan Kane, Bill Morrison,
Rick Reese, Mike Rote, Sherri Smith, Christopher Ungar, Art Villanueva, Bob Zaugh

HarperCollins Editors
Susan Weinberg, Kate Travers

Legal Guardian
Susan A. Grode

Special Thanks to
N. Vyolet Diaz, Deanna MacLellan, Ursula Wendell, Al Jean, Mike Scully, Antonia Coffman, Classietta Davis,
Bonita Pietila, Jessica Petelle, Denise Sirkot, Gracie Films, Laura Biernacki, "The Simpsons" Design Department,
Film Roman, and everyone who has contributed to "The Simpsons" over the last fifteen years.

TABLE OF CONTENTS

GREETINGS, SIMPSONS FANATICS!

Welcome to the third, but not final—oh my no, not final—tome in the seemingly endless series of official Simpsons companions, cunningly designed to meet the discerning needs of serious scholars and cartoon goofballs alike. This little baby features the inside lowdown, hidden nuggets, and secret crème filling of every single episode from Seasons Eleven and Twelve—the Wackier-Than-Ever Years.

The show tried hard to surprise everyone at the end of the century, even the most dedicated viewer. Homer accidentally gets his thumb chopped off while Marge is slicing brownies (bet you didn't see that coming), Apu's wife gives birth to octuplets (same with this), Lisa is elected president of the United States (pretty obvious when you think about it), and Maude Flanders dies (funny, funny stuff—well, weird, anyway).

Some of my favorite moments come from this era, such as the one in which farm animals go berserk after eating the tobacco/tomato hybrid, "ToMacco." I also dig Homer screaming, "Save me, Jebus!" And dolphins revolting against humanity. And Homer's eyes crusting over after laser surgery. And we even did a very special story, sweetly titled "Worst Episode Ever," in which we get to know the Comic Book Guy a lot better, even if we never learn his name. You can write down your own favorite moments on some blank page that we've got in this book somewhere.

So lean back. Enjoy. Chuckle again at the jokes you chuckled at before. Understand the parody of *Run, Lola, Run* now that you've seen *Run, Lola, Run*. And when someone says that maybe you are a little too obsessed with this show, you show 'em this book and tell 'em the voices in your head say different.

I command you!

Your pal,

MATT

EDWARD CHRISTIAN

Occupation:
Assistant VP of Finance and Distribution, PolyStar Pictures

Important duties:
Pampering stars and changing movies to suit audience opinion

Annoying habit:
Says "You know what I mean?" and "Huh?" a lot

Patent excuse for absent celebrities:
They have to attend benefits for various diseases

Drives:
A Range Rover, like all studio execs

HOW'S THE POPCORN, GUYS?

Guest Voice:
Jack Burns as Edward Christian

---

omer decides to test drive an electric car merely to get a free gift. He wrecks the car but gets two free tickets to a screening of Mel Gibson's latest film, a remake of *Mr. Smith Goes to Washington*. When Mel Gibson flirts with Marge after the screening, Homer angrily writes a negative review of Mel's film on an audience reaction card. Despite raves from everyone else, Mel obsesses over Homer's scathing review and decides he needs Homer's help to improve the film.

The Simpsons fly to Hollywood, and while Mel and Homer go into the studio to rework the movie, Marge and the kids tour Tinsel Town. Homer and Mel agree that the film's ending needs to be reshot because it has too much talking and no violence. When they show the studio executives the new ending, which has Mel Gibson exacting revenge on the Senate floor, the executives fear for their jobs. They attempt to destroy the new footage, but before they can, Homer and Mel grab the film. They flee the studio, and Homer is injured while mooning the executives.

The movie premieres with the new ending, and the audience hates it. Mel is disappointed, but Homer remains optimistic and starts planning future projects for the two of them. Mel decides he has had enough and kicks Homer out of his moving limousine.

SHOW HIGHLIGHTS

Classical Gas:
Saleswoman: *Thinking of saying goodbye to gas?*
Bart: *You betcha.*
(Bart burps.)
Marge: *Bart!*
(Marge makes a flatulent noise.)
Marge: *Well, that shut me up.*

A Breath of Fresh Air:
Homer: *Hello, I, uh, love your planet deeply and am interested in* (suppressing a laugh) *purchasing one of your electronic autos.*
Saleswoman: (handing him the keys) *Well, it's always nice to meet people concerned about the environment.*
Homer: *What kind of mint?*

The Plot Thickens:
(Homer and Marge are in bed.)
Marge: *Hey! We never opened that envelope to see what our free gift is.*
Homer: *We didn't? That's odd. Seems like we would have done that right after we left the car place.*
Marge: *I know, but we didn't.*
(Homer reaches for the envelope.)
Homer: *Well, here it is. So we can open it and find out now.*
Marge: *Perfect!*
(Homer opens it.)
Homer: *Aw, movie tickets! That hardly seems worth destroying a car.*

Got Lenny?:
Homer: *Mel Gibson is just a guy, Marge, no different than me or Lenny.*
Marge: *Were you or Lenny ever named "Sexiest Man Alive"?*
Homer: *Hmmm...I'm not certain about Lenny...*

Movie Moment:
Rainier Wolfcastle is seen filming *Saving Irene Ryan*, a reference to both *Saving Private Ryan* and the TV sitcom "The Beverly Hillbillies."

Homer on the remake of *Mr. Smith Goes to Washington*: **"At least the Jimmy Stewart version had the giant rabbit who ran the savings and loan!"**

"Thanks for coming, folks, and don't be afraid to be completely truthful when you fill out your opinion cards. Honesty is the foundation of the movie business."

Life Imitates Art:
Marge: *Look, they're making a movie! Robert Downey, Jr. is shooting it out with the police.*
(Several police officers exchange gunfire with Robert Downey, Jr.)
Bart: *I don't see any cameras.*

Homer the Movie Critic:
Homer: *Ah-ah-ah! Now, here's your biggest problem of all.*
Mel Gibson: *The filibuster scene? That was Jimmy Stewart's favorite.*
Homer: *And it was fine for the 1930s. The country was doing great back then. Everyone was into talking. But now, in whatever year this is, the audience wants action. And seats with beverage holders. But mainly action.*

An Offer He Couldn't Refuse:
Mel Gibson: *John Travolta flew me in his jet. Now I have to help him move next weekend. He deliberately waited till we were in the air to ask me!*

BLUNDERDOME

Episode AABF23
Original Airdate: 9/26/99
Writer: Mike Scully
Director: Steven Dean Moore
Executive Producer: Mike Scully
Guest Voice: Mel Gibson as Himself

FRIDAYS ARE NOT "PANTS OPTIONAL"
FRIDAYS ARE NOT "PANTS OPTIONAL"
FRIDAYS ARE NOT "PAN OPTIONAL"

THE STUFF YOU MAY HAVE MISSED

After a little heavy petting with Marge, Homer's two top hairs go a bit limp.

The sign at the film screening: Test Screening/No Internet Spies Allowed.

Sign at the Hollywood airport: George Kennedy Airport. (George Kennedy appeared as "Joe Patroni" in all of the *Airport* movies.)

Sign at Polystar Pictures gate: No Artistic Integrity Beyond This Point.

As Homer plays the "Mr. Smith" movie at fast speed, we hear one of the politicians admit to being corrupt.

Edward Christian's "Know what I mean?...Huh?" is from a famous Jack Burns and Avery Schreiber comedy routine.

A *Braveheart* poster adorns the wall of Mel Gibson's editing room.

Mel Gibson and Homer's studio cart is catapulted and "delivered" through a billboard advertising *She's Having a Baby...Again.*

Cars displayed in the Hollywood Car Museum: The Munster Mobile, The Monkee Mobile, The Bat Mobile, The Flintstones Mobile, Herbie the Love Bug, The Dukes of Hazzard "General Lee," and The Road Warrior Car.

Next to Mann's Chinese Theater is the Chinese Man's Theater

The marquee at the movie premiere: Mr. Smith Goes to Washington, A Gibson/Simpson Joint.

Movie Moment:
After their studio cart crashes, Mel says to Homer, "I'm getting too old for this crap," which is what Danny Glover often says as Mel Gibson's *Lethal Weapon* co-star.

Movie Moment:
When Mel Gibson asks Homer to come to Hollywood, Homer responds with a famous line from *Jerry Maguire* — "You had me at 'Hello.'"

Mr. Smith Goes to Washington with a Vengeance:
Mel Gibson: *Pretty cool, huh?*
Edward Christian: *You chopped off the president's head.*
Mel: *Bet you didn't see that coming.*
Robyn Hannah: *You impaled a United States senator with the American flag.*
William Milo: *Why did Mr. Smith kill everybody?*
Homer: *It was symbolism. He was mad!*
Christian: *But this was going to be the studio's prestige picture, like Howards End or Sophie's Choice.*
Homer: *Ugh. Those movies sucked. I only saw them to get Marge into the sack.* (to Mel) *P. S. Mission accomplished.*
(Homer and Mel "high five.")

Film Commentary:
Homer: *Movies aren't stupid. They fill us with romance and hatred and revenge fantasies. Lethal Weapon showed us that suicide is funny.*
Mel Gibson: *That really wasn't my intention.*
Homer: *Before Lethal Weapon 2, I never thought there could be a bomb in my toilet, but now I check every time.*
Marge: *It's true. He does.*
Mel: *Do movies mean that much to you, Homer?*
Homer: *They're my only escape from the drudgery of work and family.* (to Marge and the kids) *No offense.*

What's in a Name...Above the Title?:
Edward Christian: *Who are you, anyway?*
Homer: *Do the words "executive producer" mean anything to you?*
Mel Gibson: (surprised) *Executive producer?*
Homer: *We'll talk.*

Movie Moment:
Mel Gibson tossing away his U.S. Senator badge at the end of the *Mr. Smith* remake is similar to Clint Eastwood's tossing away his police badge at the end of *Dirty Harry.*

How Homer communicates when he's on a mission: "No time talk! Need steal car! Must save powerful but controversial movie!"

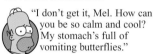 "I don't get it, Mel. How can you be so calm and cool? My stomach's full of vomiting butterflies."

Dummy Up:
(After they run over Mel Gibson's mannequin.)
William Milo: *Wait a minute...he's just a dummy!*
Edward Christian: *I know, but he sells tickets.* (long beat) *Let's go!*

A t the school's Fire Safety Day, Bart floods the gymnasium, destroying the gym floor. Homer and Marge are called in to Principal Skinner's office. Skinner believes Bart has Attention Deficit Disorder and suggests giving him a highly experimental drug called Focusyn. Homer and Marge visit the Pharm Team, makers of the drug, and are convinced that such a medication could benefit Bart.

After taking the drug, Bart becomes a model student and son. Bart is so well-behaved, Marge and Homer decide they can safely go out by themselves on an intimate date. When they come home, however, they find Bart in his room wrapped in aluminum foil with a garbage can lid strapped to his head. His room is filled with wire hangers dangling from the ceiling. Worst of all, Bart is convinced that a Major League Baseball satellite is spying on them. Concerned, Homer and Marge take

Bart back to the Pharm Team for an evaluation. The researchers decide it is necessary to wean him off the Focusyn, but Bart, desperate to stay on the medication, hastily swallows several pills and runs away.

Bart steals a tank from a local Army base. He drives the tank through town, upsetting townspeople and destroying things. Finally, he stops at the school and fires a mortar into the sky, shooting down a Major League Baseball satellite. Everyone realizes Bart was right—Major League Baseball is spying on people. Suddenly, Mark McGwire appears by helicopter, distracts the locals, and takes all the evidence. Back at home, the Simpsons continue to be observed unaware by means of an autographed "spy" baseball bat given to Bart by Mark McGwire. Marge says she will never force strange drugs on Bart again, and Bart resumes his "normal" prescription of Ritalin.

SHOW HIGHLIGHTS

Mistaken Identity:
Ralph: *And I want a bike, and a monkey, and a friend for the monkey...*
Hosey the Bear: *You're not going to start any fires, are ya?*
Ralph: *At my house, we call them "uh-ohs."*

 "Fire can be our servant, whether it's toasting s'mores or raining down on Charlie."

Summoned to the Principal's Office:
Principal Skinner: *I'm afraid I'll have to expel your son.*
Marge: *Gasp!*
Skinner: *Unless you're willing to try a radical, untested, potentially dangerous...*
Homer: *Candy bar?*
Skinner: *No. It's a new drug called Focusyn.*
Marge: *I know Bart can be rambunctious, but he's not some hyperactive monster.*
(Bart appears outside the window, dressed as a cheerleader.)
Bart: *Gimme an "F"! Gimme an "art"!*
Skinner: *Good Lord! He's gotten into the pep closet.*
Homer: *I'd say he's coming out of the pep closet.*

Just Say "No":
Bart: *I don't wanna take drugs.*
Homer: *Sure you do. All your favorite stars have used drugs. Brett Butler, Tim Allen...*
Marge: *Tommy Lee...*
Homer: *Andy Dick...*
Bart: *He's just flamboyant.*
Homer: *Yeah, and I'm a size four.*

The New & Improved Bart:
Marge: *Hmm?* (She reads a note taped to her chair.) *"Thank you in advance for a world-class meal. You're an inspiration to our entire organization. Thank you again, Bart."* Oh, what a lovely gesture.
Bart: *Cost of paper: five cents. A mother's love: priceless.*
Marge: *Aw.*
Homer: *Do I get a card?*
Bart: *No, but here's a book called* Chicken Soup for the Loser *that gave Bill Buckner the courage to open a chain of laundromats.*
Homer: *Hmm...my career has kind of lost momentum.*

Bart Gets His Head Examined:
Marge: *I understand the electrodes, but why does he have to be on a treadmill?*
Pharm Team Man: *Oh, that was his idea. He said he felt fat.*

Homer Wacks-Out on Focusyn:
Todd: *Does Mr. Simpson have a demon, Daddy?*
Ned: *Looks like it. Run and get Daddy's exorcism tongs.*
Rod and Todd: *Yay!*

Brotherly Shove:
Bart: *Joke if you will, but did you know most people use ten percent of their brains? I am now one of them. Before, my energy was all over the place. Now it's concentrated like a laser beam.* (Bart stands up and puts his hand on Lisa's shoulder.) *Well, this has been terrific. Let's do it again sometime.*
Lisa: *Are you standing up to get me to leave?*
Bart: *It's from the book.*
Lisa: (scanning the book *The Seven Habits of Highly Effective Pre-Teens*) *Hey! I'm not a "Time Burglar"!*
(Bart flips open an electronic organizer and types as he speaks.)
Bart: *Memo to self: Lock door.*
Lisa: *All right, I'll go! You don't have to be a jerk about it.*
Bart: (typing again) *Memo to self: Shut up, Lisa.*

The Proud Papa:
Homer: *I tell you, the kid's a wonder. He organized all the lawsuits against me into one class action!*
Lenny: *That's gonna save all kinds of travel time.*
Homer: *You know it.*

Parental Freedom:
Marge: *Bart's so well-behaved now. Maybe you and I can have a night out.*
Homer: *Ooh! Let's go to the water park! My ten-year ban ended yesterday.*
Marge: *I was thinking of something a little more...adult.* (She whispers in Homer's ear.)
Homer: *Oh, Marge!*
Marge: *And then afterwards...*(She whispers again.)
Homer: *Hee-hee, hee-hee! Really? With butterscotch on it?*
Marge: *I think you misheard me.*

A little known fact about Homer: **"So I gave up tap for jazz, and I've never regretted it."**

THE STUFF YOU MAY HAVE MISSED

The Fire Safety Day slogan is "Learn, Baby, Learn."

Maude Flanders's hippie belt buckle isn't a peace sign; it's a Mercedes Benz symbol.

Bart's surfboard is really a basketball backboard with the hoop still attached.

The man in the Hosey the Bear costume shakes the flood water off himself like a real bear.

The poets being studied in Mrs. Krabappel's class are Wordsworth, Auden, and Jewel (singer-songwriter-poetess).

After the Focusyn kicks in, Bart starts using reading glasses to read.

The only note for the whole week on Homer's electronic organizer reads "Buy sunscreen for legs."

When Homer says that Bart's gone from Goofus to Gallant, he's referring to the two classic characters from *Highlights* magazine.

Among the moviegoers at *Showgirls*:

Superintendent Chalmers, Apu, Abraham Simpson, Dr. Hibbert, Snake, Kirk Van Houten, Moe, Captain McCallister, Dr. Nick Riviera, Nelson, Lenny, and Krusty.

When Homer and Marge leave the movie, Homer has a teddy bear on his lap that is holding a pennant which reads "Showgirls."

One of the pills the Pharm Team man tries to give Bart is shaped like a Greek comedy mask; another is shaped like a red cross.

Officer Lou's police sketch of Bart resembles Dennis the Menace.

One of the soldiers showering at Fort Fragg has a T-shirt that reads, "I Went to the Persian Gulf and All I Got Was This Lousy Syndrome."

The readouts in the viewfinder of the Major League Baseball spy-bat as it studies the Simpsons: 2 (male symbol), Snack preference: All; 3 (female symbol); Squalor index: 97

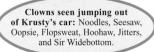

Clowns seen jumping out of Krusty's car: Noodles, Seesaw, Oopsie, Flopsweat, Hoohaw, Jitters, and Sir Widebottom.

The Right Man for the Right Job:
Comic Book Guy: *Egad! A maniac cutting a swath of destruction! This is a job for the Green Lantern, Thundra, or possibleeeee...Ghost Rider.*
Otto: *What about Superman?*
Comic Book Guy: (dismissively) *Oh, please.*

HELPER

Episode AABF22
Original Airdate: 10/03/99
Writer: George Meyer
Director: Mark Kirkland
Executive Producer: Mike Scully
Guest Voice: Mark McGwire as Himself

THE PHARM TEAM LAB RESEARCHERS

Developers of:
Focusyn

Research tools include:
Guinea pigs, miniature schoolrooms, and hand puppets

Their idea of a good time:
Augmenting chlorhexanol with phenylbutamine and maybe some cyclobenzanone

What they hear a lot of:
Concerned parents who don't want to pump their kids full of drugs

How they handle concerned parents:
Pump them full of drugs

PORK IS NOT A VERB
PORK IS NOT A VERB
PORK IS NOT A VERB
PORK IS NOT A VERB
PORK IS NOT A VERB
PORK IS NOT A VERB

Satellite Delight:
Chief Wiggum: *That's the end of your Looney Tune, Drugs Bunny. You're under arrest for astro-vandalism.*
Moe: *And may God help you if that thing carried the Spice Channel.*

The Battle of the Bart:
(Bart points the tank's turret at the school.)
Principal Skinner: *Gasp! Good Lord! He's going to fire!*
Jimbo: *All right! Scud the school, dude!*
Edna Krabappel: (without enthusiasm) *No. Stop. Think of the children.*
(Bart moves the turret toward the church.)
Reverend Lovejoy: *Not the church! Jesus lives there!*
(Bart moves turret to aim at a frame shop.)
Homer: *The frame store! You monster!*
(Bart points the turret up in the air.)
Sideshow Mel: *Not the sky! That's where clouds are born!*

IT'S NOT ABOUT SLAVERY. IT'S ABOUT HELPING KIDS CONCENTRATE. THIS PILL REDUCES CLASS CLOWNISM 44%!

WITH 60% LESS SASS-MOUTH.

The Fire Safety Day Skit by the Springfield Volunteer Fire Department Players:
(The curtains open, revealing a hippie "crash pad." Ned and Maude Flanders enter on a motorcycle, dressed as hippies.)
Ned: *Ha-ho. What a great pot party!*
Maude: *Wasn't it, man?*
Ned: *Now for a regular cigarette to make the night complete.* (He lights a cigarette and coughs.) *Oh, a-heh-heh, heh. Man, that's good.*
Maude: *Mad Dog, I've been thinking. Maybe we should get another smoke detector in case that one trips out on us.*
Ned: *Ah ho-ho-ho! Why bother, baby. One smoke detector's enough for Mad Dog. Now let's hit the sack.* (They go to bed. Ned lights his pants on fire with the cigarette.)
Ned: *Whoa! Check it out! Mad Dog's on fire!*
Maude: *Stop, drop, and roll, man!*
Ned: *Ha, ha, ha! That's for Clydes, baby. A little fire can't hurt you.*
(The curtains close. Apu walks onstage and addresses audience.)
Apu: *But Mad Dog was wrong. The fire burned through the night and cost him the use of his pants. Which just goes to show you--*
(Ned runs out from behind curtain, his pants still on fire.)
Ned: *Aaah! Sorry to break character, but these stunt pants are getting pretty toasty!*
Maude: *Uh, roll, Neddie, roll.*
(The children laugh.)
Ned: *It's not working! It just spreads the flame!*

LIFEWAYS EDITOR

Recognizable by:
His hard-boiled work ethic, loosened tie, and hairy forearms

Obvious traits:
Gruff, surly, hates spunk

Obvious role-model:
Lou Grant

Admitted mistake:
Marrying Mimi the food critic

His description of the Lifeways section content:
Chick crap

WE'RE GONNA RUN THIS ON PAGE ONE ...OF SECTION H-2.

Guest Voice:
Edward Asner as Lifeways Editor

The Springfield Elementary students go on a field trip to the *Springfield Shopper* newspaper. Homer, one of the chaperones, wanders away from the group and crashes the food critic's retirement party. The editor of the newspaper notices how much Homer likes food and offers him a chance to become the new food critic. After Homer's first review is rejected by the editor, he asks for another chance. Lisa volunteers to help Homer write the new review, and it is accepted.

Homer embarks on a new career as a food critic (with Lisa's continued help), and his enthusiasm for local restaurants leads to a sizable increase in the town's collective waistline. Other critics at the newspaper point out that all of Homer's reviews are positive and that he never pans a restaurant. Homer gives into their peer pressure and soon learns the power of writing negative reviews. No one escapes his criticism, not even Marge. Lisa refuses to continue working with him. Without Lisa's help, Homer's reviews begin to suffer. The editor tells Homer to shape up in time for the Taste of Springfield Festival, a town event in which every restaurant is represented.

Meanwhile, offended by Homer's scathing reviews, the town's restaurant owners meet and decide they must kill Homer before he destroys all of their businesses. A French chef comes up with the instrument of death: a chocolate éclair laced with poison. At the festival, Bart becomes aware of the restaurateurs' murderous plot and tells Marge and Lisa. Just as Homer is about to take a bite of the deadly pastry, Lisa saves him. The angry restaurateurs then descend on Homer and Lisa, and they are forced to flee for their lives.

SHOW HIGHLIGHTS

Extracurricular Activities:

Skinner: *I hope you all enjoy your ride to and tour of the Springfield Shopper newspaper. Groundskeeper Willie and I will stay behind to remove all traces of asbestos and the word "evolution" from our school.*
Willie: (enters wearing a Hawaiian shirt and carrying a pitcher) *Next stop, Margaritaville! Eh...(suddenly noticing the students). Oh, they're still here.*

Have Your Seen This Child?:

Principal Skinner: *Now I'd like to ask each child to pair up with a buddy, so no one gets lost.*
Bart: *Come to think of it, I haven't seen Üter since the last field trip.*
Principal Skinner: *Ptui...yeah...well, Üter? I don't remember any Üter. Neh, heh, heh. Silly name...Üter.*

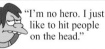

"I'm no hero. I just like to hit people on the head."

The Guided Tour:

Guide: *Welcome to the Springfield Shopper, established in 1883. The newspaper was founded by Johnny Newspaperseed, a 14-year-old boy who roamed America founding newspapers.*
Homer: *If he's so smart, how come he's dead?*
Guide: *Over the years, the Shopper merged with the Springfield Times, Post, Globe, Herald, Jewish News, and Hot Sex Weekly to become Springfield's number-one newspaper.*

A Nose for News:

Homer: *Hey, I smell cake! Cake that says ⌐sniff! sniff!⌐ "Farewell" and ⌐sniff! sniff! gasp!⌐ "Best wishes"!*
Nelson: *Your old man has an awesome nose.*
Bart: *Oh, that's nothing. He can hear pudding.*

A New Career Opportunity for Homer:

Lifeways Editor: *Hey, listen. I just had a thought. We're looking for a new food critic. Someone who doesn't immediately pooh-pooh everything he eats.*
Homer: *No, it usually takes a few hours.*

Homer's First Review...Gets Reviewed:

Lifeways Editor: *This is a joke, right? I mean, this is the stupidest thing I've ever read.*
Homer: *What's wrong with it?*
Editor: *Well, you keep using words like "pasghetti" and "momatoes"; you make numerous threatening references to the U.N.; and at the end, you repeat the words (scratching his head) "Screw Flanders" over and over again.*
Homer: *Oh. It's so hard to get to 500 words.*

Ghostwriting 101:

Lisa: *Wow, my first published article...hoo...although someone else's name is on it.*
Homer: *Heh, heh. Welcome to the humiliating world of professional writing.*

The Sweet Life:

Homer: *Can you believe it, Marge? This job is the greatest. They're paying me to eat!*
Bart: *Now if you could just get somebody to pay you for scratching your butt, we'll be on Easy Street.*

Critical Advice:

Garth Trelawny: *Listen, we've been meaning to have a talk with you about your reviews. Everything's a rave! Nine thumbs up. What the hell is that?*
Homer: *I've given out my share of bad reviews.*
Daphne Beaumont: *Oh, the only bad review you gave was to a slice of pizza you found under the couch.*
Homer: *It lost some points 'cuz it had a Hot Wheel on it.*

(Homer and Lisa dine at the Springfield Dinner Theatre.)
Homer: *This pea soup is as weak as the acting and nowhere near as hammy.*
Lisa: *Dad, that's so mean!*
Homer: *The other critics told me to be mean, and you should always give in to peer pressure.*
Lisa: *But what if someone bad tells me to...*
Homer: *Always.*

THE STUFF YOU MAY HAVE MISSED

During the couch gag, the "animated" Matt Groening signs his name upside down in order for it to appear right side up, while using his right hand. The "real" Matt Groening is left-handed.

Üter was left behind on a previous field trip to Fort Springfield in "The PTA Disbands" (2F19). He has made several appearances since that episode.

Once Homer gets the kids to the newspaper, he is seen holding a balloon from the zoo.

Homer and Lisa's first restaurant review carries the headline "Cod Is Great, Scrod Is Good."

People seen at Planet Springfield: Reverend Lovejoy, Julius and Bernice Hibbert, Principal Skinner, Edna Krabappel, Kirk Van Houten, Scott Christian, and Martin Prince's parents.

Props seen at Planet Springfield: Herbie from *The Love Bug*, the coffee mug from *Heartbeeps*, the cane from *Citizen Kane*, a script from *The Cable Guy*, an alien resembling one from *Mars Attacks!* (but pink), a model of the *Titanic*, models of an X-Wing and TIE fighters, and a statue of C3PO.

Homer's review of the meal at the Springfield Dinner Theatre has the headline "Nuts to Soup!" The headline for the review of the play is "Krusty: Worst King Lear in 400 Years."

Sign seen at the Captain McCallister's Frying Dutchman restaurant: "We Arrrr Closed!"

The slogan for the Taste of Springfield Festival is "Fine Dining in a Bee-Filled Atmosphere."

Booths at the food festival: Ugli, The Gilded Truffle, Ah, Fudge!, Much Ado About Muffins!, The French Confection, The Texas Cheesecake Depository, Phineas Q. Butterfat's 5600 Flavors Ice Cream Parlor, The Pimento Grove, The Happy Sumo, The Frying Dutchman, The Hungry Hun, and Moleman's Gruel.

TO CRITICIZE DINNER

Episode AABF21
Original Airdate: 10/24/99
Writer: Al Jean
Director: Nancy Kruse
Executive Producer: Mike Scully

I AM NOT THE LAST DON
I AM NOT THE LAST DON
I AM NOT THE LAST DON
I AM NOT THE LAST D
I AM NOT THE LAST D
I AM NOT THE LAST D

THE FRENCH CONFECTION

Restaurant reviewing Homer-style:
"So come to The Legless Frog if you want to get sick and die and leave a big garlicky corpse. P.S. Parking was ample."

The Unkindest Chop of All:
Marge: Who wants pork chops?!
Homer: Sorry, Marge. I'm afraid this gets my lowest rating ever. Seven thumbs up.
Marge: You always liked my pork chops.
Homer: Marge, I'm sorry, but your cooking's only got two moves—shake and bake.
Marge: You like Shake 'N Bake. You used to put it in your coffee.

Not Getting Paid to Think:
Lisa: Dad, you're being cruel for no reason! What will people think?
Homer: People will think what I tell them to think, when you tell me what to tell them to think!
Lisa: Not anymore! I don't want to be partners with a man who thinks like that!

Movie/Musical Moment:
Homer's song about food resembles, in part, the tune "I Feel Pretty," from *West Side Story*.

Homer's Little Helper:
Editor: Homer, what gives with this review? You say the salad tastes like "bark" and the potatoes were very "grrrowl!" This reads like it was written by a dog.
Homer: Are you crazy? A dog can't type... unfortunately.

Revenge Is on the Menu:
Luigi: Homer, he's out-a of control-a. He gave me a bad review. So my "friend" put a horse-a head in his bed. He ate-a the head and gave it a bad review! True story.
Capt. McCallister: Arr, well I've had it with Homer. His bad reviews are sinking our businesses.
Akira: Then why did you put yours in the window?
McCallister: Arr, it covered up the "D" from the health inspector.

Aye, There's the Rub:
Capt. McCallister: Lard ho! Arr. 'Tis a good sign! Homer's unfastened the top button on his pants.
Akira: Uh, no. He's been walking around like that since Thanksgiving.
McCallister: I'm surprised he doesn't just give it up and go for sweatpants.
Akira: He says the crotch wears out too fast.
McCallister: Yar! That's going to replace the whale in my nightmares.

"Only your father could take a part-time job at a small-town paper and wind up the target of international assassins."

At the Food Festival:
Marge: Homey, my women's intuition's acting up. Something bad's going to happen if you go in there.
Homer: Oh, Marge. Something bad usually happens to me when I go in anywhere. (He walks away whistling, steps in a puddle, gets hit by a flying disk, and is bitten in the neck by a bat.) Aw! A bat, now that's a new one.

Attack of the Killer Éclair:
Lisa: Dad, no! It's going to kill you!
Homer: Eh, I've had a good run.
Lisa: Eh...don't...ah...um...It's low-fat!
Homer: Nooooo! (He tosses the éclair and it explodes on impact with Hans Moleman's booth.)
Chief Wiggum: Woo! That was close! Thank God it landed in that smoking crater. (Lou and Eddie arrest the French chef.) Take him into custard-y, boys.

Opening Sequence

(Spotlights play across stage curtains.)
Announcer: Live from fabulous Centauri City, it's "The Simpsons Tenth Halloween Special!" *(The curtains open and a pumpkin-shaped spaceship lands on the stage. Kang and Kodos emerge from the ship.)* Now, please welcome your hosts—if you haven't been probed by these two, you haven't been probed—Kang and Kodos!
(The audience applauds. Kang and Kodos blow kisses and applaud back.)
Kang: Thank you, thank you.
Kodos: Yes, thank you, ladies and gentlemen.

Welcome to our tenth anniversary show. Oh, we've got a great g-- *(Kodos notices that Kang is wearing a welder's mask and is lighting an acetylene torch.)* Kang, what are you doing?
Kang: You said we were going to warm up the audience.
(The sound of canned laughter is heard; however, we see an audience populated with aliens who seem to be unresponsive.)
Kodos: *(shuddering)* Ladies and gentlemen, I have to apologize for my partner. He had to borrow a human brain.

I KNOW WHAT YOU DIDDILY-IDDILY-DID

O n a foggy night, the Simpsons are driving on a lonely road with Marge at the wheel. She accidentally runs over Ned Flanders, killing him. They bring Ned's body home, and Homer tricks Maude into thinking Ned died of a heart attack. The family believes they have gotten away with murder, until they find the message "I know what you did" scrawled on the doors and walls of their house and on their car. When an ominous figure in a black rain slicker, armed with a meat hook appears, the Simpsons flee their home. Their car breaks down, and the stranger catches them. It turns out to be Ned, who explains that just before the accident, he was bitten by a werewolf and had planned to kill them. The clouds part, unveiling a full moon, and Ned is transformed. Homer is attacked by the werewolf Ned while the rest of the family runs away.

SHOW HIGHLIGHTS

Puppetry with Homer:

Maude: *Neddy? Where have you been?*
Homer: *(moving Ned's arm and head and trying to imitate Ned's voice) Hi, Maude, diddily. I've been having fun with my pal, Homer…diddily.*
Maude: *Oh, I'm so relieved. Whenever you go on one of your late-night fog walks, I get so worried.*
Homer: *Relax, I'm fine. But when I do die, I don't want any autopsies.*

Night of the Living Ned:

Marge: *It's impossible. I killed you.*
Flanders: *You can't kill the undead, silly.*
Homer: *(poking Flanders in the eye with a stick again) He's undead, all right.*
Bart: *Are you a zombie?*
Flanders: *Oh, I wish!*

HORROR X

Episode BABF01
Original Airdate: 10/31/99
Writers: Donick Spooky, Terrifying Tim Long, and Uh, An Ogre? (Donick Cary, Tim Long, and Ron Hauge)
Director: Pete "Scary Spice" Michels

Executive Producer: Mike "Insert Scary Name" Scully, George Meyer, Al "I Still Murdered Mike Reiss" Jean
Guest Voices: Tom Arnold as Himself, Dick Clark as Himself, and Lucy Lawless as Herself

Ned Looks Dead:

Homer: (poking Ned in the eye with a stick) *He's dead!* (He pokes Ned some more.) *He's definitely dead.* (He pokes Ned several more times.)
Marge: *Oh, my God! We killed Ned Flanders.*
Bart: *You mean, you killed Ned Flanders.*
Marge: *Oh, it was an accident! An accident!*
Lisa: *We've got to go to the police.*
Bart: *They'll never believe a Simpson killed a Flanders by accident. Even I have my doubts.*

Homer takes charge as the stalker draws near: **"Okay, Marge, you hide in the abandoned amusement park; Lisa, the pet cemetery; Bart, spooky roller disco; and I'll go skinny-dipping in that lake where the sexy teens were killed a hundred years ago tonight."**

When a Stranger Calls:

(The phone rings.)
Homer: *Yello?*
Voice: *I know you're alone!*
Homer: *Oo...who is this?*
Voice: *Is this...Maude Flanders?*
Homer: *No, it's...Homer.*
Voice: *Oh, hey Homer. It's Moe. I musta dialed the wrong number.*

Golly Gee, What a Eulogy:

Homer: *When I think about Ned, I can't help but remember the look on his face when Marge drove over--*
Marge: (whispering from the pews) *Homer, shut up, shut up, shut up!*
Homer: *Oh, wait. What I'd like to say is, we're still looking for the real killers. Anyway, in conclusion, a man cannot be forced to testify against his wife.* (He winks at Marge repeatedly.)
Marge: *Stop winking!*
Homer: *We'll miss you, buddy.* (He punches Ned's corpse in the shoulder.)

DESPERATELY XEEKING XENA

When an X-ray machine used to examine Halloween candy explodes, Bart and Lisa are transformed by the radiation into superheroes. Bart becomes Stretch Dude, with the ability to elongate any body part at will. Lisa is Clobber Girl, with super-human strength. Together, a new dynamic duo is born. We see one of their adventures, "Enter the Collector," which begins with Lucy Lawless, dressed as Xena, speaking before a group of nerds. She is kidnapped by a mysterious villain known as the Collector (played by the Comic Book Guy) and taken to his lair, where he plans to make her marry him. Stretch Dude and Clobber Girl come to the rescue, but are then captured by the Collector, who attempts to dip them in hot, boiling Lucite. At the last minute, Lawless tricks the Collector, forces him into the Lucite, and rescues Stretch Dude and Clobber Girl. Having saved the day, Lawless flies the young heroes home.

SHOW HIGHLIGHTS

Costumed Super-Zero:

Milhouse: *Check it out, Lisa! I'm Radioactive Man.*
Lisa: *I don't think the real Radioactive Man wears a plastic smock with a picture of himself on it.*
Milhouse: *He would on Halloween.*

Lucy Lectures the Professor:

Lucy Lawless: *...but I'm sure that once girls get to know the real you, you'll get plenty of dates. Next question?*
Prof. Frink: *Yes, over here, ng-hey, ng-haven. In episode BF12, you were battling barbarians while riding a wing-ed Appaloosa. Yet, in the very next scene, my dear, you're clearly atop a wing-ed Arabian. Please to explain it.*
Lucy: *Ah, yeah. Well, whenever you notice something like that, a wizard did it.*
Prof. Frink: *I see, all right, yes, but in episode AG4--*
Lucy: *Wizard.*
Prof. Frink: *Aw, for glavin out loud!*

Bart's solemn vow when transformed into Stretch Dude: **"I must only use this power to annoy!"**

The "Stretch Dude and Clobber Girl" Theme Song:

Stretch Dude and Clobber Girl!
He's a human rubber band,
And she's the Hulk in pearls.
He's a limber lad.
She's a powerful lass.
He'll wring your neck,
And she'll kick your ass.
They're Stretch Dude and Clobber Girl!
Stretch Dude, Clobber Girl!
Stretch Dude, Clobber Girl!

A Sticky Proposal:

Collector: *Care for a Rollo, sweet Xena?*
Lucy Lawless: *All right, Collector, stick this in your tweezers— I'm not Xena! I'm an actress, you lunatic!*
Collector: *Oh, please, I'm not insane. I simply wish to take you back to my lair and make you my bride.*
Lucy: *Oh, dear God!*

A Dastardly End to a Massive Villain:

Collector: *Aha! Not even Xena is a match for the limited-edition, double-edged light saber from Star Wars Episode 1: The Phantom Menace!*
Lucy Lawless: *Gasp! You removed it from its original packaging!*
Collector: *Gasp! No! It's no longer a collectible!* (Dazed, he crashes through a railing and plunges into the Lucite tank.) *Oh! Oh! Oooh!*
Lucy: *What a nerd.*
Collector: (climbing out of tank, covered with Lucite) *Lucite hardening...must end life in classic Lorne Greene pose from "Battlestar Galactica." Oosh! Eeuh! Best...death...ever!*

"Soon those bratty buttinskis will be encased in Lucite for all eternity. While we're waiting, here are some names you may call me on our wedding night: *(clearing his throat, then reading from a list)* Obi-Wan, Iron Man, Mr. Mxyzptlk, and, of course, Big Papa Smurf."

Xena: *Come here, you! Xena needs xex!* (The Collector puckers his lips and leans forward. Xena grabs his lips.) *Got your lips!* (She rabbit punches him in the face then kicks him off the balcony and across the room.)
The Collector: *You tricked me...with a ruse so hackneyed it would make Stan Lee blush!*

The Collector taunts Stretch Dude and Clobber Girl as he lowers them into a vat of Lucite: **"Good night, Retch Dude and Slobber Girl. Sweet screams! Ha, ha, ha! I'm unbelievably amused."**

LIFE'S A GLITCH, THEN YOU DIE

Midnight approaches on December 31, 1999, and the Simpsons are partying and watching "Dick Clark's Springfield Rockin' Eve" on TV. Just before the clock strikes twelve, everyone realizes that as the Y2K Compliance Officer, Homer may not have made sure the power plant's computers were ready for the year 2000. As January 1, 2000, hits, the plant computer goes haywire, causing every other computer in the world to malfunction, too. Pandemonium ensues, since everything has a computer chip in it. The Earth is no longer suitable for life, and a rocket is prepared to take the best and the brightest of Earth's population to safety on Mars. This leaves Homer and Bart out. They quickly spot another rocket about to leave the planet. Homer and Bart make it aboard just before it leaves, but they soon realize everyone aboard is a second-rate celebrity and that the rocket is heading for the Sun. Unable to bear another moment with the ship's passengers, Homer and Bart eject themselves into outer space.

Homer Is Non-Compliant:

Carl: *Must've been hard, debugging all those computers, huh, Homer?*
Homer: *Doing what now?*
Lisa: *You did fix them, right, Dad? Because even a single faulty unit could corrupt every other computer in the world.*
Homer: *That can't be true, honey. If it were, I'd be terrified.*

SHOW HIGHLIGHTS

a.k.a. Homer:

Rocket Security Guard: *Name, please.*
Homer: *Certainly. I am...the, uh, piano genius from the movie Shine.*
Rocket Security Guard: *Uh-huh. And your name is?*
Homer: *Uh...Shiny McShine?*

A Cautionary Tale:

(The Simpsons walk down the street as technological mayhem erupts.)
Lisa: *Well, look at the wonders of the computer age now.*
Homer: *Wonders, Lisa, or blunders?*
Lisa: *I think that was implied by what I said.*
Homer: *Implied, Lisa, or implode?*
Lisa: *Mom, make him stop.*

Rocket Ship of Fools:

Bart: *Wait! Only that ship's going to Mars. Ours is headed for the Sun.*
Tom Arnold: *Yeah, ain't that a kick in the teeth? I mean, my shows weren't great, but I never tied people up and forced them to watch. And I could've, because I'm a big guy and I'm good with knots.*
Homer: *So we're all going to die?*
Tom Arnold: *'Fraid so but, hey, the grub's pretty good, huh? Heh, heh!*
(Tom Arnold opens a can of peaches and swallows them.)
Homer: *The Sun? That's the hottest place on Earth!*

Grampa: *Man alive, what a stink-o thousand years! Blimp wrecks, teenagers...then again, we had two TV shows with Andy Griffith.*
Marge: *And eleven with Robert Urich!*

"Hey, everybody! They're looting the mall! Hurry! I got nine shoe buffers!"

Movie Moment:

The rockets leaving a doomed Earth are reminiscent of the 1951 George Pal film, *When Worlds Collide*.

HORROR X

While at the movies, Homer is inspired by the idea of challenging someone to a duel by slapping them in the face with a glove. He goes around town slapping people and getting his way until he unknowingly challenges a real duelist, a Southern colonel. The colonel accepts Homer's challenge and chooses pistols at dawn.

Frightened by the impending duel, Homer takes his family and flees to the farmhouse where he grew up. At first, Homer cannot get anything to grow at the farm, but then he fertilizes his land with plutonium from the nuclear power plant. Almost overnight, a crop grows. It is a hybrid of tomatoes and tobacco.

Homer calls his new creation ToMacco, and it tastes terrible but is highly addictive. He sells it at a roadside stand, and it becomes an instant success, attracting the attention of the Laramie Cigarette Company. Laramie offers Homer $150 million for the ToMacco plants, but Homer demands more. The Laramie executives refuse to go any higher; however, while the Simpsons are negotiating, local farm animals eat all but one of the ToMacco plants.

The farm animals, now addicted to ToMacco, attack the family. While the Simpsons try to protect themselves, a Laramie executive arrives and whisks the plant away in a company helicopter. A ToMacco-crazed sheep causes the helicopter to crash, and the last plant is destroyed. Having failed as a farmer, Homer returns home with his family and must duel the Southern colonel. Homer is shot in the arm, but he refuses treatment until he can eat some of Marge's mincemeat pie.

SHOW HIGHLIGHTS

Let's Go Out to the Lobby:

Pimple-Faced Kid: *I'm sorry, but we're not supposed to put butter on the Milk Duds.*
Homer: *You're not supposed to go to the bathroom without washing your hands, either.*
Pimple-Faced Kid: *Touché.*
(He pumps butter into the Milk Duds box.)
Homer: *To the top, please.* (to the candies) *Swim, my pretties!*

"The Zorro Rap":

From the Z to the O
To the double R—O,
He's a dude in a mask in the barrio.
With his horse and his mask
And his big ol' sword.
He'll cut your butt from a '52 Ford.

End credits to *The Poke of Zorro*:

Cast

Zorro	John Byner
Robot Zorro	Shawn Wayans
Mrs. Zorro	Rita Rudner
Scarlet Pimpernel	Curtis "Booger" Armstrong
King Arthur	Cheech Marin
Man in the Iron Mask	Gina Gershon
Wise Nun	Posh Spice
Stupid Nun	Meryl Streep
Time Traveler #1	Stone Cold Steve Austin
Orangutan at Dance	"Puddles"
Gay-Seeming Prince	Spalding Gray
Man Beating Mule	Eric Roberts
Mule Beating Man	"Gus"
Hiccuping Narrator	Pele
President Van Buren	Robert Evans
Corky	Anthony Hopkins
Voice of Magic Taco	James Earl Jones

The producers would like to thank: the Film Board of Canada, the Philadelphia Flyers, the Makers of Whip Balm, Mr. Robert Guccione, the Teamsters Pension Fund, AAABest Bail Bonds, Mr. and Mrs. Curtis "Booger" Armstrong

Agnes Skinner, telling everyone at Moe's more than they want to know: "Seymour needs the toilet! His bladder's full! Full of urine!"

Slap Happy:

Homer: *Heavy set? What's that supposed to mean?*
Moe: *All right. Take it easy, take it easy. I'm just saying, you ain't no, uh, Tommy Tune.*
Homer: *No Tommy Tune, eh? Oh, that's it! You insulted my honor!*
Moe: *I...your what now?*
Homer: *I demand satisfaction!* (Homer backhands Moe with a glove.)
Moe: *Ooo!*
Homer: *I challenge you to a duel.*
Moe: *Hey, a duel, I, uh...isn't that a little extreme? Here, here, have a free beer.*
Homer: *Really? But you've never given anyone a free beer.*
Moe: *Yeah, I ain't never been slapped with no dueling glove before, either.*
Homer: *Wow, a free beer! And I owe it all to a little glove slap.*

"Glove Slap"
(To the tune of "Love Shack"):

Glove slap, shut your big yap!
Glove slap, baby, glove slap!
Oo, glove...that's where it's at, yeah!
Glove, baby, give it a slap!
Glove slap, I don't take crap!
Glove slap, shut your big yap!
A glove slap to a little old face
Will get you satisfaction!
Glove slap, baby...

Duel at Dawn:

Homer: *He's out there, isn't he?*
Marge: *I'm afraid so, and his wife's with him.* (The colonel's attractive wife emerges from the RV and stretches.)
Homer: *Rrrrowl!*
Marge: *Homer!*
Homer: *Hey, I'm not dead yet.* (The colonel knocks at the door.) *Oh! Oh! Save me, Marge! I saved you!*
Marge: *Why don't you have the colonel's wife save you?*
Homer: *Oh, Marge, that's in the past. Just let it go.*

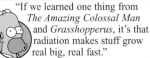
"If we learned one thing from *The Amazing Colossal Man* and *Grasshopperus*, it's that radiation makes stuff grow real big, real fast."

Movie Moment:

The Buzz Cola advertisement shown before the movie is a parody of *Saving Private Ryan*, directed by Steven Spielberg

THE STUFF YOU MAY HAVE MISSED

Movies playing at the Googolplex: *My Dinner with Jar Jar, Shakespeare in Heat, Mars Needs Towels, Facepuncher IV, That 70's Movie,* and *Das Booty Call.*

The Southern colonel sounds like Warner Brothers cartoon character Foghorn Leghorn. In the caricature of him on the RV mudflap, he looks like Yosemite Sam.

The Southern colonel's car horn plays the opening notes to "Dixie."

Chronologically, this episode must take place earlier than Season 6's "Grampa vs. Sexual Inadequacy" (2F07), since Homer's childhood farmhouse was burned down in that episode.

There's a skeleton of a farm animal standing in front of the farmhouse.

The country store sign: Sneed's Feed & Seed/Formerly Chuck's.

Things Homer's planting, seen in his hand: various seeds, a corn kernel, a gummy bear, and a piece of candy corn.

The farmer using an elephant to measure the height of his stalks of corn is in reference to a song in the musical *Oklahoma,* wherein "the corn is as high as an elephant's eye."

Chief Wiggum refers to Homer as "stranger" even though they have known each other for a long time.

The tobacco company's limousine has a sign on the lavatory door encouraging smoking, instead of a "No Smoking" sign.

Ralph Wiggum, after tasting ToMacco: "Oh, Daddy! This tastes like Grandma!"

Start Making Sense:

Lisa: *You're about to launch a terrible evil on the world! You've got to destroy this plant!*
Homer: *I know, honey. But what can I do as an individual? I wouldn't know where to begin.*
Lisa: *Just burn that plant right now and end this madness.*
Homer: *I wish I could make a difference, Lisa, but I'm just one man.*
Lisa: *Grrrr!*
Homer: *I agree, but how?!*

Movie Moment:

The ToMacco-craving animals trying to break into the barricaded farmhouse recall the zombies from George Romero's *Night of the Living Dead.*

GRUNT)

Episode AABF19
Original Airdate: 11/07/99
Writer: Ian Maxtone-Graham
Director: Bob Anderson
Executive Producer: Mike Scully
Guest Voices: The B-52's (singing "Glove Slap")

I DID NOT WIN THE NOBEL FART PRIZE
I DID NOT WIN THE NOBEL FART PRIZE
I DID NOT WIN THE NO... FART PRIZE

Field of Gleams:

Homer: *Well, Marge, have you ever seen a field glow like that?*
Marge: *It's eerily beautiful, but are you sure this is safe?*
Homer: *Of course not. But you know something? Sometimes you have to break the rules to free your heart.*
Marge: *You got that from a movie poster.*
Homer: *Well, when there's nothing left to believe in, believe in hope.*
Marge: *Where'd you get that?*
Homer: *From the producers of Waiting to Exhale.*
Marge: *Is that plutonium on your gums?*
Homer: *Shut up and kiss me.*

TV Moment:

The Simpsons farming montage music is the theme song from "Green Acres."

Homer vs. Local Yokels:

Farmer 1: *Well, well. Look at the city slicker pulling up in his fancy German car.*
Homer: *This car was made in Guatemala.*
Farmer 2: *Well, pardon us, Mr. Gucci loafers.*
Homer: *I bought these shoes from a hobo!*
Farmer 1: *Well la-dee-da, Mr. Park Avenue manicure.*
Homer: *(admiring his hand) I'm sorry. I believe in good grooming.*

At Homer's Roadside ToMacco Stand:

Lisa: *ToMacco? That's pretty clever, Dad. I mean, for a product that's evil and deadly.*
Homer: *Aw, thanks honey.*
Marge: *Well, I'm not crazy about the plutonium or nicotine, but it is very nice to see Bart eating his vegetables.*

The Fruits of Their Labor:

Bart: *Bleh! Tastes like cigarette butts.*
(Marge takes the ToMacco from Bart and inspects it.)
Marge: *That's odd. The outside looks like a tomato, but the inside is brown.*
Lisa: *Maybe the tomato seeds crossbred with the tobacco seeds.*
Homer: *Oh, great! I've got a field full of mutants.*
Bart: *Gimme!* (Bart takes it back from Marge.) *I want more.*
Lisa: *I thought you said it tasted terrible.*
Bart: *It does.* (Bart drops a ToMacco and grinds it into the ground like a cigarette butt.) *But it's smooth and mild.* (He grabs another off a plant.) *And refreshingly addictive.*
Homer: *Addictive, eh?*

Homer: *Oh, it's been a month. Why won't anything grow?*
Marge: *Maybe it needs more fertilizer.*
Homer: *I'm only one man, Marge.*

THE SOUTHERN COLONEL

Profession:
Experienced duelist

Group affiliation:
Charleston Dueling Society

Usually wears:
A dueling blouse

Mode of transportation:
A motor home, complete with all the amenities, a Confederate flag, and his beautiful wife

Never seen without:
Cigars in his breast pocket and a pocket watch

Passes time by:
Polishing his pistol and barbecuing

Bumper-stickers of choice:
"I [heart with three bullet holes in it] Dueling" and "Honk If You Demand Satisfaction"

Only Apparent Weakness:
Mincemeat pies

WHERE ARE MY MANNERS?

LENNY

Place of employment:
The Springfield Nuclear Power Plant, Sector 7-G

Job security:
He is the only one who knows how to un-jam the rod bottom dissociator

Surprising fact:
He holds a master's degree in Nuclear Physics

Doubts:
That eggs actually raise the level of serum cholesterol in the human bloodstream

Teaches:
A course on tobacco spitting at the Adult Learning Annex

Dislikes:
Women working at the plant because he can't spit on the floor.

Stonecutter member number:
12

> WHAT I DID, I DID BECAUSE OF ALCOHOL AND ANGER.

HELLO GUTTER,

Homer claims to have little time for Maggie because he is late for work, but he does have time to solve a puzzle on the back of a cereal box. That afternoon, Homer misses a tea party with Maggie and tells Marge he has to work late, when he is really going bowling. Marge and the kids find out the truth when a live news broadcast reports that Homer is just about to bowl a perfect game. The family appears at the bowling alley just in time to see Homer score 300 as a cheering crowd looks on.

Basking in the glow of celebrity, Homer enjoys making personal and TV appearances. His fame quickly begins to fade, although he is not aware of it. Not until a TV tabloid show spells it out for him does Homer realize his days of stardom are over. Homer becomes depressed, and despite the help of others, he cannot pull himself out of his funk. He goes to the top of a tall building and contemplates suicide. Before he can jump, another jumper waiting in line pushes him over the edge.

Otto is bungee-jumping off the same building, and Homer, grabbing on to him, is saved. After his near-death experience, Homer has an epiphany: he needs to dedicate his life to his children. After unsuccessfully trying to lavish his attention on Bart and Lisa, Homer focuses on the neglected Maggie. When Homer pays so much attention to Maggie, however, it frightens her. Homer begins to think there is no hope for their relationship until Maggie heroically saves him from drowning. Realizing that Maggie loves him, he spends more time with her. He takes Maggie bowling, and proving she is her father's daughter, she scores a perfect 300. Homer, however, alters her score so that she does not beat him.

SHOW HIGHLIGHTS

Springfield's Finest:
Wiggum: *All right, smart guy, where's the fire?*
Homer: *Over there.*
(He points at the flame-engulfed police station.)
Wiggum: *Okay, you just bought yourself a 317: pointing out police stupidity.*

Finding the Loophole:
Burns: *Turn around, Simpson.*
Homer: *No! I can't get in trouble if I can't see you.*
Smithers: *I'm afraid he's got us, sir.*

Music Moment:
Homer wanders the streets of Springfield contemplating suicide and singing "The End" by The Doors.

Mad About Lenny:
Homer: (on the phone) *The cooling tank just blew, and they're taking Lenny to the hospital.*
Marge: *Oh, no! Not Lenny! Not Lenny!*
Homer: *Yes, I'm going to have to work late instead of seeing you and the kids, which is what I really want.*
Marge: *Okay, sure.* (hanging up) *Kids, turn off the TV. I have some bad news about Lenny.*
Bart and Lisa: *Not Lenny!*

Perfect Idiot:
Lenny: *Hey, Homer, that's four strikes in a row! You've got a perfect game going.*
Homer: *Really?*
Carl: *Careful what you say, Lenny. You'll jinx it.*
Lenny: *Oh, right, sorry.* (Homer is just about to throw his ball.) *Miss! Miss!* (Homer frowns at him.) *Sorry, I was calling the waitress.* (To waitress while holding up a banana split) *Ah, this split you sold me is making me choke.*
Homer: (angry) *Lenny...*
Lenny: *What? I paid seven-ten for this split.*
Carl: *Will ya at least call it a banana split, you dumbwad?*
Lenny: *Hey, spare me your gutter mouth.*

"Kids, today we have to talk about Krusty Brand Chew Goo Gum-like Substance. We knew it contained spider eggs, but the Hantavirus? We-hell, that really came out of left field."

Safety First:
Brockman: (on TV) *This is Kent Brockman, live from Barney's Bowl-a-rama, where local pinhead Homer Simpson is on the verge of a perfect game.*
Lisa: *Hey! There was no accident at the plant. Dad just wanted to go bowling.*
Marge: *He shouldn't have deceived me, but I'm just so relieved Lenny's okay.*

Q&A Session:
Homer: *Any questions?* (Milhouse raises his hand.) *Yes, Bart's weird friend.*
Milhouse: *Will you be my dad?*
Homer: *Heh, heh, heh! You've got a father. He's just a dud. Next question. Yes, the girl Bart has a crush on.*
Bart: *Ohhh.*
Terri: *Do you think I could grow up to be a doctor?*
Homer: *Hey, this was supposed to be about me. Now, any other questions? Pumpkin Face? Headgear? Chicken pox? Smelly? Lazy eye?* (calling on Bart) *Spiky head? Okay, class dismissed. Rock on!*

Flavor of the Month:
Penn: *Now, before my partner Teller hits the shark-infested water, I'll need to borrow someone's crossbow. I only need one! Now, to save my partner's life, I'll need complete--*
Homer: *Hello, everybody! Did somebody say, "a perfect game"?*
Penn: *You idiot! You'll ruin everything!*
Homer: *I'm doing a walk-on. It's a show-business thing. So, how you all doing? Let's see, what's in the news today?*
Teller: *Will you shut up?*
Homer: *Hey, I thought you never talked.*
Teller: (worried) *Uh, I didn't mean to. It just slipped out. Oh, God! Now, Penn's going to beat me.*

Letting Him Down Easily:
Lisa: *Dad, what she's saying is, you've had your moment in the sun, and now it's time for you to gracefully step aside.*
Homer: *Lisa, I know what's going on here. They did it to Jesus, and now they're doing it to me.*
Marge: *Are you comparing yourself to our Lord?*
Homer: *Well, in bowling ability.*

Halfhearted Help:
Homer: *I can't believe it, Moe. The greatest feat of my life is already forgotten.*
Moe: *Geez, Homer, I never seen you so depressed. As your life partner, I'm very worried.*
Homer: *Save your tears, Moe. Save 'em in a shot glass for someone who still has a shred of hope.*
Moe: *A shred of what? I'm sorry, I was counting the cocktail radishes.*

"Children, today's local hero is Homer Simpson. Mr. Simpson bowled a perfect game without the aid of steroids, crack, angel dust, or the other narcotics that are synonymous with pro bowling."

HELLO FADDER

Episode BABF02
Original Airdate: 11/14/99
Writer: Al Jean
Director: Mike B. Anderson
Executive Producer: Mike Scully

Guest Voices: Ron Howard as Himself, Penn Jillette as Himself, Pat O'Brien as Himself, Nancy O'Dell as Herself, and Teller as Himself

Homer contemplates suicide: **"Well, world, this is it. You know, I always thought you'd die before me."**

Turning Over a New Leaf:

Homer: *That's it! Kids are the answer. I'll dedicate my life to my children.*
Ron Howard: *Really? You have children? Aw, well, look.* (holding up some money to Homer) *Here's some money.*
Homer: *No. I don't want your pity or your money.* (He takes the money and puts it in his pocket.)
Ron Howard: *Usually when you say that, you give the money back.*
Homer: *I do what, now?*
Ron Howard: *Yoink!*
(He takes back the money and drives away.)

Nelson Knows Best:

Homer: *Listen, boy. I was wondering if you could use a little more fatherly attention?*
Bart: *No need, Dad. Over the years, I've learned to find father figures wherever I can...construction workers, the Internet...and Nelson here.*
(Nelson is revealed sitting in an armchair with a newspaper in hand, pipe in his mouth, wearing a robe, ascot, and slippers.)
Nelson: *If you tie a string around your finger real tight, you can make it turn purple.*
Homer: *I can see I'm not needed here.*

Homer entertains Maggie: **"I'm Homey-Womey, the Teletubby... and I'm all man, in case you heard otherwise. Let's see what's on tummy-vision!"**

Hard to Swallow:

Dr. Hibbert: *Mr. Simpson, you're going to be fine, although you do seem to have swallowed a number of shark eggs.*
Homer: *Actually, that was before I went in the ocean.*
Dr. Hibbert: *Well, I don't want to pry into your personal life...*
Homer: *Then don't.*

Movie Moment:

When Homer bowls his perfect game, the music, the slow-motion action, the photographers' flash bulbs, the shower of sparks, and the explosive chain reaction of pins falling throughout the bowling alley recall the climax of Robert Redford's baseball movie *The Natural*.

THE STUFF YOU MAY HAVE MISSED

Waldo from the *Where's Waldo?* books appears outside the Simpsons' kitchen window while Homer looks for him on the back of a cereal box. Waldo made a previous appearance in Ned Flanders's bomb shelter in "Bart's Comet" (2F11). Bart also reads a *Where's Waldo?* book in "Treehouse of Horror III" (9F04).

After Homer pulls Mr. Burns's teeth out, another pair emerges, accompanied by the sound of a cash register.

Jacques and Lurleen Lumpkin can be seen walking together in the background when Carl asks Homer what initials he wants on the scoreboard at Barney's Bowl-a-rama.

When Marge thinks Lenny's been hurt, she makes a shrine to him that includes: a framed photo, a rose, and a candle. She also embroiders two needlepoint samplers saying "Get Well Lenny" and "We Love You, Lenny."

Written on Homer's to-do list: Before I Die I Want To: 1) End Crime & Injustice, 2) Bowl a Perfect Game, 3) See Stevie Nicks Naked. (There are already three check marks next to #3.)

Mrs. Krabappel is seen reading *Fear of Flying* (Teacher's Edition).

Celebrities in the "Springfield Squares": Rainier Wolfcastle, Krusty, Itchy & Scratchy (sharing a square), Bumblebee Man, Homer Simpson (in the center square), Princess Kashmir, Sideshow Mel, Ron Howard, and the Capital City Goofball. The host is Kent Brockman. The contestants are Agnes Skinner and Disco Stu.

When Homer and Otto fall through the manhole, they pass through levels inhabited by Morlocks from H. G. Wells's *The Time Machine*, CHUDs, and Mole People led by Hans Moleman.

The sign at the Springfield YMCA reads, "Daddy and Me Swimming Class—No Stepfathers." Kirk and Milhouse Van Houten are in attendance.

EIGHT MISBEHAVIN'

While shopping, the Simpsons run into Apu and Manjula, and Manjula enjoys playing with Maggie. Manjula and Apu decide to have a child but have trouble conceiving. With Homer's encouragement and the help of several fertility drugs, Manjula gives birth—to octuplets.

At first, Apu and Manjula receive several corporate gifts to help with the babies, but the gifts are all quickly taken away when nine children are born to a couple in Shelbyville. Raising eight children proves to be very difficult for the Nahasapeemapetilons. They get little sleep, and it costs them a fortune. The owner of the Springfield Zoo, Larry Kidkill, offers to help them raise the children if they sign a contract allowing him to put the babies on display at the zoo. They reluctantly agree but soon discover that Kidkill intends to exploit the children by putting them on display in a show called "Octopia" several times a day.

Kidkill will not allow the frantic parents to break the contract, so Apu recruits Homer to help him steal the babies back. They successfully retrieve the kids, but are followed to the Simpsons' house by Kidkill and his theater toughs. Homer makes a deal with Kidkill and replaces the octuplets himself, performing at the zoo with Butch Patrick and several poisonous cobras.

SHOW HIGHLIGHTS

Oh, She of Little Faith:
Apu: *Hello, Simpsons!*
Homer: *Hey, Apu, Manjula. You guys are still married?*
Apu: *Oh, yes, sir! Quite happily.*
Homer: *Pay up, Marge.*

Snap Decision:
Marge: *So, have you two thought about kids?*
Apu: *Well, sure we have. But the decision to have a child is not to be made lightly.* (Manjula blows on Maggie's belly.) *On the other hand, monkey see, monkey do.*

The Joys of Parenthood:
Homer: *Kids are the best, Apu. You can teach them to hate the things you hate. And they practically raise themselves, what with the Internet and all.*
Apu: *Well, perhaps it is time. I have noticed that this country is dangerously underpopulated.*

Love and Death:
Manjula: *Are you sure you want a child, Apu?*
Apu: *You know, I do. I mean, there comes a time in a man's life when he asks himself, "Who will float my corpse down the Ganges?"*
Manjula: *Oh, Apu! Take me now!* (She kisses him and turns out the light.)
Apu: *Oh, Calcutta!*

Cool Customer:
Homer: *Hey, Apu! Sitting in the ice cream cooler, eh?*
Apu: *By chilling my loins, I increase the chances of impregnating my wife.*
Homer: *Whoa-ho! Too much information! Thanks for the mental picture. Why don't you tell us what you really think?*
Apu: *Just stop spouting those hackneyed quips.*
Homer: *Could you be any more...hello?! Heh, heh, heh, heh...look, just give me some ice cream.* (Apu pulls one up between his legs.) *Ummm...how about one not touching your ass?*

Right Before Her Water Breaks:
Manjula: *Apu, do you still find me attractive?*
Apu: *Of course I do, sweetheart. You are beautiful, and silky, and manageable.*
Manjula: *You are reading that off a conditioner bottle!*

The Truth Comes Out:
Apu: *How did we get eight?*
Manjula: *Apu, I must confess. When we were having trouble conceiving, I took fertility drugs.*
Apu: *Ooh. I, too, am afraid I'm guilty of monkeying with nature. I slipped fertility drugs into your breakfast Squishee.*
Hibbert: *Mm-hmm. Well, that would only account for quintuplets. Did anyone else slip this woman fertility drugs?*
(Homer, Marge, and Bart raise their hands.)
Homer: *Mine tasted like strawberries.* (He eats a fertility pill.) *Mmm...ovulicious!*

Apu grills Butch Patrick on "The Munsters": **"If your mother was a vampire and your father was a Frankenstein, how come you are a werewolf?"**

The Stars of "Octopia":
Animal, Dazzle, Punchline, The Baron, and the rest.

Love/Eight Relationship:
Ned Flanders: *Well, morning, Apu! How are the little blessings?*
Apu: *Oh, they're a ravenous swarm of locusts. Just eating and screaming and grabbing and poking and pulling and drooling, and two have cradle rash! How do you get cradle rash when you sleep in a suitcase?*
Flanders: *They can be a handful...of joy!*
Apu: *Shut up!*
Flanders: *They'll fill your life with--*
Apu: *Shut up!*
Flanders: *Can't put a price on a miracle!*
Apu: *I can't believe you don't shut up!*

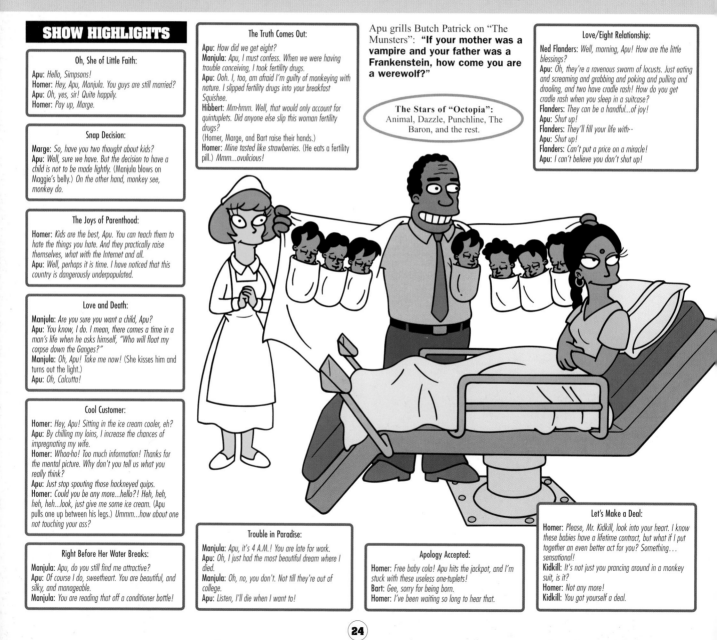

Trouble in Paradise:
Manjula: *Apu, it's 4 A.M.! You are late for work.*
Apu: *Oh, I just had the most beautiful dream where I died.*
Manjula: *Oh, no, you don't. Not till they're out of college.*
Apu: *Listen, I'll die when I want to!*

Apology Accepted:
Homer: *Free baby cola! Apu hits the jackpot, and I'm stuck with these useless one-tuplets!*
Bart: *Gee, sorry for being born.*
Homer: *I've been waiting so long to hear that.*

Let's Make a Deal:
Homer: *Please, Mr. Kidkill, look into your heart. I know these babies have a lifetime contract, but what if I put together an even better act for you? Something... sensational!*
Kidkill: *It's not just you prancing around in a monkey suit, is it?*
Homer: *Not any more!*
Kidkill: *You got yourself a deal.*

Episode BABF03
Original Airdate: 11/21/99
Writer: Matt Selman
Director: Steven Dean Moore
Executive Producer: Mike Scully
Guest Voices: Jan Hooks as Manjula, Butch Patrick as Himself

Musical Moments:

The music heard during "Octopia" includes: Guns N' Roses's "Welcome to the Jungle," Richard Wagner's "Flight of the Valkyries," and John Mellencamp's "R.O.C.K. in the U.S.A."

Homer performs his zoo act to "Highway to the Danger Zone" by Kenny Loggins.

The names of the eight new Nahasapeemapetilons:
Poonam, Sashi, Pria, Uma, Anoop, Sandeep, Nabendu, and Gheet.

Another Type of Job Security:

Marge: Apu told me all eight babies have colic, although he thinks one or two might just be going along with the crowd.
Homer: Eight kids, hmm...I'm sterile, right, baby doll?
Marge: Yes, dear. From the nuclear plant.
Homer: Beautiful!

Trying to Get the Babies Back:

Manjula: How could you do this to our children?
Kidkill: I know. The lighting cues were a mess. Don't worry, the guy's been fired.
Apu: Our babies are not circus freaks. We're taking them home now.
Kidkill: Hold on, Alpo. (He holds up a contract.) We got a contract.
Apu: Not any more! (He tries to tear up the contract.) Laminated! You monster!

THE STUFF YOU MAY HAVE MISSED

The mega-store SHØP is a parody of real-life Swedish emporium STØR.

Spoiled brat Gavin and his mom are in the SHØP food court. These characters were first seen in "Marge Be Not Proud" (3F07).

Apu and Manjula consult the Pee 'n' See Home Pregnancy Test.

When he watches Apu and Manjula perform the script he wrote, Homer is mouthing the words.

Apu and Manjula's favorite baby, Gheet, resembles Apu's brother, Sanjay.

The *Springfield Shopper* newspaper with the story of the birth of eight babies has the headline "NAHASAPEEMAPETILAN-TASTIC!"

The "Pepsi B" that Apu and Manjula get from the corporate sponsors is "for export only."

There is a picture of Babar the elephant in a Nehru jacket on the wall of the octuplets' room.

The Kwik-E-Mart doesn't accept checks, credit cards, or food stamps.

The Nahasapeemapetilons use "Wuvs" disposable diapers.

"Octopia" replaced "The Prairie Dog Experience" at the zoo.

The octuplets are displayed very much like the Canadian-born Dionne Quintuplets were at "Quintland" in the 1930s.

The sign above the octuplets' exhibit reads, "Octo Sapiens/From the Collection of Apu and Manjula."

Homer and Apu jimmy open a door that says "Danger/Newborns."

Two of Apu's pet names for Manjula are "Curry Face" and "Chutney Butt."

The set of Homer's sensational show at the zoo is inspired by the "Hansel and Gretel" Viewmaster slides he looks at earlier in the episode.

LARRY KIDKILL

Profession:
Entrepreneurial owner of the Springfield Zoo

Dares you:
To look at a kangaroo and not laugh

Mispronounces:
"Apu" and "Nahasapeemapetilon"

Seen with:
Bullying theater people and a former child star in short pants

The "pros" of him running a show with babies:
Creativity, enthusiasm, and concern about the humidity

The "cons":
His last name

LADIES AND GENTLEMEN, GET READY FOR THE EIGHT WONDERS OF THE THIRD WORLD!

Guest Voice:
Garry Marshall as Larry Kidkill

MEATHOOK AND RAMROD

Biker Affiliation:
Hell's Satans, Bakersfield Chapter

Weapons of choice:
Switchblades and switchforks

Favorite activities:
Fightin', dancin', tattooin', droolin', spittin', scratchin', and workin' on their hogs

Their reason for being so messy:
It's part of being a low-life

Diet usually consists of:
Rancid filth they find in dumpsters

Method of conflict resolution:
The Circle of Death

> I'D KILL FOR SOME WAFFLES.

> HE HAS. REMEMBER THE IHOP IN OAKLAND?

TAKE MY WIFE,

The Simpsons see a TV commercial for a new '50s-style diner and decide to go there for dinner. While dining, Homer and Marge enter and win a rock 'n' roll dance contest. Homer is extremely happy to get the prize—a vintage 1955 Harley-Davidson motorcycle. Unfortunately, Homer doesn't know how to ride a motorcycle. With a little tutelage from Bart, Homer is soon riding his "hog" everywhere—into the school, the church, and the bedroom.

Homer starts his own biker gang, the Hell's Satans. The use of the name irks a real motorcycle gang by the same name, and they invade the Simpsons' home. While the unruly gang inhabits and trashes the house, Marge takes very good care of them. When they finally leave, they take Marge with them.

Homer sets out on his motorcycle to retrieve Marge. Meanwhile, Marge is proving to be a good influence on the gang. She convinces them to find gainful employment and to give up violence. However, Homer shows up and starts a fight. Homer goes up against the leader of the bikers, wins Marge back, and takes her home.

SHOW HIGHLIGHTS

Feeling Nostalgic:
Wolfguy Jack: (on TV) *Ay! Remember the '50s? Remember television, Coca-Cola, and Dick Clark?*
Homer: *Gasp! I remember television!*
Wolfguy Jack: *Come join me, Wolfguy Jack, at Greaser's Cafe, where it's 1955 every day of the year, baby.*
Disclaimer Announcer: *Actual year may vary. Consult calendar for current year.*

Two Menaces to Society:
Bart: *Dennis the Menace?*
Jay North: *Yes, I was America's Bad Boy. I once hid my dad's hat. Ha-ha-ha-ha-ha-ha-ha-ha-ha!*
Bart: (unimpressed) *Uh-huh.*
Jay North: *And another time, I accidentally stepped in Mr. Wilson's flower bed. Ha-ha-ha! That was a two-part episode. Ha-ha-ha-ha-ha-ha-ha-ha-ha-ha!*
Bart: *I have to go.*

At Greaser's Cafe:
Wolfguy Jack: *Okay, is everybody ready for our nightly dance contest?*
Marge: *Dancing!?*
Homer: *Oh, no, you're not getting me on that dance floor. Don't try and make me. If I have to get a divorce, I will.*
Wolfguy Jack: *Our grand prize tonight is a vintage 1955 Harley-Davidson motorcycle.*
Homer: *Gasp! Oh! I need a dance partner! Ah...eh...*(looking around and then at Marge) *What about you?*
Marge: *Okay, Daddy-o.*

On the Greaser's Cafe menu:
Allen Ginsbergers, Un-American Cheese Sandwiches, and Polio Dogs.

Homer Drops Off Bart at School:
Nelson: *Sweet hog, Mr. Simpson.*
Homer: *Remember to rebel against authority, kids!* (Homer peels out.)
Principal Skinner: (over the loudspeaker) *Don't listen to him, children.*
Milhouse: *But we already did! Now I can't get it out of my head!* (Nelson clobbers Milhouse with a book.)
Mrs. Krabappel: *Thank you, Nelson.*

"The Tuesday Morning Movie":
Mother: *Oh, I don't know what's come over Jimmy. He won't do his homework, he only salutes the flag with one finger, and he comes home every night with other people's blood on his shirt.*
Father: *He's a rebel, I tell you...a rebel without a cause! Just like that boy in that popular movie we saw.*

****

Shopkeeper: *Look what you've done! You've ruined the display!*
Cop: *When will you teens learn to be uncool like everyone else?*
Jimmy: *Never, pops. Yeah, you can arrest me, but you'll never defeat the Cobras. Nothing can defeat a motorcycle gang!*

The First Meeting of Hell's Satans:
Ned: *I move we reconsider our club name. Make it something a little less blasphemous. After all, heh, heh, we don't want to go to Hell.*
Lenny: *How about the Devil's Pals?*
Ned: *N-no...see--*
Moe: *The Christ Punchers.*
Ned: *The Christ...I don't think you understand my objection.*

Musical Moment:
NRBQ plays several of their own songs ("Me and the Boys," "Want You to Feel Good, Too"), covers the '50s classic "Lucille" and "The Simpsons Theme" on the end credits, and introduces an original song (Homer's "Mayonnaise and Marmalade" motorcycle song).

Something's Missing:
Bart: *Hey, where's the food?*
Lisa: *And why aren't I at school?*
Homer: *Yeah, someone really dropped the ball here. Marge? Marge?*
Lisa: *Dad, there's a note on the back of your head.*
Homer: *Really? Read it.*
(Bart removes the note and sticks the push pin back into Homer's head.)
Bart: *"Thanks for letting us crash in your pad. We had a very nice time."*
Homer: *Aw, that's sweet.*
Bart: *"P.S. We've taken your old lady."*
Homer: *D'oh!*

Homer Gangs Up on Lisa:
Homer: *A gang...that's the answer!*
Lisa: *Answer to what?*
Homer: *Hey, don't make me hassle you, Lisa.*

Don't Tease the Man:
Homer: (on the phone) *Hello, police? Can you send a SWAT team to 742 Evergreen--*
Chief Wiggum: *Forget it, Simpson. Those pig noises you made really hurt my feelings, looking like a pig as I do.*
Homer: *But you have so much inner beauty.*
Wiggum: *Well, be that as it may, the gang is wanted in eight other states and we have a little saying around here: "Let Michigan handle it."*

> "Marge, how did you get my jacket so clean? I've tried everything to get those blood and puke stains out. I've tried hitting 'em. I've tried yelling at 'em…"

Covering All His Bases:
Homer: *Now, don't worry. I'm gonna search high and low for your mother. But, just in case I don't find her, I want you to contact this agency.* (He hands Lisa a piece of paper.)
Lisa: *"Korean Love Brides?"*
Homer: *I just don't want to be alone.*

Homer tells it the way he remembers it: **"...and those bikers saw the hard look in my eye...you know that hard look I get sometimes...and they ran away like schoolgirls, with their tails between their legs."**

On the Road:
Marge: *You know, there's more to life than boozing and roughhousing.*
Satans: (collectively) *Huh?*
Marge: *Haven't any of you ever had a dream?*
Ramrod: *Yeah, I had a dream! I was in this beautiful garden, pounding the crap out of a shopkeeper. Then--*
Marge: *No, no, I mean the dream of a good job, a loving family, and a home in the suburbs.*
Meathook: *Aw, man, to get all that you'd have to kill, like, fifty people.*

SLEAZE

Episode BABF05
Original Airdate: 11/28/99
Writer: John Swartzwelder
Director: Neil Affleck
Executive Producer: Mike Scully

Guest-Voices: Jan Hooks as Manjula,
and Jay North as Himself
Musical Guests: NRBQ as Themselves

Movie Moment:

Homer and Meathook's fight, using motorcycles as weapons, is reminiscent of many classic swashbuckling swordfights, most notably Errol Flynn and Basil Rathbone's duel in *The Adventures of Robin Hood.*

"My wife is not a doobie to be passed around! I took a sacred vow on my wedding day to bogart her forever."

Job Training:

Marge: *When you get a job interview, try not to call your employer a "punk"...or a "skank."*
Meathook: *Makes sense.*
Ramrod: *Oh, don't call them skanks.*
Meathook: *Uh...Miss Simpson? I killed my pencil.*
Marge: *Broke. You "broke" your pencil.*
Meathook: *I broke him.*

THE STUFF YOU MAY HAVE MISSED

Hans Moleman can be seen working behind the counter at Greaser's Cafe.

Herald Tribune headlines adorning the walls at Greaser's Cafe read: "Milkshakes Popular," "Beatles Unite!," "Study: Teens Rarely Pregnant," "Vietnam Situation Resolved," "Hula Hoop Mishap Kills 3," and "We All Agree: Conformity Is Best!"

Other couples in the Greaser's Cafe dance contest: Sara and Clancy Wiggum, Manjula and Apu Nahasapeemapetilon, and Edna Krabappel and Seymour Skinner.

Wolfguy Jack is a thinly-veiled caricature of the late radio great Wolfman Jack, and his girlfriend resembles Candy Clark's character, Debbie, from *American Graffiti.*

"Mental House Rock" bears a striking resemblance Elvis Presley's "Jailhouse Rock," and is performed by Hank Azaria as Johnny Bobby.

As he is learning to ride his Harley, Homer has training wheels on his motorcycle.

A sign outside the Kwik-E-Mart reads "Duff Beer Suitcase $12.95."

Homer gets his photographs printed in *Outlaw Biker* magazine.

One of the bikers uses a disconnected toilet bowl as a beer mug.

At the campgrounds, Meathook is seen reading a book titled, *Wasted Days.*

The name of the roadside biker bar Homer visits is "Poppa Wheelie's." There's a sign next to the front door that says "Ladies Puke Free!"

When the Hell's Satans bid Marge goodbye, Ramrod (played by Henry Winkler) calls her "Mrs. S." On "Happy Days," Winkler, as Arthur "Fonzie" Fonzarelli, often referred to Mrs. Cunningham as "Mrs. C."

This episode marks NRBQ's second episode of "The Simpsons." They covered The Beatles' "Can't Buy Me Love" in "The Old Man and the 'C' Student" (AABF16).

GRIFT OF THE MAGI

Bart cracks his coccyx while playing dress-up with Milhouse, and is temporarily confined to a wheelchair. When Bart returns to school he discovers that Springfield Elementary is not wheelchair accessible. Fat Tony intimidates Principal Skinner into hiring his company to install expensive wheelchair ramps. The poorly-constructed ramps collapse, the school goes broke, and Principal Skinner is forced to close its doors.

A corporation, Kids First Industries, takes over the school, and Springfield Elementary reopens with Kids First employees as teachers. The teachers do not seem concerned about educating the students. They only gather information from the children about toys. Lisa discovers that Kids First Industries is using the children's feedback to create a new electronic plush toy called Funzo. Then, Bart and Lisa learn that Funzo has been programmed to destroy other toys, eliminating its competition.

Lisa and Bart, with Homer's help, decide to save Christmas from the evil toy company by stealing and destroying all the Funzos in Springfield. They are caught in the act by security guard Gary Coleman and spend Christmas Eve with him, engaged in a philosophical conversation about the commercialization of Christmas. On Christmas morning, Mr. Burns, having been visited by three ghosts in the night, saves the school from Kids First Industries. A Christmas supper is then enjoyed by all.

SHOW HIGHLIGHTS

Going Stir-Crazy:
Bart: *Oh, I am so bored!*
Milhouse: *Oh, I can't wait till we're teenagers. Then we'll be happy.*

The Philosophy of Fat Tony:
"I don't get mad. I get stabby."

Toys for Tots:
Ralph: *Fun toys are fun!*
Teacher: *Well said, Ralph, but we're trying to come up with a name for a toy.*
Janey: *Mrs. Fun?*
Teacher: *Not bad.*
Ralph: *Fun?*
Teacher: *Ralph, there are no right or wrong answers, but if you don't pipe down, I'm giving you an "F."*
Ralph: *The before-teacher yelled at me, too.*

"And now a word from my God...our sponsor."

How the Homer Saved Christmas:
Homer: *So, who am I beating up?*
Lisa: *Nobody. You're just gonna break into everyone's house and steal their favorite toy.*
Bart: *Thus saving Christmas.*
Homer: *Now, let's see...this'll make three Christmases I saved, versus eight I ruined...two were kind of a draw...*

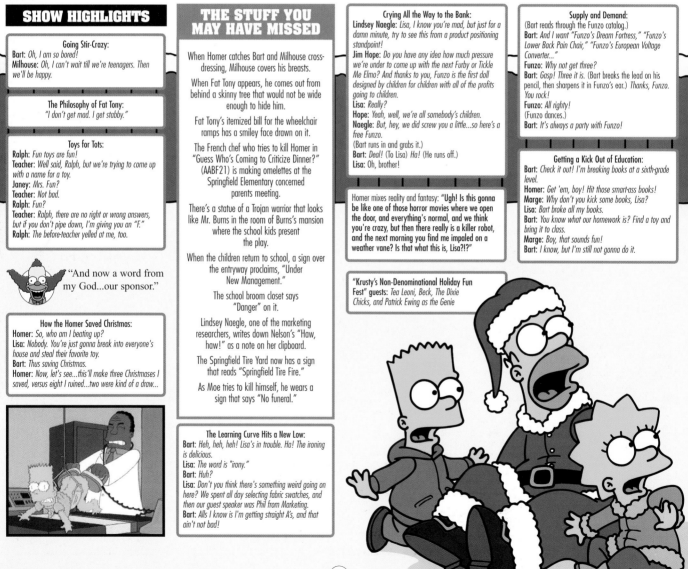

THE STUFF YOU MAY HAVE MISSED

When Homer catches Bart and Milhouse cross-dressing, Milhouse covers his breasts.

When Fat Tony appears, he comes out from behind a skinny tree that would not be wide enough to hide him.

Fat Tony's itemized bill for the wheelchair ramps has a smiley face drawn on it.

The French chef who tries to kill Homer in "Guess Who's Coming to Criticize Dinner?" (AABF21) is making omelettes at the Springfield Elementary concerned parents meeting.

There's a statue of a Trojan warrior that looks like Mr. Burns in the room of Burns's mansion where the school kids present the play.

When the children return to school, a sign over the entryway proclaims, "Under New Management."

The school broom closet says "Danger" on it.

Lindsey Naegle, one of the marketing researchers, writes down Nelson's "Haw, haw!" as a note on her clipboard.

The Springfield Tire Yard now has a sign that reads "Springfield Tire Fire."

As Moe tries to kill himself, he wears a sign that says "No funeral."

The Learning Curve Hits a New Low:
Bart: *Heh, heh, heh! Lisa's in trouble. Ha! The ironing is delicious.*
Lisa: *The word is "irony."*
Bart: *Huh?*
Lisa: *Don't you think there's something weird going on here? We spent all day selecting fabric swatches, and then our guest speaker was Phil from Marketing.*
Bart: *Alls I know is I'm getting straight A's, and that ain't not bad!*

Crying All the Way to the Bank:
Lindsey Naegle: *Lisa, I know you're mad, but just for a damn minute, try to see this from a product positioning standpoint!*
Jim Hope: *Do you have any idea how much pressure we're under to come up with the next Furby or Tickle Me Elmo? And thanks to you, Funzo is the first doll designed by children for children with all of the profits going to children.*
Lisa: *Really?*
Hope: *Yeah, well, we're all somebody's children.*
Naegle: *But, hey, we did screw you a little...so here's a free Funzo.*
(Bart runs in and grabs it.)
Bart: *Deal!* (To Lisa) *Ha!* (He runs off.)
Lisa: *Oh, brother!*

Homer mixes reality and fantasy: **"Ugh! Is this gonna be like one of those horror movies where we open the door, and everything's normal, and we think you're crazy, but then there really is a killer robot, and the next morning you find me impaled on a weather vane? Is that what this is, Lisa?!?"**

"Krusty's Non-Denominational Holiday Fun Fest" guests: *Tea Leoni, Beck, The Dixie Chicks, and Patrick Ewing as the Genie*

Supply and Demand:
(Bart reads through the Funzo catalog.)
Bart: *And I want "Funzo's Dream Fortress," "Funzo's Lower Back Pain Chair," "Funzo's European Voltage Converter..."*
Funzo: *Why not get three?*
Bart: *Gasp! Three it is.* (Bart breaks the lead on his pencil, then sharpens it in Funzo's ear.) *Thanks, Funzo. You rock!*
Funzo: *All righty!*
(Funzo dances.)
Bart: *It's always a party with Funzo!*

Getting a Kick Out of Education:
Bart: *Check it out! I'm breaking books at a sixth-grade level.*
Homer: *Get 'em, boy! Hit those smart-ass books!*
Marge: *Why don't you kick some books, Lisa?*
Lisa: *Bart broke all my books.*
Bart: *You know what our homework is? Find a toy and bring it to class.*
Marge: *Boy, that sounds fun!*
Bart: *I know, but I'm still not gonna do it.*

Episode BABF07
Original Airdate: 12/19/99
Writer: Tom Martin
Director: Matthew Nastuk
Executive Producer: Mike Scully

Guest Voices: Clarence Clemons as the Narrator, Gary Coleman as Himself, Joe Mantegna as Fat Tony, and Tim Robbins as Jim Hope

I WILL NOT SELL MY KIDNEY ON EBAY
I WILL NOT SELL MY KIDNEY ON EBAY
I WILL NOT SELL MY KIDNEY ON EBAY

FUNZO

Created by:
Kids First Industries, based on ideas by real-live kids

Guaranteed to:
Make playtime fun!
(Not a guarantee.)

Features:
Soft and cuddly with lots of firepower

Commercial tag-line:
"If you don't have Funzo you're nothin'!"

I SEE YOU! GIVE ME A HUG.

I HAVE A FLOWER FOR 'OU!

I'M VERY MAD AT 'OU!

Simpsons Cheer:
Narrator: *As for old Mr. Burns, he was visited by three ghosts during the night and agreed to fund the school with some money he found in his tuxedo pants.*
(Mr. Burns and Waylon Smithers arrive at the Simpson home with a basket of money.)
Burns: *Thank you, thank you! Humbug.*
(Moe is seen in his kitchen.)
Narrator: *While Moe, seeing what the world would be like if he had never been born, pulled his head out of the oven and replaced it with a plump Christmas goose.*
(Moe enters the Simpsons dining room and places a cooked goose on the table.)
Moe: *Yeah, Happy Holidays, there.*
All: *Merry Christmas, Moe!*
Moe: *Uh, listen, I kinda banged up that Jeep in the driveway.*
Gary Coleman: *Whatchu talkin' 'bout, Moe?*
(Everyone laughs, then Gary Coleman turns to the viewer.)
Gary Coleman: *Whatchu talkin' 'bout...everyone!*

What a Drag:
(Homer walks in on Bart and Milhouse dressed as girls.)
Homer: *What's going on?! And I want a non-gay explanation!*
Milhouse: *Uh...we're drunk. Really drunk.*
Homer: *Oh, thank God!*

Just Another Simpsons Christmas Eve:
Homer: (sings to the tune of "Tiny Bubbles") *Writhing Funzos in my sack, makes me happy, makes me hurt my back.*
Bart: *Just dump 'em in the fire, Dad.*
Lisa: *Yes, the madness ends here.*
Homer: *Ho! If I had a nickel for every time I've heard that.*

Movie Moments:
The burned Funzo that steps from the fire with its metal skeleton exposed is reminiscent of the robot in *Terminator*.

Moe seeing what the world would be like if he'd never been born is a reference to *It's a Wonderful Life*.

The last scene with Gary Coleman and Mr. Burns joining the Simpsons for Christmas dinner is a parody of the book and movie *A Christmas Carol*.

MR. SAKAMOTO

Occupation:
Acupressure Practitioner

Technique:
Always starts at the toes and works his way up

Specializes in:
Toe knuckle cracking, scalp massage, and follicle chopping

Manner:
Smooth, peaceful, relaxing, and yet strangely familiar to that of Disco Stu

MR. SAKAMOTO WANTS YOU TO BE COMFORTABLE WHILE HE DOES HIS THING.

Homer impulsively decides to take the family snow skiing on Mount Embolism. Everyone has an exciting time in the snow except for Marge, who opts to remain in the safety of the ski lodge. While she is there, a clock falls off a wall, fracturing her leg. On doctor's orders Marge must be hospitalized. Lisa confidently assures her mother that she will be able to take care of things at home, but Marge has her doubts.

Lisa is able to maintain the household briefly, but after a few days without Marge, the house becomes a total disaster. Homer and Bart will not help Lisa clean up. Lisa comes up with a wacky scheme with help from the ghost of Lucille Ball in order to get the boys to change their slovenly ways. She applies oatmeal and paint to their skin while they are asleep. In the morning, Homer and Bart are convinced they have leprosy.

Lisa's plan backfires. Instead of cleaning up their act, Homer and Bart seek help from Ned Flanders. Ned tells them he cannot take care of them, but he knows who can. When Marge comes home from the hospital, she and Lisa find out that Ned has arranged for Homer and Bart to be sent to a leper colony in Hawaii. Marge, Lisa, and Maggie rush to the islands to retrieve the boys and tell them they do not have leprosy. When they arrive, Homer and Bart have already discovered they do not have the disease, but they are willing to endure electric needle treatments to spend a vacation in paradise.

SHOW HIGHLIGHTS

Heigh-ho, Heave-ho:

Lisa: *What's in the box, Mom?*
Marge: *This box? Oh, nothing.*
Bart: *Are you sure? You sound nervous.*
Marge: *Well, anyone would be nervous with all the economic turmoil you read about in the...haaa!* (She rushes outside.)
Homer: *Get her! She's doing something!*

The Stuff That Almost Got Away:

Homer: *That was scary. We came this close to losing our spare Christmas-tree stand.* (To Marge) *You monster!*
Bart: *Look, there's the box for my Pitch Back. If I still had it, I could put it in here.*
Marge: *Oh! We'll never get rid of this useless junk!*
Homer: *Useless? This flashcube has two flashes left!*

On the Ski Slopes:

Ned: *Hi-diddly-ho, schuss-in-boots.*
Homer: *Gasp! Flanders?! That suit's a little revealing, isn't it?*
Ned: *Well, it allows for maximum mobility. Feels like I'm wearing nothing at all.*
(He shakes his booty.)
Homer: *Doy! Quit it! Must wash eyes!* (rubbing his eyes and beginning to slide rapidly downhill) *Duh-oh. Okay, don't panic. Remember what the instructor said.* (A thought bubble forms over his head with the ski instructor in it.)
Ski Instructor: *If you ever get into trouble, all you need to do is...*
(The image is replaced by one of Flanders in his ski suit and cuts tight to his wiggling bottom.)
Ned: *Feels like I'm wearing nothing at all...nothing at all...nothing at all.*
Homer: *Duuh! Stupid sexy Flanders!*

Otto's Snowboarding Class:

Dolph: *Whoa! Fat 540°!*
Nelson: *I'm gettin' aggro on this kicker!*
Bart: *Stomp that pickle revert!*
Otto: *Excellent! Your lingo is progressing nicely.*
Bart: *Can I go to the bathroom?*
Otto: *Uh, uh! Say it in "Snowboard."*
Bart: *Um...I gotta blast a dookie?*
Otto: *Dook on!*

Boogie Lodge:

Disco Stu: *Snow fox at five o'clock.* (He approaches Marge, dancing and singing.) *"Move it in, shove it out, Disco Lady." Is this seat taken?*
Marge: *Uh, I think that's an armrest.*
Disco Stu: *So, do you party?*
Marge: *You mean like a hats and noisemakers kind of party?*
Disco Stu: *Sure, baby, whatever your trip is. Disco Stu wants you to be comfortable while he does his thing.*
Marge: *Who's Disco Stu?*
Bart and Lisa: *Hey, Mom!*
Marge: *Hi, pumpkins.*
Disco Stu: *Kids?* (He retreats, singing.) *"Back away, not today, Disco Lady."*

Marge, right before the ski-lodge clock falls and breaks her leg: **"Skiing fanny-first into a crevasse isn't my idea of fun. The only risk I'm taking is running out of marshmallows."**

Housewife Down:

Dr. Hibbert: *Well, as you can see, it's a compound fracture. The leg must remain motionless—otherwise, a hunk of bone could zoom right to her brain. Ah-heh-heh-heh-heh!*
Marge: *I can't be in the hospital. Tomorrow's laundry day. And I've got to de-meat Lisa's baloney.*
Homer: *We'll be fine, honey. The main thing is for you to get better.*
Bart: *And don't worry. All the laundry and dirty dishes will be there when you get back.*

Marge's family-feeding instructions to Lisa: **"Just make sure your father eats all his meals over a tarp...but not the good tarp. I want you to get married on that someday."**

The Morning After Marge:

Homer: (yawn) *Morning.*
Lisa: *Dad! Where are your clothes?*
Homer: *I don't know.*
Lisa: *Don't tell me Mom dresses you.*
Homer: *I guess. Or one of her friends.*

A Clean Getaway:

Lisa: *Now, guys, leprosy thrives in filthy conditions. So your only chance is to clean up the house. I'll get you a couple of mops.*
Homer: *Mops? The cure sounds worse than the disease.*

BIG MOM

Episode BABF04
Original Airdate: 01/09/00
Writer: Carolyn Omine
Director: Mark Kirkland
Executive Producer: Mike Scully
Guest Voice: Elwood Edwards as the Virtual Doctor

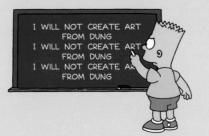

I WILL NOT CREATE ART
FROM DUNG
I WILL NOT CREATE ART
FROM DUNG
I WILL NOT CREATE AR
FROM DUNG

Little Miss Homemaker:

Lisa: *Oh! You're going to be late. Here are your lunches, and no trading your fruit for firecrackers.*
Homer: *Oh, but Lenny just got some bottle rockets.*
Lisa: *You stay away from Lenny. And where's your sweater, Bart?*
Bart: *It unraveled on a nail.*
Homer: *That's not true! He left it on the bus!*
Bart: *You're dead, squealer!*
Homer: *Aah! Lisa, help!*
Lisa: *Those boys of mine.*

"Why would God punish a kid? I mean, an American kid?"

Movie Moment:

When Bart and Homer are trying to get into the Flanders' house, crying, "Brains! Brains!," it is a reference to the zombie movie *Return of the Living Dead* (1985).

Mindless Spending:

Homer: *I got the groceries.*
Lisa: *Good! Maple soda? A cell phone full of candy?* (she pulls out a tube.) *Astronaut bread?*
Homer: *It's the bread of astronauts.*
Bart: (holding a box of cereal) *I didn't know Aerosmith made a cereal.*
Lisa: *Dad, I gave you a list.*
Homer: *Oh, yeah. Ho, ho, ho! You were way off.*
Lisa: *Hrmmm...*
Homer: (talking on the candy cell phone) *Hello, Lollipop Island? There's a little girl here who had too many sour balls.*
Lisa: *Hrmmm!*
(She walks off.)
Homer: *Anyway, where were we? Hello? Hello? They hung up!*

Appointment with the Virtual Doctor:

Lisa: (typing into a computer) *Let's see. Crusty sores?*
Homer: *Yes.*
Lisa: *Horrible wailing?*
Homer: *Yes, yes!*
Lisa: *Any exposure to unsanitary conditions?*
Bart: *Duh! We're pigs.*
Lisa: *Okay. And...diagnose.*
Virtual Doctor: *You've got...leprosy.*
Bart and Homer: *Leprosy?! Aaah!* (pointing at each other) *Unclean! Unclean!*

Who Let the Lepers Out?

Ned: *Maude! Come quick! The Simpsons are covered with cooties!*
Homer: *Help us!*
Bart: *We're diseased.*
Maude: *Oh, no! That's leprosy. Remember those scary lepers in Ben-Hur?*
Ned: (hurt) *You saw Ben-Hur without me?*
Maude: *We were broken-up then.*

An Una"peel"ing Snack:

Lisa: *Dad, Bart! I played a horrible trick on you, and I'm really sorry. You don't have leprosy. It's just oatmeal.*
Bart: *Yeah, we know.*
Homer: *I figured it out after I ate one of my chest sores.*

TV Moment:

Homer's fall off the ski jump bears a striking resemblance to the classic example of "the agony of defeat" on "The Wide World of Sports."

Livin' La Vida Leper:

Homer: *This place is a blast. All we have to do is endure two hours of blinding pain, then it's nothing but shopping and surfing.*
Bart: *Tonight, we're going to put our fake sores back on, then jump into Club Med and scare the normals.*

THE STUFF YOU MAY HAVE MISSED

The name of the newspaper Itchy reads is the *Toon Times*.

The different ski slopes on Mount Embolism are "The Widowmaker," "The Spinebuster," and "The Colostomizer."

At the ski lodge, Disco Stu appears to have been hitting on Edna Krabappel before Marge catches his eye.

When Lisa comes home from school, she finds Bart in the kitchen reading a racing form.

The Aerosmith cereal Homer buys is called "Sweet Emotions," which is named after their popular song "Sweet Emotion."

The "I Love Lucy" episode Homer and Bart watch guest-stars John Wayne.

The "Virtual Doctor" computer program is by the makers of "Dragon Quest" and "Sim Sandwich."

The Flanders' doorbell plays the hymn "Bringing in the Sheaves" by Knowles Shaw and George A. Minor.

Dr. Hibbert slices open Marge's cast with a pizza cutter.

After Ned Flanders loses his mustache, he wears a Band-Aid with happy faces on his upper lip.

The sign at the Molokai Leper Colony says "Welcome Leprous Knights of Columbus."

Easily Pleased:

Marge: *Molokai?*
Lisa: *You mean Hawaii?*
Ned: *Mmm-hmm. That's the one. They've got a top-notch leper colony there, so we shipped them right off. Ooh, cost us a bundle, too. I guess we'll have an imagination Christmas this year.*
Rod and Todd: *Yay! Imagination Christmas!*
Todd: (jumping up and down) *I got a pogo stick.*
Rod: (moving from side to side) *I got a hula hoop.*

Homer is invited to an alumni cocktail party at Springfield U. Once there, he is aggravated to learn that the party was a ploy to solicit donations for the university. To get even with the dean, Homer attempts to pull a prank with the help of his three former college roommates. However, the prank goes awry, and he gets a bucket glued to his head that refuses to come off. A short time later, the Simpsons happen upon a preacher's revival tent. Homer begs the preacher to use his power to get the bucket off, but the holy man cannot do it. The preacher asks Bart to try. Seemingly filled with God's power, Bart removes the bucket.

Convinced he now has the healing power of God, Bart plans to start his own revival. Brother Bart puts on a fantastic service in his backyard, but things turn deadly serious when Bart convinces Milhouse his poor vision is healed. Milhouse, believing he can see clearly, steps into the street and is run over by a truck that he mistakes for a dog. At the hospital, Bart attempts to heal his friend only to realize that he does not actually have any spiritual power.

Meanwhile, Homer builds a float for the homecoming game halftime show, using all of the flowers from Ned Flanders's garden. On the day of the big football game, he gets very drunk and accidentally runs over Springfield U's star place-kicker with the float. Fat Tony, having wagered heavily on Springfield U, threatens to hurt Homer if his team does not win. Homer begs Bart to use his healing power to help the injured player. Even though he does not believe he has any power, Bart tries and the "healed" place-kicker makes it back onto the field. In the final moments of the game, the place-kicker attempts a field goal that appears to miss, that is, until his now-dismembered and airborne leg gives it an additional nudge over the goal post. Springfield U wins the game, and Homer is saved.

SHOW HIGHLIGHTS

"I done spraint my elbie-bone, so it goes in the oppositty di-rection."

The Homecoming Invitation:
Marge: Hmm...there's a homecoming parade, a cocktail party...
Homer: And the big game between Springfield U and Springfield A&M. I hate Springfield U soooo much!
Lisa: You went to Springfield U. You hate A&M.
Homer: Soooo much!

Dorm Room Etiquette:
Homer: C'mon, baby! Let's matriculate.
Marge: Hee, hee, hee, hee! You college boys are only interested in one thing.
(Homer's former college roommates enter.)
Gary: Whoa! You're supposed to hang your necktie on the doorknob if you've got a girl in the room.
Doug: Or a ski hat if you've got a picture of a girl.

Revenge of the Nerds:
Homer: I'm beginning to think this alumni party was just a ruse to get our money.
Gary: That dean is going to get an indignant e-mail.
Doug: You should do it with bold, red letters.
Benjamin: My computer has 512 shades of red.

Passing the Bucket:
Dr. Hibbert: Hmm...I'm afraid it's hopeless. Beneath that bucket, he's more glue than man.
Marge: So he's stuck like this forever?
Dr. Hibbert: Oh, now don't fret. These days, the victims of comedy traumas, or "traumedies," can still lead rich, full lives.

Two Negatives Make an Affirmative:
Brother Faith: Oh, I feel it in my belly now, Springfield. Mmm. Can you feel the power?
Crowd: Yes!
Brother Faith: Do you want to be saved?
Crowd: Yes!
Brother Faith: Now, correct me if I'm incorrect, but was I told that it's untrue that people in Springfield have no faith? Was I not misinformed? (The crowd mumbles and looks puzzled.) The answer I'm looking for is, "yes."
Crowd: Yes!

Krusty K-Oed:
Brother Faith: What affliction be-plagues you, my friend?
(Krusty rasps an unintelligible whisper.) Come again?
Sideshow Mel: He paralyzed his vocal cords cramming too many "K" sounds into a punchline.
Brother Faith: (shaking his head and turning away) Oh mercy, well, I'm not sure there's anything I can do for...(whipping around and grabbing Krusty violently by the throat)
Krusty: Gaah!
Brother Faith: Feel the power! Release this clown. (He releases Krusty.)
Krusty: Have you gone completely farkachta?! I--Hey, I got my comedy K's back! (practicing) King Kong cold-cocked Kato Kaelin. Hey, you Gentiles are all right. (He kisses Brother Faith.)

O, Ye of Underachievement:
Bart: I've gotta know, how did you really get the bucket off my dad's head?
Brother Faith: Well, I didn't, son. You did. God gave you the power.
Bart: Really? Hmm. I would think that He would want to limit my power.
(Brother Faith reaches into Bart's pocket and removes his slingshot.)
Brother Faith: Oh, yes, Lord. When I was your age, I was a hell-raiser, too. My slingshot was my cross. But I saw the light and changed my wicked ways.
Bart: I figure I'll go for the life of sin, followed by a presto-chango deathbed repentance.
Brother Faith: Wow, that's a good angle. (looking heavenward) But that's not God's angle.

A Homer in Need:
Homer: Cure me! Cure me!
Brother Faith: Brother, I sense that you are feeling trapped and desperate.
Homer: Yeah! And I got a bucket on my head.

Pint-Size Preacher:
Bart: ...Then I said, "I have the power," and the bucket came off.
Ralph: Can you heal me? I can't breathe good, and it makes me sleepy.
Bart: I'll give it a whirl, Ralphie-boy. Devil...begone. (He smacks Ralph on the head.)
Ralph: Ow! (Coins fall from his nose.) My milk money! (His nose squirts milk.) And my milk.
Kids: Ew!

A Prophet Without Honor:
Lisa: Bart, I hope you don't believe your own hype.
Bart: Number of miracles performed by Bart: two. Number performed by Lisa: zero.
Lisa: How can you believe all this mumbo-jumbo? The bucket came off Dad's head because the bright lights heated it, causing the metal to expand.
Bart: Heat makes metal expand. Now who's talking mumbo-jumbo?

OFF

Episode BABF06
Original Airdate: 01/16/00
Writer: Frank Mula
Director: Nancy Kruse
Executive Producer: Mike Scully
Guest Voice: Joe Mantegna as Fat Tony

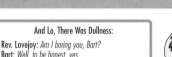

I WILL STOP PHONING IT IN
I WILL STOP PHONING IT IN
I WILL STOP PHONING IT IN
I WILL STOP PHONING IT IN
I WILL STOP PHONING IT IN
I WILL STOP PHONING IT IN

THE STUFF YOU MAY HAVE MISSED

There's an inscription on the Springfield U gate that says "If You Can Read This, You're Accepted."

This episode's Dean Peterson is not the same Dean Peterson Homer ran over during a prank in "Homer Goes to College" (1F02).

When the security men "computer-age" Homer's photo, he grows a beard, the fish he is holding turns to a skeleton, and his sweater gets holes.

In two episodes in a row, Homer sings "Aloha Oe": in "Little Big Mom" (BABF04), as he receives a treatment in the electric needle hut, and in this episode, while he shows Lisa his animated drawings of Moe doing the hula in a grass skirt.

Homer's sketch of his homecoming float depicts Godzilla being attacked with a knife by Superman.

In his sermon, Reverend Lovejoy claims the apostle Paul passed his letters like a chain letter from the Corinthians to the Thessalonians and to the Ephesians.

In keeping with his suggestion to Reverend Lovejoy of what constitutes a "fun" church service, Homer is eating chili-fries at Bart's revival.

Reverend Lovejoy's organist defects to Bart's revival.

Both Bart and Homer crowd surf during this episode: Bart, during his revival meeting, and Homer, as he is passed down to the field to retrieve his float for halftime.

The college football announcer is fashioned after Keith Jackson, who laces his commentary with colorful homespun sayings like "Whoa, Nellie!"

The Springfield U players are called the Nittany Tide, an amalgam of Penn State's Nittany Lions and University of Alabama's Crimson Tide.

Homer holds his tailgate barbecue inside the stadium.

Dr. Hibbert is the official team doctor at Springfield U.

Fat Tony has an ice pick with a laser-sight.

And Lo, There Was Dullness:
Rev. Lovejoy: *Am I boring you, Bart?*
Bart: *Well, to be honest, yes.*
Lovejoy: *(holding up the Bible) Hey, I'm doing the best with the material I have.*

Homer Builds a Float:
Ned: *Excuse me, neighbor. I couldn't help but notice, you picked pretty much all of my flowers!*
Homer: *Can't make a float without flowers.*
Ned: *Oh, sure enough. But did you have to salt the earth so nothing would ever grow again?*
Homer: *Heh-heh, heh-heh...eh-hey yeah.*

At the Hospital:
Bart: *This is my fault. I'm so sorry.*
Milhouse: *That's okay. You can just heal me again, right?*
Bart: *Well, I don't think I can.*
Milhouse: *Please? This cast is real itchy, and I tried to scratch and the fork got stuck in there and I think there was some food on the fork.*
(A trail of ants leads into the cast.)

Nepotistic News:
Kent Brockman: *Big game fever is reaching a fevered pitch as the fevered rivalry between Springfield U and Springfield A&M spreads like wild-fever.* (turns to crew) *This is writing?*
Writer: *I'm sorry, Uncle Kent. I lost my thesaurus.*
Kent: *"My thesaurus." You'll lose more than...In preparation for the big game, Springfield Stadium has caught additional-seating-capacity fever.* (crumbling his paper) *Grrr!*

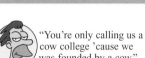

"You're only calling us a cow college 'cause we was founded by a cow."

Yo-Ho-Hum:
Captain McCallister: *You're the miracle boy with the healin' hands, arrrrn't ya?*
Bart: *Nah. I don't do that anymore.*
Capt. McCallister: *So I guess I'll have to see someone else about my cripplin' depression. Arr...arr.*
(The sea captain sadly walks away.)
Bart: *Wow, and I thought he had it all.*

Communication Error:
Doctor Hibbert: *Son, I'm afraid that leg is hanging by a thread.*
Anton Lubchenko: *Lubchenko must return to game!*
Hibbert: *Ah, heh, heh, heh! Your playing days are over, my friend. But, you can always fall back on your degree in...*(glances at the medical chart)*communications? Oh, dear Lord!*
Lubchenko: *I know! Is phony major.* (sobbing) *Lubchenko learn nothing. Nothing!*

Well-Heeled Healer:
Homer: *Poor guy. He lost his leg.*
Doctor Hibbert: *Oh, no, no. The fans will whoop it up with that leg tonight. You know, drink beer out of it and so on. But, it'll turn up in the morning, and I'll sew it back on.*
Marge: *Will that really work?*
Hibbert: *Well, I assume so...as long as I have Bart's healing powers.*
Bart: *Why won't anybody listen to me? I don't have any special powers. I am not a healer!*
Hibbert: *Fine. More money for me.*

BROTHER FAITH

Now appearing:
In revival tents across the country

Elements of a good sermon:
Flashing colored lights, dry ice, rock music, and the Holy Spirit

Heavenly insurance:
Spends his life helping people

Spiritual gifts:
Healing hands, snake handling, and dancing better than Jesus himself

TAKE THAT, SATAN!

Guest Voice:
Don Cheadle as Brother Faith

CORNELIUS CHAPMAN

Age:
108 years old

Most notable for being:
The oldest resident in Springfield…until his timely death

Famous firsts:
Built the first log cabin in Springfield and introduced the first toothbrush to its citizens

Near claims to fame:
Springfield's only basketball player for many years; helped people jump out of windows during the market crash of 1929; took one of several bullets intended for Huey Long

What he loves most about Springfield:
Cuddly infants, puppies, patriotism, and bluebirds

At the Springfield Pride Awards, the man who is supposed to receive an award for being the town's oldest citizen suddenly dies due to a kiss from presenter Britney Spears. Next in line is C. Montgomery Burns. Now that he is officially the eldest person in Springfield, Mr. Burns realizes that he has to take better care of himself. Waylon Smithers agrees and makes plans for his boss to visit the Mayo Clinic for a check-up. Homer is chosen to watch Mr. Burns's mansion while he is gone.

After the Simpsons move into the mansion, Homer acts as if he is a billionaire, despite Marge's constant reminders that he is not. Homer decides to throw a party for his friends at Moe's Tavern, but due to Springfield's Sunday blue laws, he is unable to obtain any alcohol before 2 P.M. Against Marge's orders, Homer invites all his friends on board Mr. Burns's yacht and sails out into international waters, where local laws do not apply.

At the Mayo Clinic, Mr. Burns is given several rigorous medical tests. The doctor tells him that he suffers from every disease known to man, plus a few new ones, but, luckily, his ailments all somehow keep each other in check. He leaves for home, thinking he's indestructible.

Meanwhile, Homer's yacht party is crashed by sea-faring pirates who rob all of the guests, trap them in a net, and cast them adrift in the ocean. Mr. Burns arrives home to find his mansion undamaged, thanks to a thorough cleaning by Marge and Lisa. Homer and his guests float home, and he tells Mr. Burns that pirates stole his yacht. Mr. Burns dismisses it as an unavoidable mishap. The Simpsons return home, and Homer once again faces the bleak reality of life without wealth.

SHOW HIGHLIGHTS

The Heart of Springfield:
Homer: *This is my year, Marge. Everyone knows I'm what makes this city great.*
Marge: *I don't know. There's a lot of buzz around Lenny.*

Award-Winning Humor:
Homer: *Oh, why won't anyone give me an award?*
Lisa: *You won a Grammy.*
Homer: *I mean an award that's worth winning.*
(He crosses his arms and the following legal disclaimer scrolls at the bottom of the screen:
"Mr. Simpson's opinion do not reflect those of the producers, who don't consider the Grammy an award at all.")

Music Moment:
The Coast Guard officer gets Homer's party going by sounding out the opening guitar riffs to the Doobie Brothers' "China Grove."

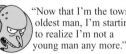 "Now that I'm the town's oldest man, I'm starting to realize I'm not a young man any more."

Useless Utensils:
Marge: *This all seems a little elaborate for Sloppy Joes. Hmm...I know what the other eleven forks are for, but what do you do with this one?*
(She holds up a long fork.)
Homer: *(in a mock-highbrow voice) Why, Marge, I believe you're supposed to scratch your ass with it.*
Marge: *Homer, watch your lang...(scratching her fanny with the fork) Oh, that's a lifesaver!*

Mr. Burns fills out a medical form:
"Let's see, 'Social Security number? Naught, naught, naught...naught, naught... naught, naught, naught, two. Damn Roosevelt. 'Cause of parents' death?' Got in my way."

Prime-Time Crime:
Marge: *Homer, did you jimmy open Mr. Burns's liquor cabinet?*
Homer: *"Jimmy" is such an ugly word, Marge, unless you're talking about Jimmy Smits. Rrrowl!*

 "Listen, I worked long and hard for this place, and no one's going to take it away from me. Not you! Not its rightful owner! Not anybody!"

Long Distance Runaround:
Homer: *Operator, get me Thailand. T...I...and so on.*
Marge: *Homer, who are you calling?*
Homer: *Everybody! I found Burnsie's address book. I called the New York Yankees and told them to bunt. Then I called the Queen of England and asked her how it was going! And then I...*
Marge: *Well, don't run up Mr. Burns's phone bill.*
Homer: *Just a second, Marge. (into phone) Hello, Thailand? How's everything on your end? Uh-huh. That's some language you got there. And you talk like that 24/7, huh?*

Party Provisions:
Homer: *Having a party, Moe. I'll need four kegs of your finest imported-sounding beer.*
Moe: *How 'bout Tuborg, the beer of Danish kings.*
Homer: *Mmm...danish.*

Captain Homer gives orders:
"Propellers! Netting! Turn! Left! Boat go there! Chips ahoy! Well done, Mr. Lenny, well done."

Going Buggy:
Burns: *Smithers, old chum, there's nothing like coming home with a clean bill of health. Oh, and sorry about your news.*
Smithers: *Thank you, sir.*
Burns: *Do they know how many eggs it laid in your brain?*
Smithers: *I prefer not to know. Frankly, one is too many.*

Diagnosis: Deadly:
Burns: *Well, Doc, I think I did pretty well on my tests. You may shake my hand if you like.*
Doctor: *Well, under the circumstances, I'd rather not.*
Burns: *Eh?*
Doctor: *Mr. Burns, I'm afraid you are the sickest man in the United States. You have everything.*
Burns: *You mean I have pneumonia?*
Doctor: *Yes.*
Burns: *Juvenile diabetes?*
Doctor: *Yes.*
Burns: *Hysterical pregnancy?*
Doctor: *Uh, a little bit, yes. You also have several diseases that have just been discovered...in you.*

The Mayo Clinic Doctor presents his findings: **"Here's the door to your body, see? And these are oversized novelty germs. That's influenza, that's bronchitis, and this cute little cuddle-bug is pancreatic cancer. Here's what happens when they all try to get through the door at once (à la Curly Howard). Woob-woob-woob-woob-woob-woob-woob! (à la Moe Howard). Move it, chowder head! We call it 'Three Stooges Syndrome.'"**

Melon-cholic Regrets:
Moe: *Aw, we're gonna die, and I never tasted cantaloupe.*
Krusty: *Eh, you didn't miss much. Honeydew is the money melon.*

The pirate captain covers his assets: **"And now we will cut you loose. For liability purposes it is the ocean that will kill you, not us."**

 "Whoo, they're poking every nook and cranny. Well, every cranny, anyway. So far, the nook is relatively...oh-nooooo it isn't!"

FAMILY

Episode BABF08
Original Airdate: 01/23/00
Writer: John Swartzwelder
Director: Michael Polcino
Executive Producer: Mike Scully
Guest Voice: Britney Spears as Herself

CLASS CLOWN IS NOT A
PAID POSITION
CLASS CLOWN IS NOT A
PAID POSITION
CLASS CLOWN IS NOT A
PAID POSITION

THE STUFF YOU MAY HAVE MISSED

The marquee at the Springfield Pride Awards reads "Please, No Rioting."

At the Springfield Pride Awards, Homer holds a pennant that says "Awards."

As Burns and Smithers talk about Homer always screwing things up, Homer can be seen on a power plant monitor, sawing into his T-437 Safety Command Console.

Smithers's suitcase is pink and round and looks like a Malibu Stacy accessory carrier.

The nude portrait that Marge painted of Mr. Burns in "Brush with Greatness" (7F18) hangs in a hallway of Burns's mansion.

The billboard next to the Mayo Clinic says "got tumor?"

The female doctor at the Mayo Clinic was seen previously as one of the Pharm Team reasearchers in "Brother's Little Helper" (AABF22).

Mr. Burns's automobile has a live fox shoulder-harness that growls as it is unlatched.

The Tyson vs. Secretariat Fight in International Waters poster at Moe's has the tag-line, "Slaughter in the Water."

Unlawful activities seen in international waters include a Wild-West shoot-out, a bullfight, a man marrying a cow, the dispensation of illegal fireworks, drinking alcohol before 2 P.M. on Sunday, nude dancing, and a monkey knife fight.

In one of the rooms in Burns's mansion, there are four embryos that look like Mr. Burns, floating in jars, and one that looks like Waylon Smithers.

Animal-head trophies mounted on the wall of Burns's mansion include a hippo and a triceratops.

Cut Adrift:
Moe: Hey, what do ya know? It floats!
Homer: That was my plan all along. Now relax and the currents will take us home.
Bart: What about the people on the bottom?
Homer: They're the greatest heroes of all. (suddenly panicking) Hey! Something's clawing at my leg! (suddenly relieved) Okay, it stopped.

SADDLESORE

The Springfield Elementary Band is entered into a competition at the state fair. After her band's performance, Lisa is sure they're going to win, but Ogdenville's school band uses brightly colored glow-sticks to enhance their performance and takes first prize. Lisa is very angry because visual aids are strictly against the rules. Marge suggests she forget about the competition and enjoy the fair. The Simpsons watch as a horse dives off a high platform into a water tank. Chief Wiggum accuses the horse's owner of animal cruelty, and the owner flees. In order to save the horse from the dog food factory, the Simpsons take the horse home with them.

The horse proves to be an expensive pet, so Homer and Bart try to figure a way it can pay for itself. First, they consider using it as a football place-kicker, but they quickly discover that using horses as kickers is against the rules. Then, they decide to try it out as a racehorse with Bart as the jockey, but it does miserably its first time out of the gate. Meanwhile, Lisa writes an angry letter to President Clinton. She believes that being a fellow sax player, he will be inclined to look into Ogdenville's cheating.

Homer and Bart decide the horse needs a new image. Later, with a bad-boy attitude and a fierce new look, the horse starts winning race after race. This angers the other jockeys, who waylay Homer, take him to their secret elfin lair, and threaten him with bodily harm if his horse does not start losing.

Homer ignores their warning and encourages Bart and the horse to win the Springfield Derby. The jockeys are furious and attack them, but with Marge and Lisa's help, the diminutive athletes are subdued. Shortly after, President Clinton arrives at the Simpson home to tell Lisa he overturned the outcome of the band competition and to give her the first-place award.

SHOW HIGHLIGHTS

Marching Orders:

Lisa: *I hate to be a killjoy, but do you really think we can win playing "Stars and Stripes Forever"? It's so beginner band, and we're advanced beginner band.*
(Ralph draws a crude picture of a cat on a bass drum.)
Ralph: *This is band?*
Largo: *Very well, Lisa. What rousing Sousa march would you have us play?*
Lisa: *Well, I thought maybe for once we could play a song that wasn't written by Sousa.*
Largo: *You mean something...just arranged by Sousa?*

War and Remembrance:

(Homer tries to pass himself off as a veteran to gain free admission to the fair.)
Homer: *Vietnam veteran.*
Pimple-faced Kid: *Do you have a military ID?*
Homer: *ID? Charlie didn't ask for ID when I fought at La Choy and Chun King. I saw my best friend's head explode at Margaret Cho!*
Marge: *Homer, give him the fifty cents.*
Homer: *Why should I? Did my country give me a parade? No man, they spat at me and --*
Pimple-faced Kid: *Just go!*
Homer: *Thank you. This closes the saddest chapter in American history.*

Horse Sense:

Chief Wiggum: *All right, show's over, folks. I'm afraid this horse is going to the dog food factory.*
Homer: *Good luck gettin' a horse to eat dog food.*
Bart: *You can't do that to Duncan. It's not his fault that his owner was a sleaze.*
Wiggum: *Look, I just want the horse to have a good home or be food. If you want to take him, fine with me.*
(Duncan the horse looks at Bart, who looks at Homer, who in turn looks at Marge.)
Marge: *Hmm. Should the Simpsons get a horse?*
Comic Book Guy: *Excuse me! I believe this family already had a horse, and the expense forced Homer to work at the Kwik-E-Mart, with hilarious consequences.*
Homer: *Anybody care what this guy thinks?*
Crowd: *No!*

Nostalgic Rock:

Bart: *Who are those pleasant old men?*
Homer: *It's BTO. They're Canada's answer to ELP. Their big hit was TCB. That's how we talked in the '70s. We didn't have a moment to spare.*

The Men That Got Away:

Chief Wiggum: *This is clearly a case of animal cruelty. Do you have a permit for that?*
Barker: *No problem, sir. It's in my car.*
(He backs away, hops in his car, and speeds away.)
Lou: *You gotta stop being so trusting, Chief.*
Wiggum: *Ah, I'd rather let a thousand guilty men go free than chase after them.*

Racing Form:

Homer: *Hey, where do you get those metal dealies for his feet?*
Jockey 1: *You mean, horseshoes?*
Homer: *Hey, what's with the attitude? I just wanted some dealies.*
Jockey 2: *You really think that horse can run a mile and a half?*
Homer: *He ran all the way here.*

Movie Moments:

The subjects of horse diving and equine place-kicking were both tackled in the Disney films *Wild Hearts Can't Be Broken* and *Gus*, respectively.

Homer claims that he has learned everything he needs to know about horse training, which includes seducing lonely women, from the Robert Redford and Kristin Scott Thomas film, *The Horse Whisperer*.

The jockeys' underground lair borrows many elements from Munchkinland in *The Wizard of Oz* and the Oompa Loompas in *Willy Wonka and the Chocolate Factory*.

Bart riding his horse to victory against all odds brings to mind classic horse-racing dramas like *National Velvet* and *The Black Stallion*.

GALACTICA

Episode BABF09
Original Airdate: 02/06/00
Writer: Tim Long
Director: Lance Kramer
Executive Producer: Mike Scully

Guest Voices: Randy Bachman as Himself, Trevor Denman as the Track Announcer, and C. F. Turner as Himself.

THE STUFF YOU MAY HAVE MISSED

Innovative product booths seen at the state fair: Miracle Shears, Drain Bugger, and the OmniGog anti-rubber band-injury system.

Duncan wears Bermuda shorts while doing his diving stunt.

When Homer and Bart are teaching Duncan the horse to kick football field goals, Homer is wearing his Tom Landry hat from "You Only Move Twice" (3F23).

The fire extinguisher Marge buys at the state fair features a picture of Lynda Carter, dressed as Wonder Woman, with George Foreman sitting on her shoulders, holding a fire extinguisher.

A sign at the Springfield Downs racetrack says "Now with E-Z Tear-Up Tickets!"

As a first-time jockey, Bart wears his Krusty the Clown pajamas and brushes Duncan's mane with a toilet brush.

The sampler Marge shows Lisa reads "Please, Pick Up Your Underpants."

After Duncan is transformed into Furious D, he has a gold tooth.

The name Furious D appears to be taken from the satirical devil rock band Tenacious D.

Those standing in line at the track's "Wuss Bets" window are: Reverend Lovejoy, Ned Flanders, Principal Skinner, and Hans Moleman.

The tree and chocolate waterfall in the elfin jockeys' secret lair bear a striking resemblance to the setting where the Keebler elves make their cookies.

According to the track announcer, the Springfield Derby is the fifth, and penultimate duel of racing's Triple Crown.

The Comic Book Guy is the continuity cop of the episode, pointing out that the Simpsons have owned a horse before in "Lisa's Pony" (8F06) and that Marge has struggled with a gambling addiction previously in "Springfield" (1F08) and "Bart the Fink" (3F12).

"Man, I got more trophies than Wayne Gretzky and the Pope combined."

Deja-vu:
Marge: Okay, Lisa, I've got Furious D across the board, boxed with the three and the eight, and wheeled up and down.
Lisa: Mom, I think you might be developing a gambling problem.
Comic Book Guy: (wearing a shirt that reads "Worst Episode Ever") Hey! I'm watching you.

The racing announcer goes around the bend: **"Could it be? In a bizarre twist, a horse is abusing a jockey! Might this be the start of a terrifying 'Planet of the Horses'? In this announcer's opinion, almost certainly, yes! And away I go!"**

Music Moments:
At the fair, Randy Bachman and C. F. Turner of Bachman Turner Overdrive perform snippets from two of their hit songs: "Takin' Care of Business" and "You Ain't Seen Nothing Yet."

The Springfield Elementary Band plays James Brown's "Living in America."

Presidential Pardon:
Lisa: You read my letter?
President Clinton: Much of it, yeah. And those glow-sticks were wrong, very wrong. So I personally overturned the results of that band contest. Congratulations.
(He gives Lisa the first-place award.)
Lisa: Thank you, Mr. President!
President Clinton: No, thank you, Lisa, for teaching kids everywhere a valuable lesson: If things don't go your way, just keep complaining until your dreams come true.
Marge: That's a pretty lousy lesson.
President Clinton: Hey, I'm a pretty lousy president.

Idle Threat:
Homer: That horse better win, or we're taking a trip to the glue factory...and he won't get to come.
Lenny: Yeah, that's a great tour. But you can't see it all in one day.

The announcer calls the race: **"And away they go! It's Chock Full o' Drugs, followed closely by Stalker, with Old Levis fading fast!"**

Duncan Gets a Makeover:
Marge: Furious D?
Bart: He's the bad boy of racing. He's got attitude and bad-itude. So show him some latitude, and you'll win his gratitude. Only in America!
Lisa: Ew, you used my bracelet for a nose ring.
Homer: (profoundly) Possessions are fleeting.

Culture Splash:
Mrs. Vanderbilt: Why, look at that disgraceful beast.
Mr. Vanderbilt: Good Lord! What has become of "The Sport of Kings"?
Bart: Get bent!
The Vanderbilts: Gasp!
(Mr. Vanderbilt drops his monocle into his drink and it breaks.)
Mr. Vanderbilt: That's my third monocle this week. I simply must stop being so horrified.

The Jockeys' Song:
Jockeys: We are the jockeys; jockeys are we. We live underground in a fiberglass tree.
Tree Jockey: 'Tween Earth and Hell, we reign supreme...
Toadstool Jockey: ...On toadstools grown by a chocolate stream.
Jockey 1: But all is not well in Jockey Town.
Woman Jockey: Your renegade horse is making us frown.
Homer: (spoken) What do you want me to do?
Jockey 2: Your horse must lose.
Homer: (spoken) My horse must lose?
Jockey 2: No win.
Jockey 3: No show.
Tree Jockey: No place.
Toadstool Jockey: Just lose the stinking race.
Homer: (spoken) And what if I refuse to lose?
Jockey 2: (spoken) We'll eat your brain!
Homer: (sung) My horse must lose!

MR. LARGO

Occupation:
Springfield Elementary School's music teacher

Attitude:
Decidedly snippy

His firm belief:
There's no room for crazy be-bop in "My Country 'Tis of Thee"

What he does not want to see in his classroom:
Outbursts of unbridled creativity

What he does want to see:
The whole band ending at the same time

DO YOU FIND SOMETHING FUNNY ABOUT THE WORD "TROMBONER"?

RACHEL JORDAN

Her calling in life:
Lead singer of the band Kovenant

Where you can see her:
In small-town churches and on tour with The Monsters of Christian Rock

Her fashion sense:
Decidedly fringe

How you can tell she's a little bit country:
Compares salvation to the Triple-A

Special talent:
Can lift heavy speakers

> THIS IS A LOVE SONG ABOUT A DUDE I MET IN A SLEAZY MOTEL...A DUDE NAMED GOD.

Guest Voice:
Shawn Colvin as Rachel Jordan

ALONE AGAIN,

While hiking, the Simpsons discover a racecar speedway built right in the middle of a bird sanctuary. A friendly professional driver gives the family tickets to watch the races, and they join the Flanders family at the top of the bleachers. Homer taunts the Fandemonium squad of cheerleaders, who are shooting T-shirts into the audience with air bazookas. They send a full salvo of shirts his way, but Homer bends over and the shirts hit Maude Flanders. She is knocked over the back of the bleachers and falls to her death.

After the funeral, everyone tries to comfort Ned and his boys. Homer decides to ease Ned's grief and secretly makes a dating tape for him. Homer shows the dating tape to Ned hoping it will cheer him up, but Ned feels it is too soon to date. Feeling lonely, he soon changes his mind and mails Homer's tape to the video dating service.

Ned goes on several dates with little success. He questions God's judgment in taking Maude away from him and decides not to go to church. Realizing the gravity of what he has done, he rushes back to church in time to watch a Christian rock band perform. He is somewhat smitten by the spiritual lead singer, Rachel Jordan, but decides it is still too soon for him to start dating. Ned happily realizes, however, that his faith has been renewed.

SHOW HIGHLIGHTS

Ah, Wilderness:

Lisa: *Now remember, we have to leave nature just the way we found it. Everything we pack in, we pack out.*
Homer: *What if I have to do my business?*
Lisa: *Use this plastic bag.*
Homer: *Aw, how come bears can crap in the woods, and I can't?*
(A bear walks out of the woods, drops a plastic bag in a garbage can, and lumbers away sheepishly.)

A Matter of Perspective:

Bart: *Oh my God! It's a racetrack!*
Lisa: *The bird sanctuary...they've ruined it!*
Homer: *No, they didn't! They just surrounded it with something wonderful like a raisin covered in chocolate, or a monkey in a cowboy suit.*

Kissin' Siblin's:

(Brandine and Cletus make out in the bed of a pick-up truck.)
Brandine: *Dang, Cletus. Why'd ya have to park next to my parents?*
Cletus: *Now, honey, they's my parents, too.*

Crash Course in Cursing:

Rod: *Daddy, can we move closer?*
Ned: *Abso-not-ly, hot Roddy! We're up here, out of range of the crashes and driver's cussing.*
Bart: (shoving Lisa) *Move your damn butt!*
Lisa: (shoving him back) *Bite me!*

At the Speedway:

Dr. Hibbert: (inspecting his free T-shirt) *Hmm...a Ford urinating on a Chevrolet.*
Mrs. Hibbert: *Don't you usually laugh at everything?*
Dr. Hibbert: (solemnly) *Yes. Yes, I do.*

Homer Dances Topless:

Homer: *I need a shirt! Gimme a shirt!*
Ralph: *Mommy has bosoms like that.*
Chief Wiggum: (sarcastically) *Yeah, I wish.*

Maude Knows Best:

Maude: *I'll get some hot dogs.*
Ned: *No foot-longs!*
Maude: *I know. They make you uncomfortable.*

The Bottom Line:

Marge: *It's hard to believe we're never going to see Maude again.*
Homer: *And poor Ned didn't get a chance to say goodbye. Well, from now on I'm never going to let you leave the room without telling you how much I love you and how truly special...*(looking at his watch) *this is really eating up a lot of time. Maybe just a pat on the butt.* (He pats Marge's posterior.) *Yeah, that works.*

Moe's Condolences:

Moe: *Look, Ned, I know we ain't hung out much, what with your insane fear of drinking and me being banned from the church and all. But, uh, but, that Maude, she was really something.*
Ned: *Aw, wasn't she? Thank you, Moe. I appreciate that.*
Moe: *No, I really mean it! Though, I mean, if it was you that died, I would have been on her so fast...*
Ned: (horrified) *What are you saying?*
Moe: *What? Nothing. She was hot. What, you can't take a compliment?*
Flanders: (speechless noise) *You monster!*
(He starts hitting Moe, who doesn't resist.)
Moe: *That's good, no. Let it out. That's it. Let it out. Send me to Maude. That's it.* (He looks heavenward.) *Here I come, baby. Oh, yeah.*

At the Funeral:

Rev. Lovejoy: *In many ways, Maude Flanders was a supporting player in our lives. She didn't grab our attention with memorable catchphrases or comical accents.*
Groundskeeper Willie: *Aye.*
Capt. McAllister: *Yar.*
Prof. Frink: *Oh, glavin! Why, glavin?*
Lovejoy: *But, whether you noticed her or not, Maude was always there...and we thought she always would be.*

Sex, Lies and Videotape:

Bart: *Why are you taping Flanders, Dad?*
Homer: *You'll see.*
Bart: *Do you even have a job anymore?*
Homer: *I think it's pretty obvious that I don't.*

"Oh, I would date Ned in a second if I was a woman or gay. He looks like a cuddler, that Ned. I...I like that. I like to be held. I like to be pampered."

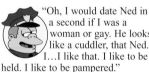

NATURA-DIDDILY

Episode BABF10
Original Airdate: 02/13/00
Writer Ian Maxtone-Graham
Director: Jim Reardon
Executive Producer: Mike Scully

THE STUFF YOU MAY HAVE MISSED

A sign seen in the forest says, "Springfield Nature Preserve—Outdoor Sex by Permit Only."

The label on Homer's bee repellent reads, "Bee-Gone—African Strength" and features a picture of a choking bee.

Two-time FASCAR Champ Clay Babcock is sponsored by Duff Beer, Garden Blast, and Kwik-E-Mart Squishees.

Headstones seen at the cemetery: Bleeding Gums Murphy, with an angel-winged saxophone; Dr. Marvin Monroe, with a stone psychiatrist's couch; Beatrice Simmons (Grampa's girlfriend) from "Old Money" (7F17); and the dilapidated monument of Frank "Grimey" Grimes from "Homer's Enemy" (4F19).

Maude's coffin has racecar sponsor stickers plastered all over it.

T-shirts for the 21-T-shirt salute at Maude's funeral feature a cartoon skeleton and read "Let 'er R.I.P."

Bart alters the "Rest in Peace" cake so it reads "Rest in Pee."

Homer keeps a bucket of "War Rocks" in his bedroom in the event of a rock fight. A rather big rock in his bucket has "Flanders" written on it.

Individual video tapes that Homer made are labeled, "Flanders—Yard," "Flanders—Frolicking," and "Flanders—59th Birthday."

Lisa owns a "My 1st Video Editor."

Ned's ATM PIN number is 5316.

Words Ned spells out while playing Scrabble by himself: Solitary, Alone, Forever, Horny, and Flanswered.

Edna Krabappel has a bottle of "Chateau Maison" wine in her ice bucket, previously introduced in "The Crepes of Wrath" (7G13).

The sign at the video dating store reads "Video Matchmaking—Yes, We Have Desperate Immigrants."

Bumper sticker on rock band Kovenant's van: "If this van's a-swayin', I'm in here a-prayin!"

Heavenly Thoughts:

Ned: *Homer, I'm having second thoughts. This feels so disloyal to Maude.*
Homer: *Oh, wake up, Ned. You think Maude isn't dating in Heaven?*
Ned: *You think she would?*
Homer: *How could she not? The place is full of eligible bachelors. John Wayne, Tupac Shakur, Sherlock Holmes...*
Ned: *Heh, heh! Sherlock Holmes is a character.*
Homer: *He sure is! Rrrowl!*

Open Bag, Let Cat Out:

Homer: *So, how'd you do tonight, Romeo?*
Ned: *Well, I just can't relate to the women of today, Homer. Ah, it's probably me. I'm about as exciting as a baked potato.*
Marge: *You're darn right you are! And you've got lots of other great qualities, too!*
Homer: *That's right, Ned. Those floozies we married in Vegas were crazy about you.*
Marge: *What floozies? What are you talking--?*
Homer: *(sternly) Marge, we're trying to help Ned.*

"Lord, I never question you, but I've been wondering if your decision to take Maude was, well, wrong… U-unless this is part of your divine plan…Oh, could you just give me some kind of sign? *(beat)* Anything? *(angry)* And after all that church chocolate I bought! Which, by the way, was gritty and had that white stuff on it! Well, I've had it!"

Something's Wrong with Ned:

Todd: *Daddy, get up! You'll be late for church.*
Ned: *Oh, you boys can go with the Simpsons. I'm not going to church today.*
Rod and Todd: *Gasp!*
Ned: *That's right. And I may not go to church tomorrow.*
(Horrified, Rod and Todd back out of the room, then flee in terror.)

Heaven Metal:

Rev. Lovejoy: *While our organist is on a much-needed vacation, we thought we'd try something new. So get down and put your knees together for the Christian rock stylings of Kovenant!*
(The band begins to play.)
Lisa: *Hey, isn't that the bass player from Satanica?*
Marge: *I think it is!*

Two Lost Souls:

Ned: *That was a lovely song. You really got to me.*
Rachel: *Been through some rough times yourself?*
Ned: *I...I recently lost my wife.*
Rachel: *I'm real sorry to hear that. We just lost our drummer...to a Pentecostal ska band.*

Musical Moment:

The background music during Ned Flanders's dating tape is "I'm Too Sexy" by Right Said Fred.

MISSIONARY:

I n order to get PBS to end a pledge drive and return to a TV show he is watching, Homer calls in anonymously and pledges $10,000. However, using a tracing system, the PBS pledge enforcement van swiftly arrives at the Simpsons' doorstep. When it becomes clear Homer cannot pay, the PBS people chase him and threaten him with bodily harm. Homer takes sanctuary in the church and pleads for help from Reverend Lovejoy. Lovejoy promptly puts Homer on a plane bound for a South Pacific island and explains that Homer can be a missionary until it all blows over.

Homer does the best he can to acclimate himself to tropical island life. He passes the time by licking toads and experiencing their hallucinogenic effects, and he befriends a native girl whom he refers to as Lisa, Jr. Back in

Springfield, Bart becomes the "man of the house" and fills in for Homer at the nuclear power plant. Homer and the islanders build a gambling casino, and he teaches the natives about gambling and other vices.

In no time, the island tribe shows strong signs of moral decay. Since they have all become such horrible sinners under his influence, Homer decides he needs to build the natives a church. Once the church is finished, Homer rings its bell with such gusto that it causes an avalanche which triggers an earthquake and volcanic activity. Lava flows into the village, destroying the church and endangering lives. Just when it appears as if Homer and Lisa, Jr. are going to perish, the action is interrupted by a Fox Broadcasting pledge drive. Bart calls in a pledge of $10,000 and saves the network.

SHOW HIGHLIGHTS

Homer Enjoys the Arts:
Bart: *You're watching PBS?*
Homer: *Hey, I'm as surprised as you. But I stumbled across the most delicious British sitcom.*
Bart: (reading the title on TV) *"Do Shut Up"?*
Homer: *It's about a hard drinking, yet loving family of soccer hooligans. If they're not having a go with a bird, they're having a row with a wanker.*
Bart: *Cheeky!*

"If you watch even one second of PBS and don't contribute, you're a thief! A common thief! Sorry, but these thieves make me so damn mad. You know who you are! Thieves!"

"Um, it's an honor to give ten thousand dollars—especially now, when the rich mosaic of cable programming has made public television so very, very unnecessary."

Homer tries some fast talk: **"Maybe your movie star banks are open crazy hours, but we in Springfield are simple folk. We like our cars fast and our banks closed!"**

The Last Resort:
Homer: *Sanctuary! Sanctuary!*
Rev. Lovejoy: *Oh, why did I teach him that word?*
Homer: *Quick! You've got to hide me from PBS! Their bloodthirsty pursuit is made possible by a grant from the Chubb Group!*

Stranger in Paradise:
(Homer drinks from something resembling a coconut.)
Qtoktok: *Are you enjoying your ox testicle?*
Homer: *Oh, yes. Very much so.*
Qtoktok: *Really? You sure you wouldn't rather have a coconut? Heh. They're delicious.*
Homer: *No, I'm good.*

Music Moments:
The Sex Pistols' "No Feelings" plays in the background during the British sitcom "Do Shut Up."

Homer hallucinates that a toad is talking while over the ham radio Marge is saying, "Hello? Hello? Hello? Is there anybody in there?" in a reference to Pink Floyd's song "Comfortably Numb" from their album *The Wall.*

Homer, running things via ham radio: **"Hmm, I see the house is falling apart without me, so here's the new order: Bart, you're the man of the house; Lisa, I'm promoting you to boy; Maggie's now the brainy girl; the toaster can fill in for Maggie; and Marge, you're a consultant."**

IMPOSSIBLE

Episode BABF11
Original Airdate: 02/20/00
Writer: Ron Hauge
Director: Steven Dean Moore
Executive Producer: Mike Scully
Guest Voice: Betty White as Herself

LISA, JR., AK, QTOKTOK

Cultural differences:
Cannot read, lack razzle-dazzle, and drink ox testicles

Low tolerance for:
Dristan mixed with holy water and inexpensive salad buffets

Never heard of:
TV, couches, or beer

Susceptible to:
Religious fervor and gambling addiction

"Wait! I'm no missionary! I don't even believe in Jebus!"

Celebrities seen answering phones at the Fox pledge telethon: Mulder and Scully from "The X-Files," Hank from "King of the Hill," Thurgood from "The PJs," Bender from "Futurama," Rupert Murdoch, and Luke Perry.

A Call from a Home:

Marge: Homer, are you all right?
Homer: I guess so, but that first month was pretty rough.
Marge: You've only been gone two days.
Homer: Really? Without TV, it's hard to know when one day begins and the other ends.
Bart: I miss you, Dad. Mom won't let me read "Hagar the Horrible."
Marge: I just don't think it's funny.

Man of the House:

Marge: Guess who I saw at the supermarket today.
Bart: Can it wait? I just got off work.
Marge: I'm sorry, honey, I just thought...
Bart: Don't you do enough yakking at the beauty parlor?
Marge: That's it, Bart. You're taking this "man of the house" thing too far.
Bart: You're right, I'm sorry. Tell you what, Saturday night we'll go out for steaks, just you and me.
Marge: Hmm. (She shrugs.) A night out is a night out.

Homer introduces the casino into tribal life: **"So, have fun, everybody! And who knows, maybe you'll hit the jackpot, get off this island, and spend the rest of your days in a tropical paradise."**

Club Microatia:

Homer: Hey, what happened to all the shirtless girls you see in all the geographical magazines?
Qtoktok: Craig and Amy gave us the gift of shame. All the naked women are on that island.
(He points to another island.)
Ak: Yeah, anything goes over there. Bouncy, bouncy!

THE STUFF YOU MAY HAVE MISSED

The head in the PBS logo has the characteristic Simpsons-style overbite.

At the department store, Marge is scooping greeting cards onto a scale from a barrel labeled "Greeting Cards $5.00/lb."

When Homer looks at his wrist and says "The banks are closed by now," he's not wearing a watch.

PBS stars seen chasing Homer: the hooligans from "Do Shut Up," Mr. Rogers, Yo-Yo Ma, Garrison Keillor, the Teletubbies, Big Bird, Oscar the Grouch, and Elmo.

Crates in the Christian Relief plane include those filled with prayer books, bibles, and inflatable pulpits. There's also a water cooler labeled "Holy Water."

The little island girl Homer renames Lisa, Jr. wears a string of pearls just like Lisa's.

When the casino is being built, Homer uses a tortoise shell for a construction helmet, à la Fred Flintstone.

Bart dresses exactly like Homer when he takes his place at the power plant.

At the festive island casino opening, Homer wears a tiger-pelt cummerbund.

During the casino riot, one native is stabbed in the back with a swordfish.

When Betty White mentions crude, lowbrow programming, the "Family Guy" logo is on the television next to her.

Bart Goes to Work:

Mr. Burns: Simpson!
Bart: Aah!
Mr. Burns: I've just reviewed your ten-year performance record, and it's appalling.
Bart: But I'm not Homer Simpson.
Mr. Burns: I think I know who Homer Simpson is. In ten short years, you've caused seventeen meltdowns. One is too many!
Bart: Yeah, but...
Mr. Burns: You sold weapons-grade plutonium to the Iraqis...with no markup!
Bart: But...
Mr. Burns: And worst of all, you took the Hamburglar's birthday off last Monday and Wednesday. Which is it? Sigh! Now, my voice is giving out, so I'm just going to poke you for the next hour or so.

Homer the Replacement:

Missionary Craig: Welcome aboard, brother! You must be Homer. I'm Craig, that's Amy. Well, see ya!
Homer: You're leaving? Wait! What do I do here?
Missionary Amy: First of all, forget everything you learned in missionary school.
Homer: ...Done.
Craig: We taught them some English and ridiculed away most of their beliefs.
Amy: So, you can take it from there. Bye!
Craig: Don't let the bedbugs bite...seriously.

Homer on church building: **"Well, I may not know much about God, but I have to say, we built a pretty nice cage for him."**

HOW CAN ACE BE ONE **AND** ELEVEN? WHAT KIND OF GOD WOULD ALLOW THAT?

PYGMOELIAN

Occupation:
Bartender at "Juggernauts" in Hollywood, CA

Nickname:
The chick with the rack

Trick-pouring talent:
Filling two mugs of beer while bouncing up and down

Other abilities:
Fluffing her hair, pouring beer on her tight blouse and jiggling from side to side, and batting her eyelashes

Turn-ons:
Sleeping with contest judges

Turn-offs:
Touching drunks

OOOH! WAH!

oe wins the "Beer-Tender of the Year" contest at the Duff Days Beer Festival and gets to have his picture printed on the front of new Duff Beer calendar. When the calendar comes out with stickers placed over his photograph, Moe realizes how truly ugly is he and opts to have plastic surgery.

Meanwhile, Bart and Lisa, fighting over Maggie's pink elephant balloon from the Duff Days beer festival, accidentally allow the balloon to escape from the house. They chase the balloon through town, and it finally comes to rest in a conference room filled with gay Republicans who are looking for a symbol to represent them.

Moe comes out of his bandages looking handsome. Now that he has a second chance, he decides to exact revenge on the people who mistreated him when he was ugly. One target is the producer of a soap opera who didn't cast Moe because of his offensive looks. Unexpectedly, the producer hires him on the spot when she sees how handsome he is. Moe's thirst for revenge is forgotten, and he soon becomes a soap opera star, living the high life surrounded by beautiful women.

Moe chances upon a top-secret book of the soap opera's upcoming plot lines and discovers that his character is going to be killed off. Once again, he vows revenge. With Homer's help, Moe gives away a year's worth of upcoming plots while on live TV. The furious producer fires Moe. Certain that he can land a role on another soap opera, he storms off slamming the set door. The entire set wall falls on him, smashing his face back into its original, repulsive form. Moe returns to the life of a homely bartender.

SHOW HIGHLIGHTS

"Are you ready for some Duff love?"

Moe gets a little confused: **"Hey, there's one thing I don't get though. When my face was crushed, why did it go back to my old face? I mean, shouldn't it have turned into some kind of third face that was different?"**

At the Duff Days Beer Festival:
Marge: *Kids, would you like a balloon?*
Bart: *Yeah, right, Mom. Then I'd like a rattle and a wowwipop. Actually, I would like a wowwipop.*
Lisa: *Those balloons won't biodegrade for ten thousand years. And if Bart gets a wowwipop, I want a wowwipop.*

Artistic License:
Homer: *Moe! The new Duff calendars are out! The ones with your picture.*
Moe: *Oh, boy! Move over, liquor license.* (He takes the license off the wall.)
Lenny: (examining the liquor license) *Hey, Moe, this license expired in 1973, and it's only good in Rhode Island...and it's signed by you!*
Moe: *Yeah, yeah. I've been meaning to get that updated, uh, for this state and...real.*

The Ugly Truth:
Moe: *Oh! Am I really that ugly?*
Carl: *Moe, it's all relative. Is Lenny really that dumb? Is Barney that drunk? Is Homer that lazy, bald, and fat?*
Moe: *Oh, my God, it's worse than I thought!* (Moe, Lenny, Barney, and Homer start sobbing.)
Carl: (to the camera) *See, this is why I don't talk much.*

What Are Friends For?:
Moe: *Aw, c'mon, look at me. I'm a gargoyle. What with the cauliflower ear, there, and the lizard lips...*
Carl: *Little rat eyes...*
Homer: *Caveman brow...*
Lenny: *Don't forget that fish snout.*
Moe: *Okay, I get it. I ain't pleasant to look at.*
Lenny: *Or listen to.*
Carl: *Or be with.*

The Importance of Being Handsome:
Moe: *Plastic surgery, huh? Eh, maybe they could dynamite Mount Crapmore here and carve me a new kisser.*
Carl: *Oh, I don't know. Plastic surgery might make you look good on the outside, but you still might feel bad in the inside.*
Moe: *But I'd look good on the outside, right?*
Carl: *Yeah, but you'd feel bad inside.*
Moe: *Plastic surgery it is!*

TV Moment:
Homer's appearance as the Angel of the Future on "It Never Ends" is a nod to Jackie Gleason's similar appearance as the Chef of the Future on an episode of "The Honeymooners."

(Dr. Velimirovic and his nurse prepare Moe, who lies on the operating table with his eyes closed, for surgery.)
Nurse: *Hoo-boy, what a mug.*
Dr. Velimirovic: *Yeah, you should see his genitals. Would you like to see them?*
Moe: *I'm awake here.*

A New Life After Death:
Moe: *Homer, did you hear that? She called me handsome. Me! It's like I've gone to Heaven.* (worried) *Wait a minute. I died on the operating table, didn't I?*
Homer: *Heh, heh, heh, heh. Yeah, but just for a minute. It's a funny story. I'll tell you sometime.*

Revealed this episode:
Carl's last name is Carlson, Snake (Jailbird) has a son (who steals Lisa's bike), and Duffman's first name is Larry.

THE STUFF YOU MAY HAVE MISSED

The tag-line on the Duff Days banner is "A Lost Weekend for the Whole Family!"

The Duff Days announcer says that Duffman had recently appeared before the House Subcommittee on Teenage Alcoholism.

According to Duffman, trick beer-pouring qualifies for course credit at Dartmouth College.

The Duff Beer Company has a Vice President in charge of Calendars and Fake IDs.

Marge lifts weights while "doing time" in the designated driver "Rockin' Fun Zone" detention facility. Also detained: Apu (bouncing a racquetball), Skinner (smoking a cigarette), and Kirk Van Houten (pushing a laundry cart).

The stickers that are piled over Moe's face on the calendar read, "Drink Duff," "Duff Enuff," "Viva La Duff," "Kiss Me I'm Duff," "Ich Bin Ein Duff," and "I'mo Duff You Up!"

The sign on the Cosmetic Surgery Group door reads ""We'll Cut You Good!"

When Bart and Lisa lose Maggie's pink elephant balloon, she spends the whole scene without a pacifier in her mouth.

The Plastic Surgeon cauterizes Moe's "leakage" with a soldering iron.

When the old "Dr. Tad Winslow" removes his eye-patch, he has a tan line.

The soap opera director is bleeped when he says, "What the fudge?"

Episode BABF12
Original Airdate: 02/27/00
Writer: Larry Doyle
Director: Mark Kirkland
Executive Producer: Mike Scully

The "It Never Ends" Title Sequence:

(We see a ticking grandfather clock half-buried in the sand on the beach. The sun is setting, and the waves crash on the shore.)
Narrator: *Like the cleaning of a house...It Never Ends.* (The theme music crescendos.)
Narrator: *With Gabriella DeFarge as Gabriella St. Farge. Allegra Hamilton as Sister Bernadette and Roxy Monoxide. And as Dr. Tad Winslow...Moe Szyslak.*

On the Set of "It Never Ends":

Helen Morehouse: *What were you thinking?*
Casting Director: *Well, you said you wanted gritty. In other words...ugly.*
Helen: *I wanted Mary Ann on "Gilligan's Island" ugly, not Cornelius on "The Planet of the Apes" ugly. TV ugly, not...ugly ugly.*

Girl Trouble:

Carl: *So, Lenny, how are things working out with you and that girl next door?*
Lenny: *Eh, it's over. She got a window shade.*

Homer and Moe Rehearse:

Moe: *I didn't bring you back to life so you could make a fool of me at the club!*
Homer: (reading from a script) *You don't love me! The only thing you love is your ear, nose, and throat pavilion.*
Moe: *I've dedicated my life to diseases of the head holes, but the one hole I've never been able to fix is the one in my soul.*
Homer: *That was amazing, Moe. I'm actually a little turned on.*

"I've been called ugly, pug ugly, fugly, pug fugly, but never ugly ugly."

Movie Moments:

The Duff Days trick-pouring contest takes place to the tune "Hippy Hippy Shake" as performed by the Georgia Satellites and in similar fashion to Tom Cruise and Bryan Brown's dazzling display in *Cocktail*.

The producer in the booth allows Homer and Moe to change the soap opera episode on live TV just like Dustin Hoffman at the end of *Tootsie*.

Thespian Love Affair:

Moe: *Yeah, hey, I've got a gift. As a child, I was bitten by the acting bug. Then it burrowed under my skin and laid eggs in my heart. Now, those eggs are hatching, and I...the feeling is indescribable.*
Homer: *I know what you mean. Our dog had that.*

Divine Intervention:

Moe: *And what do you have to tell us O Angel of the Future?*
Homer: (dressed as an angel) *You're going to die in a sky-diving accident.*
Moe: *How tragic! Tell me more.*
Homer: *Gabriella's baby shower will be invaded by terrorists...with sexy results.*
Moe: *Ooh! That's unexpected. What else?*
Homer: *Well, Sister Bernadette will leave the convent and start a softball team...with sexy results.*

When mosquitoes overrun the campground the Simpsons plan to visit, they stop at a Native-American gambling casino instead. Bart is caught sneaking into an area off-limits to minors, and he is brought before the mysterious manager of the casino. To teach Bart a lesson, the manager shows him a vision of his life thirty years in the future.

Future Bart is a fat, lazy slacker who is always broke. After getting evicted from his apartment, he decides to move in with Lisa, who is the newly elected president of the United States. Homer and Marge are also visiting the White House, and Homer keeps busy searching for Abraham Lincoln's hidden gold. President Lisa valiantly copes with her family, but when Bart becomes too distracting, she sends him to Camp David with a phony assignment.

While at Camp David, Bart is convinced by the ghost of Billy Carter that he was sent away from the White House because he was an embarrassment. Bart decides to return to the White House and prove himself. He arrives in the nick of time, and is able to save Lisa from angry foreign diplomats demanding loan repayments. The vision ends, and as the Simpsons leave the casino, Bart tells Lisa about their future.

SHOW HIGHLIGHTS

All-You-Can-Eat Prime Fib:

Casino Manager: *So, you like to sneak into casinos?*
Bart: *I wasn't going to gamble! I just wanted a Bloody Mary.*

Future Roomies:

Ralph: *I'm sick of having to dry myself with a newspaper. You could at least do some laundry. I pay the rent.*
Bart: *Dude, you know I'm good for it. I'll have plenty of money when my lawsuit pays off.*
Ralph: *You mean the spider bite at Disneyland?*
Bart: *Or the incident with the over-salted fries.*

"I can't believe 'Smell ya later' replaced 'Goodbye.'"

The Once and Future Homer:

Homer: *Oh, what a bleak, horrible future we live in!*
Bart: *Don't you mean, "present"?*
Homer: *Right, right, present. Anyway, can I get you some Soylent Green?*

Movie Moment:

Bart's encounter with the ghost of Billy Carter in the ballroom is reminiscent of one of Jack Nicholson's run-ins with the spirit world in *The Shining*.

Ongoing Sibling Rivalry:

Homer: *Oh, I'm tired of giving you money. Why can't you be more like Lisa?*
Bart: *I am so sick of hearing about Lisa! Just because she's doing a little better than me...*
Marge: *She's president of the United States!*
Bart: *President-elect.*

Bionic Homer:

Bart: *What happened to you, man? You used to be cool.*
Homer: *I'm still cool!*
Bart: *Nah, you've changed, man.*
Homer: *Well, I do have this robotic prostate, but you can't see it. (He looks down below his waist.) Oh, you can.*

The future Ned Flanders on the horrors of growing old: **"I never should have had that trendy laser surgery. It was great at first, but, you know, at the ten-year mark your eyes fall out."**

Flanders Returns a Favor:

Ned Flanders: *Bart, you're never going to grow up if I keep bailing you out.*
Bart: *Then, please, help me help myself.*
Ned: *Oh, all right, but only because you haven't outed Rod and Todd.*

"Smell ya later, Bart. Smell ya later, forever!"

In a Fiscal Pickle:

Lisa: *As you know, we've inherited quite a budget crunch from President Trump. How bad is it, Secretary Van Houten?*
Milhouse: *We're broke.*
Lisa: *The country is broke? How can that be?*
Milhouse: *Well, remember when the last administration decided to invest in our nation's children? Big mistake.*

Your Future Government in Action:

Lisa: *If I'm going to bail the country out, I'll have to raise taxes. But in my speech, I'd like to avoid calling it a "painful emergency tax."*
Milhouse: *What about "colossal salary grab"?*
Lisa: *See, that has the same problem. We need to soften the blow.*
Milhouse: *Well, if you just want to out-and-out lie...okay, how about a "temporary refund adjustment."*
Lisa: *I love it.*

Some Things Never Change:

Bart: *I knew you'd need some help keeping it real, so I figured I could be, like, your co-president.*
Lisa: *Co-president? Are you crazy?*
Bart: *Mom! Lisa won't share!*
Marge: *Be nice to your brother, Lisa!*

Getting the Skinny:

Lisa: *I want you and your pals to go away to Camp David and write up a report on coolness.*
Bart: *Well, if my country needs me...can we skinny-dip?*
Lisa: *At Camp David? Sure. They couldn't keep pants on Kissinger.*

Homer's unflattering assessment of Abraham Lincoln: **"That lying, rail-splitting, theater-going freak!"**

Bart the Diplomat:

Bart: *Guys, the thing is, we totally have the money. And we tried to wire it to you, but you know how banks screw up.*
French Ambassador: *I do not understand.*
Bart: *We tried to call you all day Saturday.*
German Ambassador: *We were there Saturday.*
Bart: *Dude, I know. I left a message with some guy named Hans.*
German Ambassador: *Hans?*
Bart: *He might have been a temp. Very surly.*
German Ambassador: *We have had a lot of turnover.*
Chinese Ambassador: *You pay now! Now!*
Bart: *What happened to you, China? You used to be cool.*
Chinese Ambassador: *Hey, China is still cool. You pay later. Later!*
Bart: *Solid. The rest of you go on home, and look in your mailboxes, 'cause I totally remember sending checks out.*

THE STUFF YOU MAY HAVE MISSED

The marquee at Caesar's Pow-Wow Indian Casino reads "Now Appearing: Carrot Scalp."

Arthur Crandall and Gabbo's truck said "As Seen on TV," but a "W" has been hand-painted on it to read "Was Seen on TV."

One of the Indian weavings in the casino manager's office is made to look like a slot machine, another like playing cards.

Future Bart's "Future Duff Beer" can has twinkling lights.

Future Nelson is dressed like Biff Tannen from *Back to the Future II*.

The Simpson home of the future has a station wagon hovering in the driveway and a huge satellite dish on the roof. The extra room Homer built onto the house in "Lisa's Wedding" (2F15) can be seen.

The virtual fudge machine looks like an old Atari game.

The Soylent Green box advertises "Now with More Girls."

Bart's band is named Captain Bart and the Tequila Mockingbirds.

There's a Hustler Superstore next door to the White House in the future.

Outside Camp David, there's a handwritten sign that reads "Beer Guy Turn Here" with a balloon attached to it.

The Bill Clinton pornography stash is labeled "Girlies What Ain't Got No Clothes."

A portrait of Ted Kennedy hangs over a fireplace in one of the White House conference rooms.

This episode aired one week shy of five years from another episode that showed the Simpsons in the future: "Lisa's Wedding" (2F15)—airdate 3/26/95.

One Nagging Question:

Bart: *Why did a vision about my future include a story about Homer and Lincoln's gold?*
Casino Manager: *I guess the spirits thought the main vision was a little thin.*

Episode BABF13
Original Airdate: 03/19/00
Writer: Dan Greaney
Director: Michael Marcantel
Executive Producer: Mike Scully

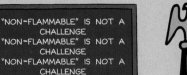

"NON-FLAMMABLE" IS NOT A
CHALLENGE
"NON-FLAMMABLE" IS NOT A
CHALLENGE
"NON-FLAMMABLE" IS NOT A
CHALLENGE

Musical Moments:

Bart tries to sell his band's tape to the nation using two tropical melodies as ad jingles: Rupert Holmes's "Escape (The Piña Colada Song)" and Harry Belafonte's "Day-O (The Banana Boat Song)."

Chaotic State of the Union:

Director: *Thirty seconds, Madame President.*
Bart: *Hey, Lis, I need a favor.*
Lisa: *Not now, Bart! I'm about to speak to a hundred million people. This speech could make or break my presidency.*
Bart: *I hear you. All I want you to do is play my demo tape in the background while you're yakking about whatever. Now, this "play" button is a little screwed up, so you gotta hold it down.*

The Presidential Veto:

Lisa: *Oh, but Bart could screw everything up.*
Secret Service Agent Kearney: *You want him... eliminated?*
Lisa: *No, just keep him out of my hair.*
Kearney: *Out of your hair...extreme severity?*
Lisa: *No!*
Kearney: *Come on, every president gets three secret murders. If you don't use them by the end of the term ⸘pfft!⸘ they're gone.*

CASINO MANAGER

Amazing ability:
Can see into the future

Where his visions come from:
His mysterious magical flame and rows of casino floor video monitors

What worries him the most:
His brother Crazy Talk

Special service:
Will offer you a second mortgage for your gambling pleasure

Where his shameless promotions come from:
Dances With Focus Groups

Rewards customers with:
Expired crab-claw coupons

YOUR LINEN SERVICE HAS BROKEN MANY PROMISES TO US. LAUNDRY BILL SOAR LIKE EAGLE!

BRANDINE DEL ROY

Careers of choice:
Dairy Queen worker/Topless dancer

Relations:
Wife and sister of Cletus the slack-jawed yokel; mother of 26

Fashion sense:
A bare midriff's a must, no matter how big the belly gets

Special talent:
Birthin' young'uns in the back of a pickup

Favorite magazine:
"Better Trailers and Sumps"

> CLETUS, WHAT ARE YOU BEATING YOUR GUMS ABOUT?

DAYS OF WINE

Barney realizes he is a disgusting drunk after watching a video of his birthday party, and he vows to get sober. He finds maintaining sobriety difficult at first, but with Homer's help he finds his way to an AA meeting. Meanwhile, Bart and Lisa decide to enter an amateur photo contest to get their picture on the cover of the new phone book. They find an old camera in the closet and set out to take snapshots.

Now that he is clean and sober, Barney makes plans to change his life. His first stop is the Springfield Flight School, where he takes helicopter-flying lessons. A few lessons later, Barney gives Homer a ride in the helicopter. While in the air, they get into a big argument which strains their relationship.

Bart and Lisa are taking pictures atop Mt. Springfield when Bart starts a forest fire by carelessly discarding a hot flashbulb. The children are in imminent danger, and Barney and Homer must band together to save them. They hop into the helicopter, but Barney is so nervous, he doesn't think he can do it sober. When a Duff beer truck comes to a sudden stop, spilling its contents in front of a weakening Barney, Homer refuses to let him give up on sobriety and drinks an entire six-pack in his place. Together, Barney and a drunken Homer save the kids. Barney's confidence and his relationship with Homer are restored, and he looks forward to an alcohol-free future, although he is now addicted to double-tall mocha lattés.

SHOW HIGHLIGHTS

Trash Talk:
Cletus: *Looky here! Cardy-board tubes!*
Brandine: *Now we can has indoor plumbing, just like they's got at the women's lockup.*
Cletus: *They spoilt you, Brandine. Sometimes I don't even know who you are anymore.*

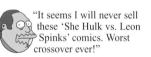
"It seems I will never sell these 'She Hulk vs. Leon Spinks' comics. Worst crossover ever!"

A Pair of Pretty Pecs:
Homer: *Well, this muscle-shirt's a pretty good find.*
Bart: *Dad, that's a sports bra.*
Homer: *All I know is, I'm finally getting the support I need.*

"Professor Barney" Speaks:
Barney: *I'm just saying that when we die, there's going to be a planet for the French, a planet for the Chinese, and we'll all be a lot happier.*
Lisa: *Mr. Gumble, you're upsetting me.*
Barney: *No, I'm not.*

With Friends Like These...:
Barney: *Oh, I'm a disgrace!*
Homer: *Disgracefully hilarious! You passed out before we could even give you your presents.*
Carl: *I still got mine! Barney, I got you what no drunk can do without—"Morning After" stationery.*
(They all laugh, except Barney.)
Moe: *And I got you helicopter flying lessons. Can you imagine this booze-bag at the wheel of a whirlybird? Ha! Ha! He'd be all, "Look at me! I'm a tanked-up loser in a helicopter!"*

"Wait a minute, Barney. You've got to be sober to fly. I mean, it's not like driving a car."

Gil Hits Bottom:
Lindsey Naegle: *We all know why we're here, don't we? To keep ourselves sober...and to network. So let's get started.*
Gil: *Well, after I lost my third job in two days, old Gil was in a pit of despair.*
Lindsey: *And that's when you realized you were an alcoholic.*
Gil: *Oh, no, I never touch the stuff. But you don't have to be drunk to know the value of Amway!*
Everyone: *Gasp!*

Wrong Place, Right Time:
Barney: *My name is Barney, and I'm an alcoholic.*
Clerk: *I feel for you, pally, but, uh, you want AA. This is Triple A.*

At the AA Meeting:
Barney: *I have a problem with alcohol, and I need help.*
Lindsey Naegle: *Well, your recovery begins today. And we promise you all the sugar cookies and second-hand smoke you can handle.*
Homer: *These sugar cookies you speak of, are they real or symbolic?*
Lindsey: *They're on that table over there.*
Homer: *Oh! I don't wanna walk that far. Anything that takes twelve steps isn't worth doing! Get it? Heh. Twelve? Heh, heh, heh. Steps? Ee-hee-hee!*

Up, Up, and Away:
Barney: *Hey, I think I'm gettin' it.*
Helicopter Pilot: *Yes, that's great. Now let's just pull ourselves out of this tailspin here.*
Barney: *Oooh! I'm sorry about that!*
Helicopter Pilot: *That's okay. That's what the diapers are for.*

& D'OH'SES

Episode BABF14
Original Airdate: 04/09/00
Writers: Deb Lacusta & Dan Castellaneta
Director: Neil Affleck
Executive Producer: Mike Scully

McBain Gets McBusted:
Lisa: *Is that Rainier Wolfcastle?*
Bart: *Check out the gut.*
Wolfcastle: *It's for a movie! I'm playing a fat secret agent.*

Homer's idea of a touch of class:
"So, you missed some big changes at Moe's. He hangs newspapers over the urinals now. You can read the sports page while you pee! Very la-dee-da!"

"Heh, heh! Nobody gets away from Moe. Nobody!"

Wasted Days and Wasted Whine:
Barney: *When I think about all the time I wasted at Moe's...*
Homer: *Wasted? What about our staring contests? And the way we always knew what football coaches should have done? Remember the day we jumped that census guy and stole his clicker?*

Music Moment:
When Homer tells the tiki, "Get outta my dreams and into my car," he's quoting the Billy Ocean song of the same name.

People Who Need People:
Homer: *Stupid Barney! Thinks he's too good for me.*
Marge: *Cheer up, Homey. You don't need friends to be happy. I haven't had a friend in years.*
Homer: *But you've got me. Who have I got?*
Marge: *You still have Lenny and Carl.*
Homer: *Aw, Lenny and Carl suck! Please don't tell Lenny and Carl I said that! 'Cause if I ever lost them as friends...*

Cross Purposes:
Lisa: *Oh, we'll never get a good picture.*
Bart: *Hey, why don't we dump spaghetti on Maggie's head?*
Lisa: *That picture's a cliché.*
Bart: *Picture?*

Barney Takes One of His Twelve Steps:
Barney: *Moe, I've come here to make amends for my disgraceful behavior over the last twenty years.*
Moe: *No, that's okay, Barn.*
Barney: *No, it's not okay. I broke barstools, befouled your broom closet, and made sweet love to your pool table...which I then befouled.*
Moe: *Well, that would explain the drop-off in play.*

News as It Happens:
Kent Brockman: *This is a Channel 6 news bulletin. Fire has broken out on Mt. Springfield, trapping two youngsters and their camera.*
Homer: *Oh, no! That's Bart and Lisa!*
Kent: *Unfortunately, fire trucks are unavailable to fight the blaze as they're all being used to film the new Burt Reynolds movie, Fireball and Mudflap. I caught up with Burt on the set. (Cut to Kent and Burt sitting on a movie set.) So, Burt, tell us a little about Fireball and Mudflap.*
Burt Reynolds: *I play Jerry "Fireball" Mudflap, a feisty Supreme Court justice who's searching for his birth mother while competing in a cross-country fire truck race. It's...garbage.*

"We should be safe up here. I'm pretty sure fires can't climb trees."

Drunken Homer to the Rescue:
Bart: *You did it, Dad!*
Homer: *You can't prove I did it.*
Lisa: *No, you saved our lives.*
Homer: *I could do a lot of things if I had some money.*
Lisa: *What?*

Movie Moment:
At Moe's Tavern, Homer is ridiculed like Dean Martin's town drunk in *Rio Bravo*, who danced in a bar while being called a rummy and having coins thrown at him.

KILL THE ALLIGATOR

omer gets a self-evaluation magazine and goes around giving tests to friends and family members. When he finally tests himself, the results confirm that he has only a few years left to live. This frightens Homer, causing him to lose sleep. Sleep deprivation leads to neurotic behavior, so the power plant psychiatrist suggests he take a vacation in Florida. When the Simpsons arrive in a small Florida town, the place is swarming with college students on Spring Break. Before Marge can stop him, Homer joins the festivities.

While Marge and the children see the sights, Homer parties with the college kids. Homer has a drunken, rowdy day, and he sleeps so well that he feels sane again the next morning. He wants to party some more, but he discovers that Spring Break is over. Undaunted, Homer takes the family out to the swamps on an airfoil and parties there, but he accidentally runs over the town's most famous resident, a giant alligator named Captain Jack. The angry town sheriff arrests the whole family for murdering the alligator, but when he is not looking, the Simpsons escape.

On the run from the law, the Simpsons take jobs in a backwoods diner, and for a while they enjoy a simple country existence. Before long, the sheriff catches them, and they are sentenced to hard labor on a chain gang. The family is put on a work furlough at a posh garden party. They attempt to escape during the party, but their plan is foiled. Fortunately, Captain Jack makes an appearance at the party. It seems Homer only stunned the town's famous reptile. The Simpsons are released and told to never to return to Florida.

SHOW HIGHLIGHTS

Homer the Rebel:
Bart: *Here's the mail, Dad. That'll be three dollars for on-couch delivery.*
Homer: *(paying him) And three makes three.*
Bart: *This isn't real money! It's printed by the Montana Militia.*
Homer: *(threateningly) It'll be real soon enough.*

Getting Testy:
Homer: *Oo, my first issue of Self-Test Monthly. Finally, I get to find out what makes me tick.*
Bart: *I'm betting it's hunger and rage.*
Homer: *Yeah, but in what ratio?*

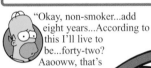

"Okay, non-smoker...add eight years...According to this I'll live to be...forty-two? Aaooww, that's horrible! I won't even live to see my children die!"

Reliving Bad Memories:
Homer: *Okay, Flanders. Your love quiz score is 61. That makes you a "Frigid Frieda." I took off thirty points for all that crying you did.*
Ned: *Well, it was a little insensitive of you giving me a sex test, being that my wife just passed away.*
Homer: *No way! When?*
Ned: *Six months ago! You were at the funeral. You fell into the grave!*
Homer: *Oh, yeah. I saw a gopher. What a day!*

Thanks for Nothing:
Homer: *Okay, last question. Who is your favorite Backstreet Boy?*
Lenny: *Oh! The little rat-faced one.*
Carl: *No, no, no. Nick! He's so good to his mother.*
Homer: *According to this, you're both idiots.*
Lenny: *Hey, thanks. What do we owe ya?*

Music Moments:
Homer sings the words to Kid Rock's "Bawitdaba" during the Spring Break concert, and Kid Rock sings the song over the closing credits.

The classic college party song "Louie, Louie" plays during Homer's airfoil ride through the Florida swamps.

When a college girl presses her breasts against the Simpson's car window and Marge exclaims, "Take 'em off the glass! Take 'em off the glass!" it is a reference to the rap song/video "Put 'em on the Glass" by Sir Mix-A-Lot.

The Numbers Don't Lie:
Marge: *Now what's wrong?*
Homer: *I've only got three more years to live.*
Marge: *Well, maybe you added it wrong; let me have it. (tallying his score) Gasp!*
Homer: *See? And these quizzes are never wrong, Marge. They're put together by the finest scientists in the magazine business.*

What's in a Nickname?
Psychiatrist: *What you need is a good, long rest. I suggest Florida.*
Homer: *Florida? But that's "America's Wang"!*
Psychiatrist: *They prefer "The Sunshine State."*

On the Way to Florida:
Lisa: *Mom! Bart's sitting next to me!*
Bart: *Mom! Lisa's growing!*
Marge: *Quiet, you two! You know your father's had a breakdown.*
Homer: *My pockets hurt!*

Smokey and the Party Animal:
Homer: *Guess how many boobs I saw today, Marge? Fifteen!*
(He passes out.)
Marge: *I hope he didn't cause too much trouble, Sheriff.*
Sheriff: *Aw, boys will be boys. I reckon he was just blowin' off a little steam.*
Homer: *(coming to) Heh, heh, heh! Doesn't he talk funny?*
(He passes out again.)

SPRING BREAK 4-EVER

AND RUN

Episode BABF16
Original Airdate: 04/30/00
Writer: John Swartzwelder
Director: Jen Kamerman
Executive Producer: Mike Scully

Guest Voices: Joe C. as Himself, Robert Evans as Himself, Kid Rock as Himself, and Charlie Rose as Himself

I AM NOT HERE ON A FARTBALL SCHOLARSHIP
I AM NOT HERE ON A FARTBALL SCHOLARSHIP
I AM NOT HERE ON A FARTBALL SCHOLARSHIP

THE SOUTHERN SHERIFF

Recognizable by:
His red neck

Tools of the trade:
Handcuffs of every size

Preferred method of correction:
Whipping

Unusual ability:
When he throws his hat to the ground, it bounces back onto his head—but only when nobody's looking

Surprising fact:
Thinks Kid Rock's "Fists of Rage" is a good song

Swamp Meet:

Lisa: *Look at the size of that gator.*
Marge: *Is he a man-eater?*
Park Guide: *Only convicts and hobos.*
Bart: *Do you have any hobo chunks we could throw to him?*

Jekyll and Hyde:

Marge: *Did you really have to handcuff the children?*
Sheriff: *No, ma'am, I did not.*
Marge: *You seemed so understanding before. What happened to "boys will be boys"?*
Sheriff: *You see, during Spring Break, the beer companies pay me to look the other way. The rest of the year, I'm a real hard-ass.*

The Big Chase:

Sheriff: *Pull over!*
Homer: *There's no good place!*
Sheriff: *There's lots of good places! What about over there?*
Homer: *No shade!*

Simple Plan:

(Homer speeds toward the railroad crossing with the family in tow.)
Marge: *Homer, no! You'll kill us all.*
Homer: *Or die trying!*

"This family has hit a new low. We're on the run from the law, totally lost, no car, no money, no clean clothes, and it's all your fault."

Movie Moments:

The jewel in Sepulveda the MTV VJ's palm starts to flash on her birthday in a nod to the classic science-fiction thriller *Logan's Run.*

The chain gang, the whip, and the guard in the mirrored sunglasses are all elements from the Paul Newman prison film *Cool Hand Luke.*

A giant alligator appearing in the middle of a garden party is reminiscent of the John Sayles–penned horror film *Alligator*, but with far less fatal results.

Help Wanted:

Velma: *You took the signs out of the window? That's pretty presumptuous. How do you know I'm going to hire you?*
Bart: *Sorry. I just want to be a broom boy so bad.*
Velma: *I like your attitude. You're hired. How 'bout you, missy? You wanna be a mop girl?*
Lisa: *Not really, no.*
Velma: *I like your honesty. You're hired. (To Homer and Marge) And you two haven't said a word. I like that. You're hired.*

Homer's Country-Life Song:

Jimmy crack corn and I don't care.
Jimmy crack corn and I'm not there.
We built this city on rock 'n' roll.
Something something day!

The Simpsons Down-Home:

Bart: *I'm getting used to this country life. Teacher says I'm whittling at a tenth-grade level.*
Marge: *And y'all hardly ever bicker any more.*
Lisa: *Too hot to bicker, I reckon.*
Homer: *You know, killing that 'gator was the best decision I ever made.*
Bart: *Got that right.*
Marge: *Dern tootin'.*
Lisa: *Boy, howdy.*

A Rush to Judgement:

Southern Judge: *Well, first up is the State of Florida vs. the Simpson family.*
Homer: *Your honor, I'd like to represent myself. (speaking to the jury) Drunken hicks of the jury...*

Sweet-Talkin' Marge:

Marge: *My goodness, what a lovely suit, sheriff. Is that seersucker?*
Sheriff: *Nah, not on a civil servant's salary. It's nearsucker.*
Marge: *Well, the fabric really brings out the red in your neck.*
Sheriff: *Yup, it's coming along, huh? You should see it in August after the horseflies been gettin' at it. Whoo, man!*
Marge: *Dang, I wish I could, but in August, our chain gang has to dig for tar.*
Sheriff: *Well, now, heh-heh. I might could switch you to dead-animal pickup.*

THE STUFF YOU MAY HAVE MISSED

Homer's Quiz Master hat is an orange traffic cone with a question mark painted on it.

As Homer rocks back and forth in his sleeping bag, it makes the picture of a cowboy riding a horse on the bag appear to gallop.

While in the car on the way to Florida, Homer holds a pennant that says "Mental."

The billboard that says "Welcome to Palm Corners" has a picture of an alligator sleeping contentedly on a pillow.

College boys switch the marquee of "The Royal Fart Inn" to read "The Royal Frat Inn."

While on vacation, Maggie has a butterfly pin in her hair instead of her usual blue bow.

The MTV-style VJs, Sepulveda and Cienega, are both named after streets in Los Angeles.

As Homer finds out Spring Break is over, a shopkeeper is putting out a "Back to School Sale" sign.

In the swamp, Homer is attacked by turtles, baby alligators, leeches, and an eel.

The trailer behind the diner has corn cob curtains over the kitchen sink, just like Marge's at home.

Palm Corners is in Six Toe County.

The ice sculpture at the judge's soirée is of an electric chair.

YOU IN A HEAP O' TROUBLE, SON!

Guest Voice:
Diedrich Bader as the Southern Sheriff

LITTLE VICKI VALENTINE

Résumé:
Formerly, a too-cute child star; currently, a pushy dance instructor

Credo:
People go to a children's dance recital expecting a certain level of professionalism

The key to great dancing:
One word: tappa-tappa-tappa

Wartime service:
Tapped Morse Code messages to the Allies till her shoes were filled with blood

Craziest act of desperation:
Destroyed Buddy Ebsen's credit rating

Her advice to parents:
Don't live through your child

> I'M EVER SO PISSED!

LAST TAP DANCE

The Simpsons spend the afternoon at the Springfield Mall. Marge needs to buy Bart some supplies for his upcoming camping trip, and Homer's eyesight has gotten so bad that he needs to see the optometrist, where he opts for laser eye surgery instead of glasses. Marge and Lisa go to see a new film at the mall's movie theater about Latin dancing. Lisa is enamored by the movie's plot and decides that she wants to learn how to dance.

Marge enrolls Lisa at a dance studio run by a former child star. Before long, it becomes obvious that Lisa is not a naturally gifted dancer, and the teacher isn't very helpful. Frustrated, Lisa feels like quitting, but doesn't want to disappoint Homer and Marge.

Meanwhile, Bart and Milhouse realize they do not want to spend a week at camp being beaten up by Nelson. They jump off the bus, go to the mall, and camp there instead. At night, when the mall is closed, they have the run of the place and make a big mess.

The mall manager calls the police when he sees the destruction Bart and Milhouse have caused. Chief Wiggum is convinced a giant rat is to blame, so he lets loose a mountain lion in the mall. Luckily, Bart and Milhouse outwit the mountain lion and escape.

Across town, Lisa's dance class is performing a recital. However, the dance instructor will not allow Lisa to participate because her dancing is below par. Wanting to help, Professor Frink provides Lisa with a new invention: self-tapping dance shoes. Delighted, Lisa joins the recital, but her shoes dance out of control, ruining the show and frightening the audience away. When it seems as if Lisa's dream of being a Broadway baby has come to an end, Marge and Homer encourage her to become a writer of depressing, curse-ridden plays, for which she is grateful.

SHOW HIGHLIGHTS

> "Well, looks like we got everything for Bart's camping trip: Blair Witch repellent, antler saw, and deep-woods Scrabble."

Shop till You Drop:
Marge: Come on, Bart. While your dad gets his glasses, we'll go shop for your trip.
Bart: Ooh! I hate shopping. Just get me a deck of cards, and I'll win whatever I need from the other kids.
Marge: But you need to try things on. Every brand has a different idea of "husky."
Bart: (dropping to the ground) I'm in tantrum position. T-minus five...four...three...(his eyes begin to fill with tears) remembering dead cat for real tears...and...
Marge: Fine, you win. I'll do your shopping for you.
Bart: Tantrum averted...but now I can't forget the cat! (He begins to cry.)

The Eyes Have It:
Optometrist: That pair's popular with celebrities like Val Kilmer.
Homer: Ooh, my favorite Door.
Optometrist: And Yoko Ono.
Homer: Ew! She ruined the Plastic Ono Band!
Optometrist: Maybe you're a candidate for laser eye surgery.
Homer: Will it get me out of having to choose glasses?
Optometrist: Well, yes, but I must warn you it's an experimental procedure and we still don't know the long-term effects.
Homer: Less yappin', more zappin'!

Tango de la Muerte:
Eduardo: Now that my severed foot has been reattached, I must win back the coveted dance title "Loco Legs."
Coach: As your wise, but alcoholic dance coach, I know that somewhere your father is looking down on you and smiling. Oh, there he is!
(An older man on a balcony above grins at them and gives them a "thumbs up.")

Cautious Optimism:
Marge: I remember Little Vicki Valentine. Her perky smile and dancing brought America right out of the Depression.
Lisa: Well, I think World War II helped a little, Mom.
Marge: Don't smart mouth, Lisa.

Little Big Deal:
Little Vicki Valentine: A great big sunshine hello to you.
Marge: Hi, Little Vicki!
Little Vicki: Ha, ha, ha! That was such a long time ago. I'm just plain Vicki now.
Marge: All right, I'd like to sign my daughter up for lessons, Vicki.
Little Vicki: Little Vicki.

Where Do We Go from Here?
Milhouse: I don't want to go home. My grandma's sleeping in my bed, and she has skin like a basketball.
Bart: Wait a minute. Everybody thinks we're at camp this week. We can stay wherever we want!
Milhouse: Yeah! Like the Four Seasons! Each room has its own safe.

A Sweet Discovery:
(Bart and Milhouse fall from an air shaft into barrels of candy.)
Milhouse: (horrified) Worms!
Bart: Gold! Wait...(disappointed) This is just chocolate...(thrilled) chocolate!
Milhouse: And these are Gummi worms! (excitedly) Gummi!
Bart: Warheads? Jelly Bellies? We're like two kids in a candy store!

Letter Home:
Homer: Hey, we got a postcard from Bart. "Dear Mom and Homer, I'm having fun." Aw, it sounds like he's having fun!
Marge: Why does it have a picture of Vitamin Barn?
Homer: Didn't you ever go to camp? (reminiscing) The old vitamin barn.

Off the Beat:
Lisa: What am I doing wrong, Little Vicki?
Little Vicki: Well, you're falling a lot. Maybe you should work on that.
Lisa: Yeah. Well, no offense, but maybe I need a little more instruction than just: tappa-tappa-tappa.
Little Vicki: Why, back when I was your age, I had forty-three movies under my belt, and I had to do it without tappa-tappa-tappa. I would've killed for tappa-tappa-tappa.
Lisa: Sorry. I'm just frustrated.
Little Vicki: Well, you'll never save Grandpa's farm with that attitude! You've just got to turn that frown upside-down! (Lisa attempts a smile.) That's a smile, not an upside-down frown! Work on that, too!

Screams from a Mall:
Chief Wiggum: We'll catch that mall rat.
Lou: Sure hope this ACME kit works.
Wiggum: Gosh, that cheese looks good. Think I could grab it before that anvil hits?
Lou: Oh, I don't know, Chief. It's a million to one.
Wiggum: I like those odds! (He reaches for the cheese and the anvil hits him in the back.) Oh! My mistake was grabbing the cheese.

Movie Moments:

The "dancer meets ugly ducking, transforms her into a beauty, and together they win the dance contest" plot of *Tango de la Muerte* has been seen in many movies, most recently in *Strictly Ballroom*.

Chief Wiggum's warning to the mall manager to close the mall on President's Day weekend echoes that of Chief Brody to the mayor of Amity to close the beaches on Memorial Day weekend in *Jaws*.

Little Vicki Valentine is loosely based on 1930s child star Shirley Temple. The movie Lisa watches on television evokes memories of Shirley Temple and her most famous dance partner, Bill "Bojangles" Robinson, in such films as *The Littlest Rebel*, *The Little Colonel*, and *Rebecca of Sunnybrook Farm*.

IN SPRINGFIELD

Episode BABF15
Original Airdate: 05/07/00
Writer: Julie Thacker
Director: Nancy Kruse
Executive Producer: Mike Scully

THE STUFF YOU MAY HAVE MISSED

Homer's optometrist works at "Eye Caramba."

Baby Gerald's mother only has one eyebrow, too.

In *Tango de la Muerte*, the sign outside where the contest is being held reads "Tonight: Contesto de la Dance, Tomorrow: ¡Revolucion!"

Movie posters seen in Little Vicki's studio are *Little Vicki for President*, *Little Vicki vs. Big Rhonda*, and *Hell Hath No Little Vicki*.

According to the banner on the bus, Bart and Milhouse are heading for "Camp Franks 'n' Pranks."

Among the children taking dance lessons from Little Vicki Valentine are Alex Whitney, who was first seen in "Lard of the Dance" (5F20), and Allison Taylor, who first appeared in "Lisa's Rival" (1F17).

The salesman at Stan's Keyboards is playing on a MORG keyboard, which appears to be named after two musical influences—the Moog synthesizer and the popular professional Korg keyboard brand.

The trap the police set at the mall is from ACME, the same company where Looney Tunes' Wile E. Coyote gets his equipment to catch the Roadrunner.

The dancing Martians pop out of their craters and giggle just like the Munchkins do in *The Wizard of Oz*.

Lisa's runaway shoes may have been inspired by Hans Christian Andersen's fairy tale "The Red Shoes," in which a ballerina is tormented by slippers that will not stop dancing.

The Show Must Go On:

Little Vicki: *Heavens to Betsy! The star of the show is sick! Whatever will we do? There's only one person who can get us out of this pickle...Lisa?*
Lisa: *(hopefully) Yes?*
Little Vicki: *Help me into Ralph's costume.*
Lisa: *Sigh!*

On the Spaceship Lollipop:

Little Vicki: *Lean, muscular children of Mars! We bring you candy!*
(The Martians giggle.)
Allison Taylor: *Let's walk over to them.*
Little Vicki: *Why walk when you can dance?*
(We see Marge and Homer in the audience.)
Marge: *Where's Lisa?*
Homer: *Shhh! This plot is hard enough to follow as it is.*

Try a Little Less Tenderness:

Prof. Frink: *Jesus, Mary, and glavin! These shoes are in the "off" position!*
Lisa: *You mean I danced all by myself?*
Marge: *See, honey? All you needed was to believe in...*
Homer: *What are you talking about, Professor Frink? They're clearly in the "on" position. See? "On."*
Prof. Frink: *I was merely trying to spare the girl's feelings, you insensitive clod.*
Homer: *Oh...oh! Well, now that I look even closer...*
Lisa: *Forget it, Dad.*

ach student in Bart's class is given a camera to use to make a video project. Bart tapes Otto the bus driver proposing marriage to his girlfriend Becky and volunteers the Simpsons' house for their wedding. On the day of the wedding, Marge learns that Becky does not like Otto's heavy-metal music and encourages Becky to make Otto choose between her and his music. Otto chooses music and the wedding is off.

Marge feels bad about breaking up the wedding, so she lets Becky move in until she gets over it. After a while Marge begins to resent the competition of another woman in the house. After talking to her sisters, she is convinced Becky is trying to kill her and take her place. When Marge meets the family at an ice cream parlor, she

discovers Becky giving artificial respiration to Homer. Misinterpreting Becky's actions for a kiss, Marge attacks her and is arrested by the police.

A board of psychiatrists declares Marge legally insane, but before she can be sent to a mental hospital, she escapes. Everyone in town believes she is crazy, even her family. Failing to find any "real" evidence against Becky, Marge returns home just in time to witness Becky performing a satanic sacrifice on Homer, Lisa, and Maggie. When it is revealed that Bart was just making a music video for school, Marge thinks she really is crazy until Becky admits she was planning to kill Marge and take over the family after all. A doctor arrives with two orderlies and subdues Marge with tranquilizer darts, assisted by Homer.

SHOW HIGHLIGHTS

Principal Skinner, encouraging the future Spielbergs: **"Now be careful with those video cameras, children. In order to buy them, the school board had to eliminate geography.** *(He padlocks a globe.)* **This globe will never spin again."**

A Match Made by Milhouse:

Otto: *Today's the day I ask my girlfriend to take a ride on the matrimony pony.*
Milhouse: *(sing-song) Otto's got a girlfriend! Otto's got a girlfriend!*
Otto: *That's right, I do.*
Milhouse: *Uh...I know you do...baby!*

Popular Science:

Marge: *Let's see...candles, flowers, place cards, rice...*
Lisa: *Oh, Mom, you're not supposed to throw rice anymore. Birds eat it, their stomachs swell, and they explode.*
Bart: *Why am I just learning this now?* (He takes the rice box and his video camera and exits laughing.)

Compensation Miscommunication:

Reverend Lovejoy: *And now, ahem, as for the matter of my honorarium...*
Otto: *What?*
Rev. Lovejoy: *You know, my emolument.*
Otto: *Huh?*
Rev. Lovejoy: *Pay me! Three hundred dollars.*
Otto: *Three hundred? I could've gotten Rick Dees for that.*

Here Comes the Grudge:

Lisa: *Isn't it wonderful to have a hip female influence in the house?*
Marge: *Yes. Well, I guess I'll go roll socks. It's not hip, but it has to be done.*
Becky: *Actually, you could just tie them at the ends. That way the elastic doesn't wear out.*
Marge: *Yes. I hate when things get worn out. Mmm... socks...welcomes...*

Crazy Talk:

Lisa: *Oh, I really miss Mom.*
Bart: *The kids are saying if you say "Bloody Margie" five times, she'll appear. But then she gouges your eyes out.*
Homer: *I hear she mates with men, then eats them.*

Selma on matrimony:
"Always a bridesmaid, only occasionally a bride."

Marge Simpson Living:

Marge: *Now, Lisa's going through this phase where she doesn't eat any meat, so I usually sneak a little meat juice into her vegetables.*
Becky: *Wow, you're a real-life Martha Stewart! I mean, without the evil.*

Movie Moment:

Homer assembles a tool to suck out the innards of the wedding cake as James Bond–like spy music is played.

Otto serenades Becky by holding a boom box above his head the same way John Cusack woos Ione Skye in *Say Anything*.

Patty's declaration about Lisa that "the bitterness is strong in this one" is much like Darth Vader's impression about Luke Skywalker in *Star Wars*.

Strained Relations:

Admiral: *Son, your mother and I don't approve of this marriage, as we have not approved of any part of your life to date.*
Otto: *Well, the important thing is you came.*
Admiral: *We're leaving.*
Otto: *Drive safe!*

MAD MARGE

Episode BABF18
Original Airdate: 05/14/00
Writer: Larry Doyle
Director: Steven Dean Moore
Executive Producer: Mike Scully

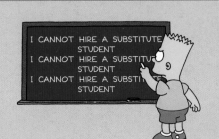

I CANNOT HIRE A SUBSTITUTE STUDENT
I CANNOT HIRE A SUBSTITUTE STUDENT
I CANNOT HIRE A SUBSTITUTE STUDENT

Lazy Patrol:

Chief Wiggum: *Let me tell you what I tell everybody who comes in here. The law is powerless to help you.*
Marge: *Do I have to be dead before you'll help me?*
Wiggum: *Well, not dead...dying. No, no, no, no. Don't walk away. How about this? Just show me the knife...in your back. Not too deep, but it should be able to stand by itself.*

I'm Ready for My Close-up, Mr. Simpson:

Bart: *Tonight, on the Discovery Channel, "Inside Lisa's Nose." What will we find? Boogers or Nazi gold?* (uses his camera to zoom in on Lisa's nostril)
Lisa: *Bart, quit it!*
Bart: *No way.*
Lisa: (to the camera) *Bart sleeps with Raggedy Andy.*
Bart: *Cut, cut, cut!*

Performance Anxiety:

Bart: (aiming his camera into the bathroom) *So, any words for the bride and groom?*
Skinner: *Not now, Bart! I'm trying to urinate.*
Bart: *You don't seem to be trying very hard.*

TV Moment:

Krusty the Clown's comedy bits making fun of Marge are similar to Conan O'Brien's phony celebrity interviews and Jay Leno's "Dancing Judge Itos."

Try a Little Tenderness:

Marge: *Becky, I know you must feel awful, but at least this didn't happen after you were married.*
Homer: *Yes, better now than when you're too old and fat to get another man.*

Law & Order:

(Marge is arrested by Chief Wiggum.)
Marge: *I thought you said, "The law was powerless."*
Chief Wiggum: *Yeah. Powerless to help you, not punish you.*

Suspicious Minds:

Patty: *Look, honey. Never let an attractive woman into your house. All they ever do is usurp your family and then kill you.*
Selma: *Like that documentary, The Hand That Rocks the Cradle.*
Marge: *That was a movie.*

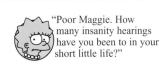
"Poor Maggie. How many insanity hearings have you been to in your short little life?"

THE STUFF YOU MAY HAVE MISSED

The colorists in the couch gag are all Asian.

One of Bart's classmates drops his video camera and says "D'oh!"

At Woodstock '99, two guys are beating up an ATM machine.

Marge shows Becky an issue of *Obsessive Bride* magazine.

After Homer gets his tongue stuck to the wedding ice sculpture, he frees himself by leaving a little piece of his tongue behind.

Homer sings the David Bowie song "Changes" with altered lyrics while changing the car's oil.

When Becky pulls Homer's head out of the ice cream, he has a clown face thanks to a banana, a cherry, and two flavors of ice cream.

At the ice cream parlor, Becky wears the same style dress and pearls that Marge wears to church, only in blue.

Members of the panel of psychiatrists at Marge's sanity hearing include Dr. Foster (with toupee) from "Hurricane Neddy" (4F07) and Dr. Zweig from "Fear of Flying" (2F08).

Kent Brockman profiles "Wet T-shirt Month" at Juggernauts, the same bar chain that employs Titania from "Pygmoelian" (BABF12).

At the Old Springfield Library, there's a banner that reads "We Have Books About TV."

While making Bart's music video, Becky wears a Vampirella costume.

Becky's name appears to be a reference to *The Hand That Rocks the Cradle* star Rebecca DeMornay.

BECKY

Occupation:
Usurper/Drive-thru window cashier at Der Krazy Kraut

Turn-ons:
Putting a little rosemary into gravy

Turn-offs:
When her boyfriend calls their lovemaking "The Headbanger's Ball"

Special talents:
Passionate painter, great karate-kicking control, and can really bring out the mung in beans

MMM, YUMMERS.

Guest Voice:
Parker Posey as Becky

Done in the style of the popular VH1 biography show "Behind the Music," the episode begins with the history of the Simpson family and how they got into show business. The first part of the pseudo-documentary follows the family from their meager beginnings to their phenomenal success. Homer's crude video "pilot" leads to a television show, a recording contract, a lot of awards, and countless wealth.

As the Simpsons' fame continues, chinks begin to show in their armor. Homer becomes addicted to prescription painkillers after a hilarious stunt causes him injury, Marge makes some unwise business investments, and Bart goes to rehab. Soon after, the IRS investigates and takes away their house. Then, at the Iowa State Fair, the family gets into a big argument and splits up.

None of the Simpsons will speak to each other, so Fox is forced to put the show on hiatus. The members go their separate ways: Homer pursues a career in the legitimate theater; Bart gets his own show, an action-adventure series; Marge puts together a nightclub act; and Lisa writes a tell-all book. Reconciliation appears hopeless until country singer Willie Nelson puts on a fake awards show in order to bring the family back together. In an emotional reunion, they hug and forget about past wrongs. Once more, they look forward to the many years of Simpson episodes to come...or not.

SHOW HIGHLIGHTS

The Narrator's introduction to the retrospective: **"They were the first family of American laughter... surfing a tidal wave of hilarity... onto the sands of Superstar Bay. But behind the chortles, this funny five-some was trapped in a private hell."**

The Lives of Stars:

Homer: *Everybody wanted a piece of us.*
Marge: *They told us what to wear, how to dress, which clothes we should put on.*
Bart: *The cops found me driving on the sidewalk.*
Lisa: *I had no business hosting the Oscars. After the show, Meryl Streep spit on me!*

TV or Not TV?:

Ned: *I'd see 'em sitting on that couch all day long, just staring at that Hollywood hogwash.*
Homer: *Our favorite show was "Hollywood Hogwash," but we also loved "The Dreck Squad"...*
Marge: *"The Malarkeys," "Dumbin' It Down"...*
Lisa: *"Sheriff Lowbrow"...*
Bart: *"Home Improvement"...*
Homer: *...but we never saw people like us on TV.*

Early "Simpsons" Test:

Homer: *"My Funny Family." Take One. And...action! Honey, I'm home. The boss is coming to dinner and I need a clean shirt.*
Marge: *I haven't done the laundry yet.*
Homer: *Mama mia! Now I'll have to do it!* (He crosses to a nearby washing machine and pours in a liberal amount of detergent.)
Lisa: *Dad, that's too much detergent!*
Homer: *Not now! I'm busy turning on this washing machine.*
(Soap suds begin to fill the room. Bart enters the front door wearing a fake mustache and a sash with "Boss" written on it.)
Bart: *Simpson! Where's my dinner?*
Homer: *Mama mia!*

Differing Viewpoints:

Marge: *Okay, the material was a little corny, but Homer and I had real chemistry on-screen.*
Homer: *Every day I thought about firing Marge. You know, just to shake things up.*

Rehearsal Footage:

Homer: *Son, let's go out for frosty chocolate milkshakes.*
Bart: *Cowabunga, dude!*
Director: *And...cut.*
Bart: *Dad, I've never said "cowabunga" in my life! Your script sucks!*
Homer: *Why, you little...!* (grabbing Bart by the throat and choking him)
Director: *Hey, that's funny!*

Homer, on choking Bart: **"...and that horrible act of child abuse became one of our most beloved running gags."**

"Yeah, I've seen all the overnight sensations... Brad Hall, Rich Hall, Rich Little, Little Richard...but the Simpsons blew 'em all away. They even had a hit record! Meanwhile, 'Krustophenia' sits on the shelf!"

Homer comes clean: **"I want to set the record straight. I thought... the cop...was a prostitute."**

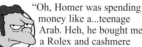

"Oh, Homer was spending money like a...teenage Arab. Heh, he bought me a Rolex and cashmere jeans. I felt kinda guilty 'cause I was always trying to score with his wife. So, when do we start filming? *(being told from off-camera that he has been filmed all along)* Ohhh."

Moments from "Behind the Laughter" taken from previous episodes of "The Simpsons":

Title Sequences:

Marge as a policewoman shooting her gun on the obstacle course from "The Springfield Connection" (2F21); Homer at Cockamamie's collectible shop from "Homer's Phobia" (4F11); Homer battling the lard vacuum from "Lard of the Dance" (5F20); Bart being chased by Homer while holding the change jar à la *Raiders of the Lost Ark* from "Bart's Friend Falls in Love" (8F22); Lisa playing her new sax with an inscription from Homer on it from "Lisa's Sax" (3G02); Maggie liberating her fellow babies' pacifiers at the Ayn Rand School for Tots from "A Streetcar Named Marge" (8F18); Bart falling down the well from "Radio Bart" (8F11).

Citizens of Springfield Interviewed:

Ned Flanders—Neighbor; Krusty the Klown—Embittered Comedy Legend; Moe Szyslak—Local Hothead; Lenny & Carl—Nuclear Technicians; Seymour Skinner—Educator; Comic Book Guy—Comic Book Guy; Clancy Wiggum—Interim Police Chief; Anonymous Tipster (Apu); Abe Simpson—Coot; Dr. Julius Hibbert—Meddler.

Homer Greatest "Hits":

Jumping the Springfield Gorge on Bart's skateboard from "Bart the Daredevil" (7F06); skiing downhill and hitting snow mounds with his crotch from "Little Big Mom" (BABF04); being punched in the face by Groundskeeper Willie from "Lard of the Dance" (5F20); trapped in a runaway cherry picker and scraping his head on an overpass from "Lost Our Lisa" (5F17); parasailing and crashing through the glass ceiling of the Baldwin/Basinger house from "When You Dish upon a Star" (5F19); using his body to stop a wrecking ball from "Sideshow Bob Roberts" (2F02); being hit over the head with a chair while in the bathtub from "A Milhouse Divided" (4F04).

"Trendy" Guest Stars (In Order of Appearance):

Butch Patrick from "Eight Misbehavin'" (BABF03), Buzz Aldrin from "Deep Space Homer" (1F13), Tom Kite from "Scenes from the Class Struggle in Springfield" (3F11), Stephen Hawking from "They Saved Lisa's Brain" (AABF18), and "Sir" Gary Coleman from "Grift of the Magi" (BABF07). (According to this episode, Gary Coleman has been knighted.)

Other Moments:

"The Principal and the Pauper" (4F23), the episode when Seymour Skinner reveals that he is an imposter, is used as an example of a show that has a "gimmicky premise" and a "nonsensical plot."

Homer is seen on screen during the episode with a plunger stuck on his head. The same incident, but not the same footage, occurred in the opening moments of "The Front" (9F16).

The dialogue from the "Delaware" scene of "The Simpsons" that the family watches in the editing room comes from the opening scene of "Simpsons Tall Tales" (CABF17), the final episode of Season 12. However, it appears that only the soundtrack is used, since the opening scene of "Simpsons Tall Tales" takes place at the Springfield Airport and not the family's living room.

More of Homer's Greatest "Hits" (Closing Credits):

Being beaten up by Bart's big brother, Tom, from "Brother from the Same Planet" (9F12); being hit in the stomach by a cannonball in "Homerpalooza" (3F21); getting butted by reindeer while holding Bart over his head in "Homer's Phobia" (4F11); being strangled by Willie with the vacuum hose in "Lard of the Dance" (5F20); getting crushed by a car that falls off a transport truck in "Homer Simpson in: 'Kidney Trouble'" (AABF04); being hit over the head with a chair while in the bathtub in "A Milhouse Divided" (4F04); flying upside down in a plane and being dragged through rose bushes from "I'm with Cupid" (AABF11); skiing downhill and hitting snow mounds with his crotch from "Little Big Mom" (BABF04); being trapped in a runaway cherry picker and getting his head caught in a drawbridge from "Lost Our Lisa" (5F17); jumping out of Moe's car, while attempting to steal it, and rolling back in from "Dumbbell Indemnity" (5F12).

LAUGHTER

Episode BABF19
Original Airdate: 05/21/00
Writers: Tim Long, George Meyer, Mike Scully, and Matt Selman
Director: Mark Kirkland
Executive Producers: Mike Scully, George Meyer, and Al Jean
Guest Voices: Jim Forbes as the Narrator, and Willie Nelson as Himself

I WILL NOT OBEY THE VOICES IN MY HEAD
I WILL NOT OBEY THE VOICES IN MY HEAD
I WILL NOT OBEY THE VOICES IN MY HEAD

THE STUFF YOU MAY HAVE MISSED

Magazine covers the Simpsons are featured on include: *TV Guide*, *Rolling Stone*, *Coin Laundry News*, and *Short Hair Ideas*.

Words that are seen during the "Behind the Laughter" title sequences are: Success, Fame, Beer, Candy, Money, Drugs, Women, Donuts, Sex, Milhouse, Lawsuits, Redemption, Hormones, and Graphics.

The major networks Homer tries to sell his demo tape to: ABC, NBC, and Telemundo.

The girls screaming wildly at Bart on TV, as though he were one of the Beatles, are inmates in a hysteria ward.

The various Bart sayings printed on T-shirts read: "Good Grief, Man," "You Bet Your Sweet Bippy, Man," and "Life Begins at Conception, Man."

Headline reviews in the Hollywood trades *Daily Variety* and *The Hollywood Reporter* read: "Yellow Fever" and "Bumptious Brood Boffo!" respectively.

The *Krustophenia* record cover is a parody of The Who's album *Quadrophenia*.

The Simpsons records that go mega-platinum are *Simpsons Boogie*, *Lovely to Love Your Lovin'*, and *Simpsons Christmas Boogie*.

Ozzy Osbourne bites the top off of a Grammy and the trophy starts spurting blood à la his alleged dove- and bat-biting incidents.

The Queen of England is eating a TV dinner while watching "The Simpsons."

The people at the parade like the Simpsons more than Santa Claus, the Pope, and an astronaut.

Walk of Fame stars near to the Simpsons include: Milton Berle (with a symbol of a TV), Joan Jett (a typewriter), Nelson Mandela (a race car), and the Cheerios Honey Bee.

While the Comic Book Guy is being interviewed in The Android's Dungeon, there is a toy version of the Iron Giant on the shelf behind him. *The Iron Giant* was written and directed by former "Simpsons" director Brad Bird.

Richie Rich appears as Bart in an episode entitled "Disorder in the Court."

The opening act for the Simpsons' show at the Iowa State Fair is "Jimmy Carter's Habitat for Hilarity."

The costumes the Simpsons wear for their show at the Iowa State Fair are very similar to the Partridge Family's performing outfits.

When the Simpsons show is put on hiatus, it is replaced by a reality show called "Peepin' It Real," with footage taken from the dressing room at Ann Taylor.

At the Thanksgiving dinner, Marge is represented by her lawyer (Mr. Burns's lawyer), Lisa by hers (Gloria Allred), and Bart by his (a Christopher Darden look-alike). Homer's lawyer is not featured. Also, Grampa and Maggie are seated at the children's table.

After helping to reunite the Simpsons, Willie Nelson's braids fly up just like Pippi Longstocking's pigtails.

Stool Pigeon:
Narrator: *Then, another bombshell. An anonymous tipster alerted Uncle Sam that the Simpsons were evading their income taxes.*
Apu: *(in silhouette) Yes, I finked on Homer. But you know, he deserved it. Never have I seen such abuse of the take-a-penny/leave-a-penny tray.*

Smackeroos for Smacks:
Lenny: *Even Bart was throwing dough around. He paid me and Carl a thousand bucks to kiss each other.*
Carl: *Hey, did we ever get that money?*

"One time, Lisa bought a first edition of 'Susan B. Anthony Man.' Her check bounced higher than Rubber Girl."

Trouble on the Set:
Lisa: *Dad, I want to go to bed. Aren't there child labor laws?*
Homer: *Who told you about those laws? Was it Marge?*
Marge: *Hey, you've been riding me all day. Why don't you poop in your hat?*
Kang: *Are you going to need us tonight?*
Kodos: *I have ballet tickets, not that they'll do much good now.*

Revealed this episode:
The Simpsons are from northern Kentucky.

The Narrator chronicles the family's fall from grace: **"The Simpsons' TV show started out on a wing and a prayer, but now the wing was on fire and the prayer had been answered...by Satan."**

Marge learns an important lesson: **"When people reach for their diaphragm, they don't want to see my picture."**

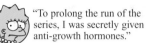

"To prolong the run of the series, I was secretly given anti-growth hormones."

Movie Moment:
The image of the plastic grocery bag getting blown by a gentle updraft comes from a similarly metaphorical scene in the film *American Beauty*.

Back to "Normal":
Homer: *We put all the craziness behind us, and now it's time to get back to what matters—the show...and the Sunday comic strip.*
Marge: *Which Homer writes himself.*
Bart: *(sarcastically) So you know it's great!*
Homer: *Why you little...! (grabbing Bart by the throat and choking him)*
Narrator: *So whether choking their son or poking some fun, the Simpsons will keep on gagging for years to come.*

A Bright Future:
(The family views "dailies" on a monitor over an editor's shoulder.)
Marge: *I can't believe it! We won another contest!*
Homer: *The Simpsons are going to Delaware!*
Lisa: *I want to see Wilmington!*
Bart: *I want to visit a screen-door factory!*
Homer: *(aside to the editor) This'll be the last season.*

22| "BRO
DESCRIPTION

NED DRESSED AS BAD ASS
BIKER

KN/SA

Eyeball
from side

FUNZO
ROUGHS

Bottom jaw
slides up and
down

size
relationship

Other eyeball options:

Enclosed highlight
in black pupil

Pupil inside
blank iris ring

BABF07   Act III
Funzo

- Raymond Persi and Joe W.

BABF13   Act I
"Rat Pack" Totem Pole
- Joe

FINAL   11·18·99

Harness: white canvas

Sketch for possible
feeding position

Note: Apu is shirtless.

BABF03   Act II
Apu with Baby
Bottle Harness

- Joe

FINAL   7·22·99

ROUGH

fated
3-6-00

BABF17   Act III
Johnny Tightlips

- Joe

DIRECTORS
APPROVAL

Opening Sequence

The episode begins with a parody of the classic TV series "The Munsters," with "The Simpsons" theme song being played to similar electric guitar strains as "The Munsters" theme. Homer, looking like Herman Munster, crashes through the front door. At first, he is embarrassed and then he laughs with child-like delight and exits. Marge, dressed as Lily Munster, emerges cautiously from the doorway and checks the weather while holding a six-pack of Duff. Homer comes back, kisses her on the cheek, takes her by the arm, and they walk off together. Bart, as Eddie, enters holding a large slingshot and practices taking aim with it before walking off. Next comes Lisa, as Marilyn, holding a book with the title "Copyright Law." As she exits, Grampa Simpson, dressed as a vampire like his counterpart, appears with a bubbling beaker that holds his dentures. He pops the fake fangs in his mouth. The family suddenly joins him in the doorway when they see that an angry mob is approaching holding torches, axes, baseball bats, and boards with nails in them. The townspeople attack the family, and when the dust clears, we see everybody but Lisa lying dead or dying on the ground. Homer is on fire, Marge (with a garland of garlic around her neck), and Grampa have stakes through their hearts, and Bart's head is caught in a hunter's trap. Lisa exits, nonchalantly whistling, having been overlooked because she appears normal.

G-G-GHOST D-D-DAD

Homer's daily horoscope predicts his death, and after several near-fatal encounters, he chokes on a piece of broccoli and dies. Up in Heaven, St. Peter looks at Homer's file and discovers that he did not do any good deeds in his lifetime. Homer is sent back to Earth for twenty-four hours so he can perform one good deed and thus pass through the Pearly Gates. Homer has little success performing a good deed, but eventually and accidentally he manages to save a baby's life. Happily, Homer returns to Heaven, but St. Peter was not paying attention and missed the good deed. Homer is sent to Hell for all eternity.

SHOW HIGHLIGHTS

Getting into the Spirit:

Ghost Homer: *Marge, you gotta help me! I have to do one good deed to get into Heaven.*
Marge: *Well, I've got a whole list of chores: clean the garage, paint the house, grout the tu--*
Ghost Homer: *Whoa! Whoa! Whoa! I'm just trying to get in! I'm not running for Jesus.*

Homer's unusually specific horoscope: **"Today you will die, and you may get a compliment from an attractive coworker."**

Comic Strip Snit:

Homer: *Hey! Who cut out "Beetle Bailey"? I need my Miss Buxley fix.*
Marge: *(holding a pair of scissors and the excised strip) I don't like you ogling her! Why don't you read "Cathy"? She's hilarious.*
Homer: *Eh. Too much baggage.*

Movie Moment:

The child in distress, rolling down the steps of a government building in a baby carriage, resembles a scene from the classic silent film *Battleship Potemkin* (1925), directed by Sergei Eisenstein. This famous scene was also recreated by Brian DePalma in *The Untouchables*.

Slither and Yawn:

Lenny: *Homer, if I may compliment you...*
Homer: *Yes? Go on.*
Lenny: *That is one handsome rattlesnake you got biting your arm there.*
Carl: *Yeah, that's quite fetching. But, uh, aren't you worried about the deadliness?*
Homer: *Nah, he'll get tired of biting in an hour or so.*

Missed It by That Much:

Homer: *Did you see that? I did the deed! Open up.*
St. Peter: *Oh, I'm so sorry. I wasn't looking.*
Homer: *Hey! I thought you guys could see everything!*
St. Peter: *No, you're thinking of Santa Claus.*
Homer: *Well, I'll be damned.*
St. Peter: *I'm afraid so, yes.*

Death by Vegetable:

Dr. Hibbert: *(shaking his head) Hmm. Another broccoli-related death.*
Marge: *But I thought broccoli was--*
Dr. Hibbert: *Oh, yes, one of the deadliest plants on Earth. Why, it tries to warn you itself with its terrible taste. Ah-heh-heh-heh-heh-heh.*

"Ha, ha! Your dad is dead! Mine's just in jail!"

THE STUFF YOU MAY HAVE MISSED

Marge takes issue with yet another comic strip in this episode. In "Missionary: Impossible" (BABF11), she claimed that "Hagar the Horrible" was not funny.

Homer's astrological sign is Taurus.

Apparently, Springfield has had a Planet Hollywood, a Planet Hype, and a Planet Springfield.

The Pearly Gates are electrified.

St. Peter plays Solitaire and reads the newspaper while waiting for souls.

After the baby carriage is hit by a station wagon and a bus, it bursts into flame.

Satan laughs just like Nelson Muntz.

Things that almost kill Homer: **a nasty paper-cut, a tree felled by lightning, a falling globe from a Planet Hollywood being torn down, a pickax to the forehead, a poisonous snake bite, and an**

HORROR XI

Episode BABF21
Original Airdate: 11/01/00
Writers: Rob LaZebnik, John Frink, Don Payne, and Carolyn Omine
Director: Matt "Groening" Nastuk

Executive Producers: Mike "Insert Scary Name" Scully, George Meyer, Alimony Jean

SCARY TALES CAN COME TRUE

The Simpsons are a peasant family, living near the deep, dark woods. Homer loses his job as an oaf, so he throws Bart and Lisa into the woods so that he will have two less mouths to feed. Marge becomes irate because she reasons that they could have sold the kids, and so Homer enters the forest to find them. Meanwhile, with the help of a book of fairy tales, Bart and Lisa are able avoid many dangers in the woods. However, Lisa neglects to check her book when they meet an old lady who lives in a gingerbread house, and the children soon find themselves in the clutches of an evil witch. Just when the witch is about to cook Lisa, Homer finds them. The witch turns him into a half-chicken, half-fish creature with broomstick hands, but Homer is able to force her into the oven and save the day. Upon the witch's death, her spell on Homer is partially reversed. Safely back at home, the family, though still poor, is able to subsist on the eggs that Homer can now lay with his half-chicken body.

SHOW HIGHLIGHTS

Thinking with Their Stomachs:
Bart: *Wow! A house made of gingerbread.*
Witch: *Come on in, my darlings. The best candies are inside.*
Lisa: *Wait! Let me check the book.*
(The witch cackles.)
Bart: *Eh, she seems nice. I'm gonna go with my gut and trust her.*
Lisa: *You're probably right.*

"Son, I don't like you watching that fire. It's too violent."

Unemployed Oaf:
Homer: *I lost my job as an oaf today.*
Marge: *What? Oh, why are the oafs always the first to go?*
Bart: *Maybe you can be a dunce, Father.*

"Imaginary" Boyfriend?

Witch: *Stop your jabbering and sweep! This house is filthy!*
Bart: *So, what do you care? It's not like you have friends.*
Witch: *I have a boyfriend.*
Bart: *Yeah, right.*
Lisa: *(snickering) Sure.*
Witch: *What? I do.*
Lisa: *Oh yeah? What's his name?*
Witch: *Uh, George...(looking around and spying the cauldron) Cauldron.*
Lisa: *George Cauldron? Maybe he can fix me up with Ed Ladle.*

Getting Ready for Dinner:

Witch: *Sweep faster! (poking Lisa with a stick) It's almost time for your beating!*
Lisa: *Oh, this is horrible!*
Bart: *(eating a slice of pie) Horribly delicious.*
Lisa: *You know, she's only fattening you up so she can eat you.*
Bart: *Eh, what are you gonna do?*
(He squirts gravy over his head with a baster.)
Lisa: *Well, at least stop basting yourself!*

"Aw, geez. I came on too strong again. Uh, I'm so desperately lonely."

TV Moment:

Suzanne the witch's "invention" of a boyfriend is reminiscent of Eve Plumb (as Jan Brady) making up a boyfriend (named George Glass) in a similar fashion in an episode entitled "The Not So Ugly Duckling" on "The Brady Bunch."

Deconstructing Homer:

(Homer suddenly appears, eating through the gingerbread house)
Homer: *Mmm...sugar walls.*
Lisa: *Father, I knew you'd rescue us.*
Homer: *Rescue you, stuff myself with candy...it's all good.*
(He takes a bite out of a big candy cane in the corner and the roof starts to cave in.)
Witch: *Oh! That's a load-bearing candy cane, you clumsy oaf!*

THE STUFF YOU MAY HAVE MISSED

The giant pumpkin the Simpsons live in has the same bay windows as their "normal" house on Evergreen Terrace.

When Homer comes home from his job as an oaf, he's got one foot stuck in a bucket.

The Three Bears have a bear-shaped doorknocker.

When the Three Bears come home, they are humming the song "Teddy Bears' Picnic." Bart once performed the same song at Moe's Tavern in "Burns Verkaufen der Kraftwerk" (8F09).

Maggie is put on sale for "2 Chickens or Best Offer."

When the half-chicken, half-fish, part-broomstick Homer faces off with the witch, he scratches the floor like a fighting rooster.

Homer tells it like it is: **"Oh, I'm no dunce. I was born an oaf, and I'll die an oaf."**

HORROR XI

NIGHT OF THE DOLPHIN

A t a marine amusement park, Lisa takes pity on a sad-looking, performing dolphin and releases it into the ocean. Once back among its kind, the dolphin is revealed to be the king. With the aid of an army of loyal subjects, the king dolphin executes a plan to attack the humans on land. With the humans in Springfield surrounded, the king explains that dolphins were once land-dwellers until they were forced to live in the water. King Snorky decrees that humans will be banished to live in the ocean and that the dolphins will stay on dry land. A huge battle follows, but ultimately the dolphins win and the humans are put out to sea.

SHOW HIGHLIGHTS

Chief Wiggum uses his questionable deductive powers: **"Hmm. Bottlenose bruises, blowhole burns, flipper prints. This looks like the work of rowdy teens. Lou, cancel the prom!"**

Homer rallies the humans: **"Wait! Stop! We can outsmart those dolphins. Don't forget: we invented computers, leg warmers, bendy straws, peel 'n' eat shrimp, the glory hole, and the pudding cup! I'm not gonna let a few hoop-jumping, tuna munchers push me around!"**

"Arr, I'm the sea captain! Arr."

The announcer at Marine World: **"Folks, we're heating up the lobster tank, so hurry on over if you want to pet 'em before you eat 'em!"**

Dolphin Disses the Depths:

Marge: *But you seem so happy in the ocean. All that playful leaping.*
King Snorky: *We were trying to get out! It's cold, it's wet...every morning I wake up phlegmy.*
Lisa: *Plus all that sewage we keep dumping.*
King Snorky: *Gasp! That was you?!*
Homer: *It was her all right! Take the one who wronged you!*
King Snorky: *I, King Snorky, hereby banish all humans...to the sea!*

A Monarch's Shame:

Dolphin 1: *Your Majesty! You are free at last!*
King Snorky: *They made me do tricks—Like a common seal!*
Dolphin 1: *Can you put it behind you?*
King Snorky: *No! Here is my secret plan:* (inaudible whispers).
(He whispers to all the dolphins conspiratorially. A small crab nearby overhears the plan and scuttles away.)

"Hey, you gotta hand it to those dolphins. They just wanted it more."

The End of Life as We Know It:

Lisa: *I kinda wish I hadn't freed their leader, and, you know...doomed mankind.*
Marge: *Oh, honey, I wouldn't say doomed. It's gonna be an adjustment, no question.*

Movie Moments:

Snorky the dolphin's triumphant escape from the marine park echoes that of the killer whale in *Free Willy*.

Lenny's drunken ocean swim and subsequent attack by dolphins directly brings to mind the first chilling moments in *Jaws*.

The title of this episode and King Snorky's first spoken words are derived from the movie (and book) *The Day of the Dolphin*, wherein George C. Scott and Trish Van Devere portray scientists who have trained a pair of dolphins how to speak and understand English.

As the citizens of Springfield leave the Town Hall, there appear to be dolphins everywhere—lining the rooftops, the telephone lines, and the jungle gym bars—just like the threatening birds in Alfred Hitchcock's eco-thriller *The Birds*.

"Aaah. Mmm...alcohol and night swimming! It's a winning combination! Uh-oh, sharks! The assassins of the sea. Hey, you're not sharks, you're dolphins... the clowns of the sea. Ow! Owww! Hey, what's the gag?"

THE STUFF YOU MAY HAVE MISSED

The tag-line for Marine World is "No Longer Educational!"

During the Marine World show, Snorky wears a hula skirt and lei.

The gate Lisa opens to let Snorky out has a sign that reads "Authorized Personnel Only (No Dolphins)."

When the dolphins are marching on Springfield, they sing a military cadence.

Krusty Burger serves donut burgers and party-size buckets of flan.

One of the invading dolphins is hanging out by a roadster, flipping a coin.

One of the dolphins beats Homer with a net full of oranges.

Apparently, the statue of Jebediah Springfield floats.

Mayor Quimby attempts to restore order: **"People, please! We're all frightened and horny! But we can't let some killer dolphins keep us from living and scoring."**

Closing Sequence

(Kang and Kodos orbit Earth in their flying saucer.)
Kang: Can you believe it, Kodos? They left us out of the Halloween show.
Kodos: Are you sure the space phone is working? *(Kang picks up the receiver on a phone. A dial tone sounds. Kodos gets anxious.)* Hang up! They could be trying to call right now.
(Kang hangs up the phone.)
Kang: I knew we should have sent them a muffin basket.
(The phone rings. They both reach for it. Kodos answers.)
Kodos: Kang and Kodos Productions. Uh-huh...yes...just a second. *(covering the phone)* Do we want to do a commercial for something called Old Navy?
Kang: *(shrugging)* Hm. Work is work.

Episode BABF20
Original Airdate: 11/05/00
Writer: John Swartzwelder
Director: Shaun Cashman
Executive Producer: Mike Scully

A TALE OF TWO

A badger takes over Santa's Little Helper's doghouse, and after failing to get it out himself, Homer tries to call to Animal Control. When his call will not go through, he learns that the Simpsons' section of town has a new telephone area code. This change upsets Homer, and at a town meeting, he reveals that the rich side of Springfield gets to keep the old area code, while the "Joe Twelve-Packs" have the inconvenience of learning a new code. Homer stirs up emotions at the meeting, and the blue-collar people follow Homer in his pledge to start a separate town just for those with the new code.

Homer is made mayor of the non-rich side of town, now renamed "New Springfield." The other side is called "Olde Springfield." The two towns coexist uneasily side-by-side. New Springfielders do not feel welcome in Olde Springfield, and Olde Springfielders make fun of their poorer neighbors. The two towns attempt to sabotage each other by blocking one another's electricity, beer,

and water supplies. Finally, Homer has a wall built, dividing the two towns. But when everyone in New Springfield realizes that they have no supplies or chance of survival, they climb over the wall and desert Homer and his family.

To make people realize the importance of New Springfield, Homer talks The Who into playing there instead of in Olde Springfield, where they are scheduled to perform. The Olde Springfielders are irate at losing their concert, so they attack Homer and New Springfield. Roger Daltrey of The Who convinces everyone to buy speed-dialers to relieve the stress of punching in area codes, so that they can live in peace again. Everyone agrees to this solution, and with a mighty power chord from Pete Townshend that brings down the wall, The Who launch into their concert. As the townspeople dance happily, an army of badgers in the hills decide to invade the reunited town.

SHOW HIGHLIGHTS

Fun Factoid:
This episode marks the 250th episode of "The Simpsons" and the season premiere of Season 12. In conjunction with the airing of this episode FOX purchased the domain name whatbadgerseat.com and set up a phony site (linked to thesimpsons.com) for the curious viewer who might want to see if the site truly existed.

"It's not fair! I've been a fan of The Who since the very beginning, when they were the Hillbilly Bugger Boys."

TV Moment:
Homer imagines himself as a mayor, walking down the street in a Western town, wearing a cowboy hat and firing a rifle, in a parody of the opening credits of the Western show, "The Rifleman," starring Chuck Connors.

"Homer stole our rock performers! That fat, dumb, and bald guy sure plays some real hardball."

By the Numbers:
Marge: *The phone company ran out of numbers, so they split the city into two area codes. Half the town keeps the old 636 area code, and our half gets 939.*
Homer: *939?! What the hell is that?! Oh, my life is ruined!*
Marge: *Geez, you just have to remember three extra numbers.*
Homer: *Oh, if only it were that easy, Marge.*
(The badger appears at the window and growls.)
Homer: *Go away! We got bigger problems now!*
(Embarrassed, the badger leaves.)

Sidekicked:
Krusty: *I opened for The Who at Woodstock. I came out in a Beatle wig with a ukulele. Hendrix said he almost plotzed! His exact words.*
Sideshow Mel: (sarcastically) *Oh, I never tire of that story.*

Canned Laughter:
Bart: *C'mon, Lis. There's got to be a way to lure that badger out.*
Lisa: (consulting her computer) *Well, according to whatbadgerseat.com, badgers subsist primarily on a diet of stoats, voles, and marmots.*
Bart: (digging through kitchen cabinet) *Hmm. Stoats...stoats...*
Lisa: *Stoats are weasels, Bart. They don't come in cans.*
Bart: (holding up a can confidently) *Then what's this?*
Lisa: *That says "Corn," Bart.*
Bart: (deflated) *Must you embarrass me?*

Us vs. Them:
Kent Brockman: (on TV) *...and while we speak in a well-educated manner, they tend you use lowbrow expressions like, "Oh, yeah?" and "C'mere a minute."*
Homer: *Oh, yeah? They think they're better than us, huh? Bart, c'mere a minute!"*
Bart: *You c'mere a minute.*
Homer: (shaking his fist at Bart) *Oh, yeah?*

SPRINGFIELDS

Guest Voices: Gary Coleman as Himself, The Who as Themselves

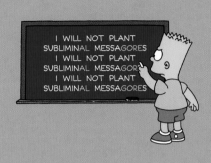

PHONY McRING-RING

Who he is:
Mascot and president of the telephone company

Method of communication:
Speaks in words you can understand

Explains that:
More area codes are great and you won't mind paying the extra hidden fees

Knows you are worried about:
Remembering all those numbers

Technical data states:
Scientists have discovered that even monkeys can memorize ten numbers

---

Music Moment:
The Who sing parts of two songs in the episode: "The Seeker" and "Won't Get Fooled Again." Other songs mentioned but not played are: "My Generation," "Squeeze Box," "Magic Bus," and "Pinball Wizard."

Retaliation Communication:
Lenny: *There's nothin' like revenge for getting back at people.*
Carl: *I don't know. Vengeance is pretty good.*

"I'm not sure which one's better. The 6 is closer to the 3, so you've got convenience there, but the 9 has less to do with Satan, which is a plus in this religious world of ours."

Badgered Homer:
Homer: *It's a badger, all right. Or possibly a griffin. Bart, do you have any dynamite in your room?*
Bart: *Tons.*
Homer: *Get it.*
Lisa: *No, Dad! We don't want to kill him. Let's call Animal Control.*
Homer: *Great idea! Then we can call a doctor about this.*
(He pulls up his shirt to unveil a gaping wound in his abdomen, revealing his internal organs.)
Lisa: *How did the badger do that without ripping your shirt?*
Homer: *What am I, a tailor?*

Homer Makes a Request:
Homer: *Now, these are the tunes I want you boys to play.*
Roger Daltrey: *(looking at list) Wait a minute. Homer, a lot of these are Grand Funk Railroad songs.*
John Entwistle: *And we don't know "Pac-Man Fever."*
Homer: *Oh, come on! It plays itself!*

THE STUFF YOU MAY HAVE MISSED

Todd's woodpecker laughs like the cartoon character Woody Woodpecker.

The phone number for Animal Control is (555) X-TERM-N-8. The ad in the yellow pages depicts a housewife battling a massive octopus with a broom.

Homer has "Lenny = White, Carl = Black" written on his palm, so he can tell them apart.

The Who is scheduled to perform at Springfield's historic Yahoo Search Engine Arena.

The winner of The Who concert tickets is Mr. Burns, who in this episode has the same phone number as the Simpsons (555-0013) but with a different area code. In "Lisa's Date with Density" (4F01), Mr. Burns's phone number was revealed to be 555-0001.

The Vanderbilts, the rich snobs from "Saddlesore Galactica" (BABF09) are seen together at the town meeting. Mr.Vanderbilt drops his monocle while being horrified once again.

The mortise that appears on Kent Brockman's newscast of Homer, Moe, Lenny, and Carl drinking beer is inspired by the design of The Who's 1971 album *Meaty Beaty Big & Bouncy*.

After the bullies steal his pants, Bart is seen two scenes later still in his underpants.

The four Olde Springfield "Indians" who sabotaged the Duff Beer delivery to New Springfield by pouring it into the river are Chief Wiggum, Sideshow Mel, Apu, and Principal Skinner.

As the citizens of Olde Springfield pick up gold from the riverbed, they are joined by several old-time prospectors with their mules.

Fat Tony's company, Lowball Construction, built the wall that divides Springfield in three days. In "Grift of the Magi" (BABF07) Fat Tony builds the Springfield Elementary handicapped access ramps through another construction company, Valdazzo Brothers Olive Oil.

Recycled items used to build the Springfield Wall include: the Angel statue from "Lisa the Skeptic" (5F05), a Santa Claus statue, and the Olmec Indian God of War statue, Xt'Tapalatakettle, from "Blood Feud" (7F22).

Seen climbing over the trash wall to escape New Springfield are the badger from the opening scene and Lionel Hutz. Since Phil Hartman's untimely passing, Lionel Hutz and several of the characters he made famous are used sparingly in crowd scenes. However, no new stories feature the characters because they have been officially "retired."

Homer takes a bottle of chloroform from a store called "Just Chloroform."

The Who are staying at the Hotel Pillowmint.

The Who concert is presented by Lemon Pledge.

The Olde Springfieldians get their catapult from Rent-A-Pult.

Pete Townshend has a volume-level setting of "Whuh-oh!" on his amplifier.

Homer uses chloroform to silence Marge at the end of the episode. He has silenced Marge in a similar fashion in two previous episodes: in "Mayored to the Mob" (AABF05) by applying a nerve pinch to her neck and in "It's a Mad, Mad, Mad, Mad Marge" (BABF18) by shooting her with a tranquilizer dart.

ARE YOU STUPIDER THAN A MONKEY?

SOPHIE

Who she is:
Krusty the Clown's illegitimate daughter

Family traits:
Telltale green hair; says, "Hey! Hey!" instead of "Hello"

Found Krusty by:
Typing "pathetic clown" into a computer search-engine

Her mother's taste in interior design:
Artwork depicting clowns being tortured and killed

Special talents:
Playing the violin and softening a clown's hard heart

> YOU KNOW, FOR A CLOWN, YOU'RE NOT REALLY A LOT OF FUN.

Guest Voice:
Drew Barrymore as Sophie

Marge forces Bart and Homer to spend the day doing chores together, and they believe they can accomplish all their tasks by using fireworks. While trying to remove a jammed tape from a VCR, the pair blow up Lisa's room, ruining everything. Because it is her birthday, Homer lets Lisa decide what the family should do for the day. She chooses to go to a book festival, where a plethora of novel activities are taking place. Krusty is there, signing his latest book, and he gets a big surprise when one of his fans, a little girl named Sophie, declares that she is his daughter.

Sophie's paternity claim turns out to be true. During the Gulf War, Krusty met her mom while he was performing for the troops. Krusty enlists Homer to help him with some fatherly tips, and with a little prompting, Krusty and Sophie spend a day at the beach bonding. As the sun goes down, Sophie plays her violin, showing Krusty that he is not the only one with talent in the family. That night while playing poker, Krusty wagers Sophie's violin and loses it to Fat Tony.

When Sophie finds out Krusty has lost her violin, she is very upset. Her mom does not like Krusty, and Sophie is forced to admit that her mom was right—she is better off not knowing him. Krusty does not want his little girl to hate him, so he gets Homer to help him sneak into Fat Tony's compound to get the violin back. Despite the fact that there is a mobster summit taking place at the compound, Krusty and Homer are able to retrieve the violin. Krusty returns the musical instrument, and he and Sophie make amends. Homer, on the other hand, ends up on the run from the mob.

SHOW HIGHLIGHTS

The Fruit of Valour:
Homer: *Hee-hee-hee-hee, heh-heh-hee!* This watermelon won't know what hit it!
Bart: I love our Tuesdays together, Dad.
(They blow up a watermelon with fireworks.)
Marge: (from a window and covered in watermelon) Don't you two have a list of chores to do?
Bart: Hey, we just took care of that dangerous melon that was threatening our garden.
Homer: Yeah, we're heroes! (angrily) But where's our parade?

(Milhouse, dressed in Elizabethan fashion, holds a sheaf of coupons.)
Milhouse: Hear ye, hear ye! One dollar off on all poetry books! (He is suddenly swarmed by a mob of excited people who leave him trampled into the dirt and sobbing.) Their hands were everywhere.

Mum's the Word:
Louie: Johnny Tightlips! Where'd they hit ya?
Johnny: I ain't sayin' nothin'.
Louie: But what'll I tell the doctor?
Johnny: Tell 'im to suck a lemon.

Bagged Dad:
Krusty: Listen, honey, a lot of kids think of me as their daddy, but I'm just a simple TV legend. Here, have a key chain.
Sophie: No, I'm sure you're my father. You met my mom during the Gulf War.
Krusty: Was your mother an Israeli flight attendant?
Sophie: No.
Krusty: Cokie Roberts?
Sophie: No, she was a soldier. Chestnut brown hair, kind of shy, thirty-two confirmed kills.
Krusty: Oh! Oh! Oh! Oh, boy! Now it's comin' back to me.

THE STUFF YOU MAY HAVE MISSED

The title of this episode is a play on the name of the Detroit rap group the Insane Clown Posse.

When Santa's Little Helper's house is blown up, it implodes like a building being demolished.

This is the second episode that takes place on Lisa's birthday; the first one being "Stark Raving Dad" (7F24).

The sign for the Festival of Books reads "This Banner Available on Audio Tape."

The title of Reverend Lovejoy's cookbook is "Someone's in the Kitchen with Jesus."

Free food samples at Reverend Lovejoy's book-fair booth include "Stig-muffins" and "Sister Mary Magdalene's Chocolate Orgasms."

Professor Frink's instant book-absorbing invention is called the InfoCram 6000.

"For Dummies" books sold at the Festival of Books include: *Cow Tipping for Dummies, Animation for Dummies, Network Programming for Dummies, Christianity for Dummies,* and *Moby Dick for Dummies.*

Krusty's book is titled *Your Shoes' Too Big to Kickbox God.*

During his USO show, Krusty holds a golf putter à la Bob Hope.

As the sand covers them during the storm, the Cincinnati Bengal Cheerleaders go from being in a pyramid formation to being a pyramid.

As the night of Krusty's lovemaking passes, the blazing oil wells melt like candles.

The pallet of Duff Beer being air-dropped for the Desert Storm soldiers has a parachute that reads "Duff Cares."

While eating ice cream cones, Krusty and Sophie sit atop a surfing horse.

During the poker game, Krusty's bow tie starts spinning rapidly when he realizes he has four aces.

License plates on the mobsters' limousines read: BAGMAN2, MOB MOM, and KILLER. KILLER's limo has "Just Made" written on the trunk, along with tin cans tied to the bumper.

Music Moment:
NRBQ's "I Like That Girl" plays over the Krusty-Sophie beach montage and the end credits.

Bart walks among rows and rows of "For Dummies" books: **"Finally, books for today's busy idiot."**

Homer Says "Grace":
Homer: Dear Lord, bless this humble meal...and, did you hear about Krusty? Whoo, man! I mean, I knew he was a player, but geez, a kid...
Marge: Homer, that's not a prayer. That's gossip.
Homer: Fine, I'll just discuss heavenly matters. So, how's Maude Flanders doin' up there? She playing the field? Ooh, yeah? Really? All those guys? (noticing the family staring at him) Amen.

POPPY

Episode BABF17
Original Airdate: 11/12/00
Writers: John Frink and Don Payne
Director: Bob Anderson
Executive Producer: Mike Scully

Guest Voices: Stephen King as Himself, Joe Mantegna as Fat Tony, Jay Mohr as Christopher Walken, Amy Tan as Herself, and John Updike as Himself

I WILL NOT SURPRISE THE INCONTINENT
I WILL NOT SURPRISE THE INCONTINENT
I WILL NOT SURPRISE THE INCONTINENT

Revealed this episode:
Fat Tony's real name is Marion.

Krusty gets romantic **"There was your mother, lookin' like a beautiful mirage. Maybe it was the anthrax in the air, maybe it was the fact the Arab women weren't bitin'. Whatever it was, it was magic!"**

The Clown Comes Clean:

Krusty: *Now look, Sophie, I know you think your daddy's perfect...*
Sophie: *No, I don't.*
Krusty: *...but I did a bad thing. I lost your violin in a poker game.*
Sophie: *You what?!*
Krusty: *But, don't worry! I got you an even better one!*
Sophie: *This is a ukulele.*
Krusty: *Yeah, the thinking man's violin!*

A Pause in the Action:

Krusty: *You gotta help me! My daughter found out I'm a jerk!*
Marge: *Oh, Krusty, I'm sure she just needs time to get used to you.*
Homer: *Marge, may I play devil's advocate for a moment?*
Marge: *Sure, go ahead.*
(Cut to the Kwik-E-Mart, where Homer is losing a pinball game called "Devil's Advocate.")
Homer: *Stupid game! Now, what were we talking about?*
Krusty: *My daughter's violin!*

"Welcome to my home. To answer your first question: yes, we do have pasta. If you need money laundered, just set it outside your door. You can pick it up in the morning."

Proud Papa:

Krusty: *My little girl's sharp as a tack. I tried the "got your nose" bit on her—didn't fool her for a second!*
Homer: *My uncle still has my nose.*

The Joys of Fatherhood:

Krusty: *You know, Homer, I've spent my whole life entertaining kids, and I just realized I don't know the first thing about 'em.*
Homer: *Well, I won't lie. Fatherhood isn't easy like motherhood. But I wouldn't trade it for anything... except for some mag wheels. Oh, man. That would be sweet.*

Perfunctory Pals:

Homer: *Why don't we just break into Fat Tony's compound and get it back?*
Krusty: *Really? You'd help me take on the mob?*
Homer: *For a casual acquaintance like you? Absolutely.*

Unexpected Relations:

(A young girl approaches Krusty at his book-signing.)
Krusty: *Yeah? Name?*
Sophie: *My name is Sophie.*
Krusty: *Hey! Good luck with that.*
Sophie: *I'm your daughter.*
Krusty: *Whaa?!*
Sophie: (hugging him) *I finally found my daddy!*
Krusty: *Ohhh. I think I just seltzered myself!*

The Family Genes:

Krusty: *Hey, I know that song. My dad used to play that when I was a boy.* (tearing up) *It's beautiful.*
Sophie: *Do you play?*
Krusty: *No, I guess musical talent skips a generation. Like diabetes. You might wanna watch out for that, too.*

"Listen, kid, I'm not the kind of dad who, you know, does things, or says stuff, or looks at you. But the love is there."

Mystery Solved:

Fat Tony: *I have learned that someone in dis room is a squealer.*
Louie: *We've narrowed it down to either Johnny Tightlips or Frankie the Squealer.*
Frankie: *Ok! It's me! I can't help it! I just like squealin'! It makes me feel big!*

B art needs money for a new video game console, so he starts working for a Thai restaurant, hanging menus on doorknobs. He becomes so proficient at his work that soon there are Thai menus hanging everywhere around town. This truly annoys Lisa, who feels all the menus are a wasteful use of trees. Lisa's ecological thoughts are further spurred when she meets a handsome teenage activist protesting at Krusty Burger. The activist, Jesse Grass, is soon arrested, and Lisa is smitten by his good looks and eco-radicalism.

Lisa joins Jesse's band of protesters, known as "Dirt First." She attends a Dirt First meeting, and Jesse gives an impassioned plea for someone to sit in a giant tree in the Springfield Forest that is about to be cut down. Lisa volunteers, but after several days of sitting up in a tree, she finds that being away from her family is a great hardship. Late one night, she decides to visit home for just an

hour, but accidentally sleeps there all night. Rushing back to the tree the next morning, she finds the giant redwood lying on its side.

Lisa is relieved to learn that the tree was not felled by loggers but by lightning. Everyone thinks Lisa died in the lightning storm, and a rich Texan who has the logging rights to the area where the giant tree once stood promises to make it a wilderness preserve in her memory. At first, Lisa does not tell anyone that she is alive, in order to save the other trees, but when the rich Texan goes back on his word and plans to make an amusement park there called "Lisa Land," she comes out of seclusion. Her appearance distracts everyone, so Jesse cuts the guy wires around a sign made from the felled tree with a giant Lisa head on top. The tree trunk with Lisa's head goes sliding down the mountain into Springfield, cutting a swath of destruction along its way. Eventually, the trunk makes it to the Pacific Ocean and floats off into the sunset.

SHOW HIGHLIGHTS

Krusty the Clown makes it through another show: **"Five...four...three... two...one! Well, that's all the time we have! So long, kids!"**

The Power of Advertising:
TV Announcer: *Krusty the Clown is brought to you by the new Gamestation 256! It's slightly faster—to the max!*
Bart: *256?! Oh, and I'm stuck with this useless 252?* (kicking the game into the roaring fireplace)
252 Unit: (melting in the flames) *Don't destroy me! I can still make you happy—to the max!*

Making Money the Old-Fashioned Way:
Homer: *You want money? Get a job like your old man!*
Bart: *Well, maybe I should.*
Homer: *Oh, so now you're smarter than your old man, eh?*
Bart: *I guess.*
Homer: *I like your attitude! Take what you need.* (Bart opens the wallet, but it is empty.)

You Thai Now:
Mr. Thai: *You quitta! Quitta boy! Quitta boy!*
Bart: *I'm sorry.*
Mr. Thai: *Now restaurant fail. Children go to state college. Serious students powerless against drunken jock-ocracy. Baseball hats everywhere.*
Bart: *Hey, man. This job is too dangerous.*
Mr. Thai: *Menu boy no be coward like shrimp! Menu boy be brave like prawn!*

 "Menu boy must move silently, like ghost. Leave no footprint, only lunch specials."

Different Philosophies:
(Bart spins a door hanger on his finger.)
Lisa: *Bart, do you know how many trees died to make those menus?*
Bart: *I 'unno. A million?*
Lisa: *You're ruining the Earth!*
Bart: *True, but I gots to get paid. Money equals funny, sister!*

Lisa Left Speechless:
Marge: *Bart, it's so sweet of you to take the family out to Krusty Burger.*
Bart: (holding a money clip) *Hey, some people in this family are do-ers* (looking at Lisa) *and some are don't-ers.*
Lisa: (pointing her finger at Bart) *Don't you call me a--* (Bart quickly hangs a menu on her finger.) *Unh!*
Homer: (to Lisa) *Take that, Lisa's beliefs.* (The family laughs, except for Lisa.)

Krusty the Clown gets out of his limo and several clowns follow: **"Get back in. It's only funny with a small car."**

Taking Pride in One's Work:
Chief Wiggum: *That's nice work with the bag-zooka.*
Officer Lou: *Ya gotta love what you do, Chief.* (patting the bag-zooka affectionately) *Mm-hmm.*

Marge's opinion of Jesse Grass: **"I can't believe how young he is. He'd be cute if he weren't so idealistic."**

No Reason or Rhyme:
Marge: *That was the boy Lisa likes.*
Lisa: *No, I don't!*
Bart: (singing) *"Lisa and Jesse, sittin' in a tree, K-I-S-S-I-N-G!"*
Lisa: *Shut up!*
Homer: (joining in) *"First comes love, then comes"...um...damn it, I know this!*

Domestic Disputes:
Lisa: *I'd like to visit a prisoner.*
Chief Wiggum: *Yeah, sure.*
Lisa: *Aren't you coming with me?*
Wiggum: *Hey, I get enough flaming toilet paper thrown on me at home.*

What's in the News?
Homer: (reading the paper) *Sheesh! Look at these refugees. How 'bout a smile?*
Marge: *They've undergone terrible hardships!*
Homer: *Well, moping won't make it better.*

Rebel with a Cause:
Jesse: *This planet needs every friend it can get.*
Lisa: *Oh, the Earth is the best. That's why I'm a vegetarian.*
Jesse: *Heh-heh...well, that's a start.*
Lisa: *Uh, well, um, I was thinking of going vegan.*
Jesse: *I'm a level-five vegan. I won't eat anything that casts a shadow.*

Lisa's Crusade:
Lisa: *Mom, Dad, there's something I have to do. You're not going to like it, but I really believe it's the right thing.*
Homer: (whispering) *Marge, she's going to narc on our stash!*
Marge: *We don't have a stash.*
Homer: (playing along, his eyes darting back and forth) *No...of...course not.*

Homer-erotic:
Homer: *This is your fault, with your non-threatening, Bobby Sherman–style good looks! No girl could resist your charms!*
Jesse: *This was her choice, Mr. Simpson.*
Homer: *I'm sorry. I wasn't listening. I was lost in your eyes.*

HUGGER

Episode CABF01
Original Airdate: 11/19/00
Writer: Matt Selman
Director: Steven Dean Moore
Executive Producer: Mike Scully

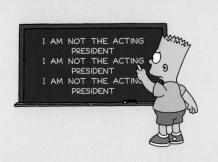

JESSE GRASS

Who he is:
An idealistic, dreadlocked dreamboat, who's Birken-stock is on the rise

Leader of:
The eco-radical group "Dirt First"

Not afraid of:
Tabasco hosings or dressing up like a cow

Firm believer in:
Yoga; pocket mulching in addition to home composting; not using redwoods as promotional tools; and the idea that one day he will have super powers

Major accomplishments:
Successfully blocked the St. Patrick's Day Parade, which every year steps on several lizards; got the prison to install a solar-powered electric chair

Bart's Letter to Lisa: **"Dear Lisa, You rock! Mom is calling rescue agencies. Dad is building a giant ladder, but it is of poor quality. We miss you, Bart."**

Movie Moment:
Bart's gravity-defying ability to hang take-out menus and the percussive techno music that accompanies his exploits are inspired by *The Matrix.*

Kent Brockman reports on Lisa's cause: **"It's Day 4 for Springfield's li'lest tree hugger. Hee-hee. Excuse me, that's littlest tree hugger. And whether you love or hate her politics, you've gotta go gawk at this crazy idiot."**

Homer Considers Playing God:
Homer: *Oh, no! Lisa's gone! And nothing will bring her back.* (stroking his chin) *Unless...*
Lisa: *Dad, I'm not dead!*
Homer: *Oh, praise God! You're alive!* (stroking his chin again) *Unless...*

"You are not pretending to be dead, young lady. This family has had nothing but bad luck when it comes to farce."

A Principal Mourns:
Principal Skinner: *So, Bart, our school policy is to give students in your situation...straight A's.*
Bart: *Get out! What's the catch?*
Principal Skinner: *The tragic loss of your sister.*
Bart: *Oh, yes. Ghastly business, that.*

"Homer, uh, booze is on the house, seeing as how Lisa is, um...how do I put this...riding the midnight train to slab city."

THE STUFF YOU MAY HAVE MISSED

The amusing headline that Marge wants to send to Jay Leno ("Ketchup Truck Hits Hamburger Stand") is followed by a less-than-amusing subheading that reads "Six Dead."

Marge's "thrift" song sounds a little bit like "Just Don't Look," the jingle that stopped the giant advertising icons from wreaking havoc on Springfield in the "Attack of the 50-Foot Eyesores" segment from "Treehouse of Horror VI" (3F04).

Lisa finds a struggling fish with a door hanger around it, as if it had been trapped by a carelessly discarded six-pack ring.

Bart reads a comic entitled, "Itchy and Veronica." The cover pictures Itchy and Veronica sitting in a booth at the malt shop and drinking through two straws from the brain of Archie's severed head.

Lisa's window to the world from her perch in the giant redwood includes: Shelbyville, St. Louis, the Mississippi River, the Rockies, Hollywood, the Canadian and Mexican borders, the Pacific Ocean, Hawaii, Mt. Fuji, the Himalayas, Paris, the Atlantic Ocean, and New York City. Her view is influenced by the much-imitated *New Yorker* cover "View of the World" by Saul Steinberg.

Upon returning from the forest, Lisa finds her family sleeping peacefully in front of the fire, including a blissful Homer with his hands around the throat of an equally blissful Bart.

The TV memorial to Lisa's memory reads "R.I.P. Lisa Simpson—Earth Angel."

The Channel 6 News caption calls Jesse Grass an "Eco-Hunk."

When everyone thinks Lisa is dead, the Springfield Elementary flag is at half-staff and Principal Skinner wears a black armband.

The Omni-Pave sign depicts a steamroller chasing a fleeing flower.

The runaway log crashes through Kentucky Fried Panda, which Homer says was "Finger Ling-Ling Good." Ling-Ling was one of two giant pandas given to the USA by China in 1972 and housed at the National Zoo in Washington D.C.

Outside the Hemp City store is a giant bong. Inside is a sign that says "Hemp, Hemp Hooray!"

Under the *Springfield Shopper* headline about Lisa being alive, there's another headline that reads "Hemp City Reduced to Stems and Seeds."

The wandering log's trip across America takes it past Mount Rushmore, over purple mountains, alongside a tornado, down Lombard Street in San Francisco, and under the Golden Gate Bridge.

Lisa shows her dedication to Jesse and his causes: **"I'll write you letters...on rice paper...with a soy pencil!"**

Bumper sticker seen on Homer's car: "My child is a dead honor student."

A Clone of His Own:
Mayor Quimby: (on stage) *And now, Branford Marsalis will play, using Lisa's very own saxophone.* (Quimby presents the sax to Branford Marsalis and a grieving Milhouse runs up.)
Milhouse: *Don't touch it! They can clone her from the spit!* (Milhouse begins to sob, grabs the sax, and runs off.)
Mayor Quimby: (calling after him) *Good luck, Milhouse.*

YOU CAN'T SILENCE THE TRUTH WITH BEANBAGS.

Guest Voice:
Joshua Jackson as Jesse Grass

MR. COSTINGTON

Title:
President of Costington's Department Store

Store Slogan:
"Over a Century Without a Slogan"

Secret Shame:
A shoe-sniffing problem, which prevents him from visiting the third floor of his own store

Holiday ad campaign:
"Costington's Department Store— The thing downtown that's open. Right next to the men's shelter."

Annual sponsor of:
A Thanksgiving parade with second-rate giant helium balloons, including: Rusty the Clown, Funky Winkerbean, and the Noid.

I'VE JUST HAD A CRAZY THOUGHT.

HOMER VS.

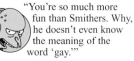

The Simpsons are struggling financially, and Homer asks Mr. Burns for a raise. Instead, Mr. Burns asks Homer to be his "prank monkey," wherein he will give Homer extra money to play mean-spirited pranks on people for his own personal amusement. Homer readily agrees.

Their first stop together is the Android's Dungeon, where Homer buys a very expensive comic book and eats it in front of the Comic Book Guy, causing the hefty collector to collapse. Homer then dresses in a diaper and lies on the floor of a sports stadium restroom, asking to be changed. Homer will not tell Marge how he is making the additional money. He is just happy to be providing for his family. Things turn nasty, however, when Burns has Homer dress as a panda bear at the zoo. First, he gets zapped several times by zoo handlers with electric prods,

and then a real panda has its way with him. Lisa witnesses the panda fiasco and helps Homer realize that he has given up his dignity for money.

Homer tells Mr. Burns that he is through performing pranks, and he uses his ill-gotten money to buy toys for the needy children of Springfield. This impresses the owner of a big department store so much, he asks Homer to be Santa in the store's Thanksgiving parade. Homer enjoys being Santa in the parade until Mr. Burns comes along and tries to bribe him into pulling an evil prank on the unsuspecting citizens lining the parade route. Homer refuses, deserting his Santa post, and keeping his dignity intact. Mr. Burns, now dressed as Santa, decides to pull his "Merry Fish-mas" prank by himself: scooping up fish guts, tossing them onto the crowd, and watching as hungry seagulls attack the people.

SHOW HIGHLIGHTS

Afternoon Delight:
Principal Skinner: Ah...Head Lice Inspection Day! While the kids are out getting their nits picked, we can have our own private "cootie call."
Mrs. Krabappel: Oh, you talk too much. Let's do it on Martin's desk.
Principal Skinner: It is usually the cleanest.

Process of Elimination:
Marge: When did this happen? When did we become the bottom rung of society?
Homer: I think it was when that cold snap killed off all the hobos.

Planning for the Worst:
Financial Planner: You haven't set aside anything for the future!
Chief Wiggum: You know how it is with cops. I'll get shot three days before retirement. In the business, we call it "ret-irony."

Out of Touch:
Smithers: I need some time off. As you know, I've been writing a musical about the Malibu Stacy doll.
Burns: A show about a doll? Heh-heh-heh, whe-bu-! Why not write a musical about the common cat? Or the king of Siam? Hoo-heh-heh-heh! Give it up, Smithers!
Smithers: Actually, sir, we've been booked into a small theater in New Mexico.
Burns: Whoa, whoa! Slow down there, maestro. There's a "new" Mexico?

Mr. Burns comments on Smithers's absence: **"Well, with the old ball and chain gone, maybe I can finally have a little fun at the office."**

Clear Explanation:
Burns: What is this? Some sort of force field around these vegetables.
Homer: That's the sneeze guard. You have to lean under it to get salad or sneeze on stuff.

It's Only Money:
Homer: Mr. Burns...I was wondering if I could get a raise.
Mr. Burns: What kind of a raise?
Homer: (uncertain) Whopping?

Pranks for the Memories:
Burns: I don't want to hear your whining. I'm a bored and joyless old man. Give me a larf.
Homer: A larf? Okay, let's see what's in the news today...
Burns: Oh, for the love of...peh! (picking up a pudding dish) Hurl this at that! (pointing at Lenny)
Homer: At Lenny? But he's a war hero.
Burns: Well, let's decorate him, then.
Homer: No!
Burns: Not even for four dollars?
(Homer hurls the dish at Lenny.)
Lenny: Ow! My eye! I'm not supposed to get pudding in it!
Burns: Nah-ho-ho-ho-ho-ho! That was capital! My lung is aching.
Homer: I liked when I threw the pudding.

Comic Book Guy, after eating his 100th marshmallow peep: **"Oh, if only the real chicks went down this easy."**

Tit for Tat:
Homer: I'd like to buy a mint condition Spider-Man #1, please.
Comic Book Guy: And I'd like an hour on the holodeck with Seven-of-Nine.

"Sold Separately"
(from *Malibu Stacy: The Musical*)
(Smithers, dressed as Beachcomber Ken, and an actress playing Malibu Stacy are sitting on the hood of a red Corvette.)
Ken: Sold separately.
    Sometimes I feel like I've been sold separately. But out-of-the-box I find you... Poseable...
Malibu Stacy: Lovable...
Ken/Malibu Stacy: ...Just like me.

"You're so much more fun than Smithers. Why, he doesn't even know the meaning of the word 'gay.'"

Can I Borrow Some Child Support?
Milhouse: Hey, Dad! Can I have some money for a Panda Cone?
Kirk: Gah! What do you do with the $68 I send your mother every month?
Milhouse: Weekday Dad wanted a DVD player.

Movie Moments:
The plot of this episode is similar to *The Magic Christian*, in which Peter Sellers and Ringo Starr go around getting so-called respectable people to do outlandish stunts for money at the risk of their dignity.

The seagull assault on the citizens of Springfield at the end of the episode is reminiscent of the attack on the seaside town in Alfred Hitchcock's *The Birds*.

The appearance of Mr. Burns's Jolly Roger flag and "Happy Pranksgiving" float evokes memories of Delta House's piratical raid on Faber College's homecoming parade in *Animal House*.

Point Illustrated:
Burns: Monty says, monkey do. What could be better?
Homer: Well, you could treat me with a little respect.
Burns: Oh, shut up, you tub of guts.
Homer: Ye–see? That's what I'm saying.

A Fistful of Humiliation:
Burns: Well, a little dough-re-mi will smooth this over.
Lisa: He doesn't want your dirty money!
Burns: Oh, come now. Everyone has his price.
Lisa: Not my dad!
Homer: Shh-shh! The grown-ups are talking, honey.

DIGNITY

Episode CABF04
Original Airdate: 11/26/00
Writer: Rob LaZebnik
Director: Neil Affleck
Executive Producer: Mike Scully
Guest Voice: Leeza Gibbons as Herself

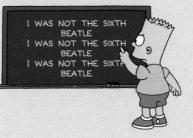

Homer's Evolution:

Homer: *Yes, I may be naked and reeking of panda love, but I've got to stop this before it goes too far.*
Mr. Burns: *Take that back...for* (counting his cash)...*$903.*
Homer: *I retract my statement.*
Mr. Burns: *Ha!*
(He shoves a handful of cash into Homer's mouth.)
Lisa: *Daaad!*
Homer: (to Burns) *I mean, screw you!*
Mr. Burns: (impressed) *Well, well, it looks like my monkey has evolved into a man.* (Homer smiles proudly.)...*a poor man.*
(Mr. Burns walks away.)
Homer: *Wha--? Oh, why did he have to say that extra thing?*

What's My Line?

Lisa: *I'm so proud! My dad will be the grand finale of the Thanksgiving Day Parade.*
Bart: *Wanna rehearse, Dad?*
Homer: *I don't need to rehearse. Ho, ho, ho! Merry...line?*
Bart: *Christmas.*
Homer: *What?* (reaching for the script) *Let me see that!*

"Yes, whether you're Christian, or just non-Jewish, everybody loves Santa Claus."

A Little Touchy:

Poor Kid: *Hey, lady! Santa Claus is gonna be here, right? He just has to!*
Lisa: *Something tells me he is.* (touching him on the back)
Poor Kid: *Don't touch me! Nothing gives you that right!*

I Will Float No More Forever:

Kent Brockman: *Here's a float saluting the Native Americans, who taught us how to celebrate Thanksgiving.*
Leeza Gibbons: *Interesting side note on this float—the papier-mâché is composed entirely of broken treaties.*
Kent Brockman: *Ha, ha, ha, ha, ha! They're good sports.*

THE STUFF YOU MAY HAVE MISSED

For help with their money woes, Marge and Homer go to "Let's Get Fiscal Financial Planning."

The computer simulation of Homer's future gravesite features an elderly Nelson Muntz kicking over the headstone and saying, "Ha! Ha!"

Carl mistakes the word "conquer" for the word "concur" on his word-a-day calendar.

Mrs. Vanderbilt, the wealthy dowager that Homer shocks twice in the episode, first appeared in "Saddlesore Galactica" (BABF09) and then as one of Bart's door-hanger victims in "Lisa the Tree Hugger" (CABF01). She is outfitted in the same Chanel suit Marge wore in "Scenes from the Class Struggle in Springfield" (3F11).

When Homer dresses up as a panda at the zoo to perform in "Panda-monium," he is called Sim-Sim.

The counterman at Costington's puts on a rubber glove before inspecting Homer's basket of "dirty, dirty" money. He first appeared as the maître d' at the dinner theater in "Mayored to the Mob" (AABF05), and is based on Frank Nelson, a popular character actor who appeared as a regular on "The Jack Benny Program" and was often featured on "I Love Lucy."

This is the second time Homer has dressed as a department store Santa. The first time was in the premiere episode "Simpsons Roasting on an Open Fire" (7G08).

Dr. Hibbert and Ruth Powers appear to be "making eyes" at each other during the Thanksgiving parade.

The Native American float features a smiling Indian with a bobbing head that resembles the controversial Cleveland Indians mascot.

Lenny receives several injuries in this episode. He previously suffered from an eye injury in "Saddlesore Galactica" (BABF09) when he fell victim to a rubber-band misfire.

Because he does not have a computer, Homer misses an e-mail telling him he does not have to go to work. So, he immediately goes out and purchases a computer, and after a few false starts, designs his own web page. Homer is not sure what to put on his web page until he hears some juicy gossip about Mayor Quimby misappropriating funds intended for pothole repair. He decides to post it on the Internet under the assumed name of Mr. X. When Quimby is exposed and Mr. X makes the morning headlines, Homer feels a sense of power.

As Mr. X, Homer garners praise, fans, and even wins the Pulitzer Prize. To collect the Pulitzer, however, Homer must publicly admit that he is Mr. X. After everyone knows who he really is, Homer finds it impossible to get any good scoops because nobody will talk to him. His web page starts becoming unpopular, since it no longer features hot gossip, so Homer starts making up stories. Once more, Mr. X attracts attention, including the unwanted attention of kidnappers, who trap Homer in a truck and take him away.

Homer is drugged, and when he awakens, he finds himself on a mysterious island. Everyone there is a prisoner because they each have information that a powerful secret organization does not want shared with the world. Homer learns that, by sheer accident, one of his fabricated stories is apparently true. While Homer is on the island, he is replaced at home by a doppelganger with a German accent. Homer escapes the island, defeats his double, and is reunited with his family. However, the entire family is unexpectedly drugged and taken back to the island, where they happily adapt to their new lifestyle.

SHOW HIGHLIGHTS

Homer with a comforting thought:
"Don't worry, head. The computer will do our thinking, now."

The First Command:

Homer: (speaking into the computer mouse) *Computer, kill Flanders.*
Ned: *Did I hear my name? My ears are burning.*
Homer: (whispering to the mouse) *Good start. Now, finish the job.*
Ned: *Ho-ho, you're busy. Catch ya later, computater!*
Homer: *Oh, $5,000 for a computer, and it can't handle a simple assignment!*

Homer goes online: **"Oo! A dancing Jesus! Dee-dee-dee-dee-dee, dee-dee-dee! If there's a better use for the Internet, I haven't found it!"**

"If you have committed a crime and want to confess, click 'yes.' Otherwise, click 'no.' You have chosen 'no,' meaning you committed a crime, but don't want to confess. A paddy-wagon is now speeding to your home. While you wait, why not buy a police cap or T-shirt? You have the right to remain fabulous!"

Double Talk:

Bart: *I got suspended from school today.*
Homer: *No kiddin'. What do you think of my page, Lisa? Be honest. It's great, isn't it? Go ahead and say it's great if you want to.*
Bart: *They found a switchblade in my locker.*
Lisa: *Well...a web page is supposed to be a personal thing. You've just stolen copyrighted material from everyone else. They could sue you for that.*
Bart: *I took a swing at a cop.*
Homer: *They can't sue me if they don't know who I am. I'll just call myself Mr. X.*
(He types the new name into his web page.)
Bart: *I'm just mad all the time.*
Homer: *Yep, you can't go wrong with Mr. X.*

Fudging and Drudging:

Bart: *I heard Mayor Quimby spent the street-repair fund on a secret swimming pool for himself.*
Homer: *Get out. Who told you that?*
Bart: *Nelson.*
Homer: *Hmm. That's the kind of dirt that belongs on my web page!*
(He begins typing.)
Lisa: *You can't post that on the Internet. You don't even know if it's true.*
Homer: *Nelson has never steered me wrong, honey. Nelson is gold.*
Bart: *You know, it might have been Jimbo.*
Homer: *Beautiful! We have confirmation.*

"What's this? Stolen funds? Pothole money used for swimming pool? There's no emoticon for what I'm feeling!"

Online with the Skinners:

Principal Skinner: *Our mayor's corrupt? Mr. X has done this town a great service, despite his poor grammar and spelling.*
Agnes: *Seymour! Are you looking at naked ladies?!*
Principal Skinner: *No, mother!*
Agnes: *You sissy!*

Breakfast Epiphany:

Homer: *I did it! I changed the world. Now I know exactly how God feels.*
Marge: *Do you want turkey sausage or ham?*
Homer: *Bring me two of every animal.*

"But we must never forget that the real news is on local TV. Delivered by real, officially licensed newsmen like me, Kent Brockman. Coming up: how do they get those dogs to talk on the beer commercials? Cowboy Steve will tell you!"

Yellow-Skinned Journalism:

Homer: *Aaooww, nobody's visiting my web page anymore. My counter is actually going down!*
(A cyber-tumbleweed bounces across his web page.)
Lisa: *Well, you can't post news if you don't have any.*
Homer: *That's a great idea. I'll make up some news!*
Lisa: *Uuuh! At least take off your Pulitzer Prize when you say that.*

MENACE SHOES

Episode CABF02
Original Airdate: 12/03/00
Writer: John Swartzwelder
Director: Mark Kirkland
Executive Producer: Mike Scully

NUMBER 6

His situation:
Prisoner on a mysterious island

His crime:
Invented a bottomless peanut bag

Mission for the last thirty-three years:
Building escape boats made of toilet paper rolls, toothpicks, plastic forks, scabs, and dynamite

Number of escape boats stolen from him:
Three

Pressure Conference:
Chief Wiggum: *In the interests of public safety, we have confiscated every donut, bagel, cruller, and bear claw in the city...and some coffee.*
Reporter #1: *This morning Mr. X reported that your own department...*
Wiggum: *I know! I know! But I assure you, the police do not take prisoners out of their cells and race them...anymore.*
Reporter #1: *What about using the electric chair to cook chicken?*
Wiggum: *Uh, yeah, all right! This press conference is over!*

Keep It to Yourself...
Carl: *The public should be warned. I wish Mr. X were here.*
Homer: *(slyly) Oh, I don't know, Carl. He might be closer than you think.*
Carl: *Are you him? Are you Mr. X?*
Homer: *No!*
Carl: *But you talked in that real sly voice. Hey, hey, everybody! Homer's Mr. X!*
Homer: *I am not! (slyly) Or am I?*
Lenny: *Are you?*
Homer: *No!*

"Look, you can drug me all you want, but my family won't rest until they find my drug-bloated corpse."

TV Moment:
The mysterious island segments of the episode are an homage to the cult-classic TV show "The Prisoner" (1968–69), created, produced, and starring Patrick McGoohan. McGoohan plays a spy who attempts to retire, but is instead trapped in a quaint but creepy village by the sea.

"Hey, Mr. X, I got a tip for ya! In science class they're dissecting frozen hobos, and I have the bindles to prove it."

Homer's Demand:
Number 2: *Hello, Number 5. How's every little thing?*
Homer: *Who are you, and why are you holding me here? I want answers now, or I want them eventually!*

The Secret Plot:
Number 2: *I'll be blunt. Your web page has stumbled upon our secret plan.*
Homer: *That's impossible. All my stories are bull plop. Bull plop!*
Number 2: *Oh don't be cute. I'm referring to the flu shot exposé. You see, we're the ones loading them with mind-controlling additives.*
Homer: *But why?*
Number 2: *To drive people into a frenzy of shopping. That's why flu shots are given just before Christmas.*
Homer: *Of course! It's so simple. Wait, no it's not. It's needlessly complicated.*
Number 2: *Yes it is.*

Examples of Mr. X's Grade-A Bull-Plop: **New race discovered living six inches under Denver, all named Morton or Mortenson; Spanish and Italian are the same language; flu shots used for mind control.**

Double Take:
Fake Homer: *Marge, honey-fraulein, I'm home!*
Marge: *You're not my husband!*
Fake Homer: *Ja, please forgive my unexplained two-week absence. To make it up to you, we will go out to dinner at a sensibly-priced restaurant, zen have a night of efficient German sex.*
Marge: *Well, I sure don't feel like cooking.*

A Tactical Error:
Number 2: *Why did you think a big balloon would stop people?*
Female Scientist: *Shut up! That's why.*

"Once you get used to the druggings, this isn't a bad place."

THE STUFF YOU MAY HAVE MISSED

After Homer checks the price of a computer, he takes a sip of coffee so he can spit it out in surprise.

Homer attaches a rear-view mirror, can holder, raccoon tail, and compass to his new computer monitor.

Things seen on Homer's first web page: screaming mouths, alarm clocks, bells, inchworms, flying toasters, and a dancing Jesus.

As Mr. X's web page first comes up, we can briefly see that Homer is Mr. X. Also, the web page's slogan is, "All The Muck That's Fit to Rake." Homer's Mr. X persona and web page are inspired by Matt Drudge's "Drudge Report."

In the "lost civilization" room housing Mayor Quimby's secret swimming pool, a city worker can be seen sculpting a fountain out of "Pothole Cement."

Hans Moleman is trapped under the floorboards at Moe's Tavern.

Due to the withering effects of the flu, Todd Flanders reaches out his hand toward the unseen spectre of his dead mother.

Some of the peculiarities seen on the island are: a flamingo wearing a bowler hat, a penguin smoking from a long cigarette holder, a peacock wearing an old-fashioned football helmet, an ostrich with a blue neck ribbon, and a koala that covers its face with a masquerade mask.

When Homer says, "I am not a number! I am a man!" he is quoting Patrick McGoohan's famous line from the TV show "The Prisoner."

According to a sign, the Springfield Forest has been "Witch-Free Since 1998."

The Mysterious Leader's lava-lamp has a frog in it. He also has a novelty drinking bird and a wind-up cymbal-clapping monkey in his office.

This episode marks the second appearance of "The Prisoner"–inspired "anti-escape orb." It first appeared in "The Joy of Sect" (5F23) as Marge made her escape from the Movementarian compound.

THEY KEEP US HERE BECAUSE WE KNOW TOO MUCH. NUMBER 27 THERE KNOWS HOW TO TURN WATER INTO GASOLINE. NUMBER 12 KNOWS THE DEADLY SECRET BEHIND TIC TACS.

Guest Voice:
Patrick McGoohan as Number 6

DEVON BRADLEY

His résumé:
Character actor, dancer, and singer

Dramatic range:
Old fogies, FBI agents, and con men

His specialties:
Grand entrances and ironic exits

Where you can catch his act:
At the courthouse, doing street improv, or at the dinner theatre in *Dreamcoat*

I'M A TRIPLE-THREAT!

Guest Voice:
Edward Norton as Devon Bradley

On the way home from an evening at Magic Palace, the Simpsons' car is struck by a sturgeon that falls from a Russian space lab orbiting in outer space. The repairs to the car are very costly, so Bart suggests making some money by performing magic tricks from his new magic kit. Homer agrees, and they try performing the act at the Springfield Squidport, but the pickings are slim. Homer angrily leaves Bart behind and drives off. Bart looks so pathetic that a lot of passersby drop money into his magician's hat. When Homer sees how much money Bart makes, he decides they should play on people's sympathy and try to con them out of even more money.

The con game proves to be very lucrative, and Homer decides that he and Bart should continue grifting even after the car repairs are paid for. Grampa talks them into letting him in on the action, since he's an experienced grifter, and under his guidance, they attempt to pull a scam on the folks at the Springfield Retirement Castle. Just when it looks like Homer and Bart are going to get away with it, an undercover FBI agent arrests them.

Before long, Homer and Bart find out that the FBI agent is really a con man, too, when he steals their car. Homer and Bart make up a story about being carjacked to explain the missing car to Marge, but the next morning Groundskeeper Willie is arrested for the car theft and is brought to trial. When Willie is convicted, Homer admits to all the conning he and Bart have been doing. Marge reveals that the car theft, arrest, and trial were just one big con to get Homer and Bart to give up their grifting ways. Lisa attempts to explain how the con was elaborately conceived and executed by the entire town, but Otto suddenly bursts into the courtroom with his surfboard. He declares that "Surf's up!," and everyone goes surfing.

SHOW HIGHLIGHTS

Marge, after downing several Long Island Iced Teas: **"I'd like to visit that Long Island place. If only it were real."**

Too-Steady Neddy:
Homer: *Come on, pony-up, Flanders. The kid's not turning tricks for nothin'.*
Ned: *Oh, no. I could never support the Black Arts.*
Homer: *Black Arts?*
Ned: *Yeah, you know: magic, fortune-telling, Oriental cooking...*

Father/Son Falling-Out:
Homer: *Sixty cents? I would've made more if I'd gone in to work today!*
Bart: *Don't blame me! I've gotta compete with TV and the Internet.*
Homer: *A good son would come through for his dad.*
Bart: *A good dad wouldn't miss his son's little league games!*
Homer: *I told you! I find them boring.*
Bart: *Well, I showed up for all your stupid interventions!*

The Con Is On:
Homer: *We could make a fortune!*
Bart: *But wouldn't that make us con artists?*
Homer: *Well, yeah, but God conned me out of sixty-five hundred bucks in car repairs.*
Bart: *So in a way, we'd just be balancing out the universe.*

Homer and Bart's First Con:
Kent Brockman: *(knocking Bart's cake out of his hands) Oh, excuse me!*
Bart: *(pretending to be blind) What happened? Where's my cake? It's all right, isn't it?*
Kent: *Uh...*
Homer: *(grabbing Bart) What have you done, you clumsy little ox?! Gasp! That cake was for your deaf sister!*
Kent: *Sir, it was my fault.*
Homer: *No, no! Don't protect him. (to Bart) You'll work off that cake in the acid mines!*

Bart Simpson, grifting by guilt trip: **"My bar mitzvah cake! Oy! I'll never be a man!"**

 "In the Depression you had to grift. Either that or work."

Homer and Bart Get Busted:
Homer: *Hello. Is the lady of the house in?*
Ned Flanders: *Oh, no, Homer! Remember? Maudie got called up to Heaven.*
Homer: *Oh, of course, of course. It's just that...*
Ned: *What?*
Homer: *Well, before she died, she ordered this bible especially for you.*
Ned: *Why, there's my name. In gold!*
Homer: *Now, you weren't home, so we had to pay the deliveryman.*
Ned: *Well, I'll just reimburse you right...wait a minute! This seems an awful lot like that movie Paper Moon.*
Bart: *Run, Dad!*

Grampa makes a clean getaway: **"Call me mint jelly, 'cause I'm on the lam!"**

Easily Justified:
Bart: *Dad?*
Homer: *Yes, son?*
Bart: *Why are we still grifting? The car's paid for. Doesn't that balance out the universe?*
Homer: *In a way, but I also remembered some other stuff, like my bike that was stolen in third grade...plus the baldness.*
Bart: *Okay, I'm sold.*

THE STUFF YOU MAY HAVE MISSED

The marquee at the Magic Palace says "The Great Linguini $5.99."

Diablo the Magician pulls a full-sized white tiger out of his breast pocket, and then levitates it into the air.

The tag-line on the sign at Dentz auto-body repair reads "Blackest Fingernails in Town."

Bart reads about scams in a book titled *A Child's Garden of Cons*, written by Grifty McGrift, a.k.a. Abraham Simpson.

After being repaired, the Simpson car has a license plate in a gold frame that reads "I GRIFT." Also, it has gold wheels, a gold-chain steering wheel, gold door handles, a gold grill, a gold lion hood-ornament, and a fox tail hanging from the antenna.

When Homer and Bart arrive to deliver a ten million dollar check, their car has a sign on the roof that reads "Prize Patrol."

After the "FBI Man" takes Homer and Bart into custody, their car has an "Evidence" sticker on its windshield.

In court, Homer holds a pennant that reads "Justice."

In the last scene, many of the characters from this episode are seen in the ocean, including: the two Russian cosmonauts, Diablo the magician, and the sturgeon that wrecked the Simpsons' car.

MONEY CAPER

Episode CABF03
Original Airdate: 12/10/00
Writer: Carolyn Omine
Director: Michael Polcino
Executive Producer: Mike Scully

Abraham Simpson—Inside Man:

Homer: *Which one of you youngsters is Abe Simpson?*
Grampa: *I'm Abe Simpson.*
Homer: *You've just won ten million dollars from that Publishers Cleary dealie!*
Grampa: *Whaa?!*
Crazy Jewish Man: *Everybody, come quick! Abe Simpson is rich!*
Grampa: *I can't believe it! I can finally afford a young, crazy, stripper wife!*
Old folks: *Yay!*

Flim-Flamming the Fed:

Bart: *Please, FBI Man, don't throw us in jail! We just made one mistake.*
Homer: *Yeah, we're not criminals. We're just two crazy, mixed-up kids.*
FBI Man: *Hmmm. Okay, tell you what—I'll let you turn yourselves in. Maybe they'll go easier on you.*
Homer: *You'd do that for us?*
FBI Man: *Well, I did ruin the boy's birthday cake.*

Doin' Time:

Homer: *Chief, I'd like to scare my son straight. Could I show him a jail cell?*
Chief Wiggum: *Oh, sure. I'll put you in the "Rick James Suite"—it's super freaky.*

Tangled Web-Weaving:

Marge: *You were carjacked? In the church parking lot?*
Homer: *Absolutely. We had stopped in for a quick prayer, when...Bart, would you call him a crazy-man?*
Bart: *Definitely. Well, crazy about carjacking.*

Railroaded in Court:

Prosecutor: *Will you tell the court your whereabouts at the time of the carjacking?*
Groundskeeper Willie: *I was alone in me Unabomber-style shack. I had nothing to do with that carjacking.*
Prosecutor: *Carjacking? Who said anything about a carjacking?*
Jury: *Gasp!*
Willie: *But didn't ya just say--?*
Prosecutor: *I'll ask the questions here, Carjacker Willie!*
Defense Attorney: *Objection!*
Judge: *I'm going to allow it. It characterizes the defendant as a carjacker.*

Homer confesses: **"Stop! This has gone on just long enough! Nobody carjacked me. I tried to pull a con and got conned myself. And then I lied to you all!** *(sobbing and then stopping suddenly)* **So did Bart."**

SKINNER'S SENSE

A big storm hits Springfield, turning it into a winter wonderland. Most of the area schools and establishments are closed, but not Springfield Elementary. When Bart and Lisa arrive at school, they discover that only a few children and Principal Skinner are there. The students are upset since it is the last school day before Christmas, but Skinner does his best to make the day productive. When the bell rings for everyone to go home, Skinner and the students discovered that they have been snowed-in, and that they are trapped inside the school.

Homer and Ned Flanders make an effort to rescue the kids, but Homer crashes the car into a fire hydrant. The hydrant sprays the car with water, the water freezes, and they are trapped inside. Meanwhile, at Springfield Elementary, Skinner is having discipline problems. He puts on his old Army uniform and orders the children to keep in line. Unfazed, Bart attempts to dig a tunnel through the snow to freedom, but Skinner discovers it before he can escape. Trying to maintain his control, Skinner decides to collapse the escape tunnel, and he is partially trapped in the resulting cave-in. The kids take the opportunity to seize control of the school.

The children subdue Principal Skinner by tying him up in a dodgeball sack. They run wild and torment him by trashing the school, burning books, and breaking into their permanent records. Skinner puts the school hamster, Nibbles, in a hamster ball and sends it out into the snow to find help. Ned and Homer, still trapped in the frozen car, succumb to the hallucinogenic effects of fumes from the car's running engine until the hamster ball crashes through the windshield, saving them. They are able break free from the fire hydrant, and Homer once again loses control of the car. The vehicle crashes into the salt silo at the cracker factory. The silo skids down the hill and deposits its salty contents in front of the school, melting the ice and freeing the trapped students. Bart and Skinner agree to speak no more about what took place at the school, and everyone is free to go home and celebrate the Christmas season.

SHOW HIGHLIGHTS

"Children, I'm proud of you. Most of our students didn't bother to show up on this last day before Christmas break. But you've kept intact my Cal Ripken–like streak of school openage."

Kent Brockman's weather report: **"Roads closed, pipes frozen, albinos virtually invisible. The Weather Service has upgraded Springfield's blizzard from 'Winter Wonderland' to a 'Class 3 Kill Storm.'"**

At Cirque de Purée:
Marge: *Finally! A circus full of whimsy and wonder.*
Homer: *(sarcastically) Oh, yeah. That's way better than fun and excitement.*
Lisa: *(reading the program) As French-Canadians, they don't believe in refunds or exploiting animals for entertainment.*
Homer: *Oh, I wanted to see 'em fire a gorilla out of a cannon!*

Problem Solving:
Marge: *This is terrible! How will the kids get home?*
Homer: *I 'unno...Internet?*

Skating Around the Issue:
Nelson: *I can cut a trail through this snow. I'm part Eskimo.*
Skinner: *I don't care if you're Kristi Yamaguchi. No one leaves the building!*
Bart: *This stinks! We'll miss the Itchy and Scratchy where they finally kiss.*
Skinner: *I don't care if they're kissing Kristi Yamaguchi. You're not going home.*

Selective Memory:
Ned: *Hey, whatever happened to the plow from your old snowplow business?*
Homer: *I never had a snowplow business.*
Ned: *Sure you did. Mr. Plow. You're wearing the jacket right now.*
Homer: *I think I know my own life, Ned! (singing) "Call Mr. Plow, that's my name. That name again is Mr. Plow."*

Vietnam Flashback:
Soldier 1: *Sarge, let's make a break for it while the guards are partying with Jane Fonda.*
Skinner: *Nope! Too dangerous. We're all going to sit tight and reminisce about candy bars.*
Soldier 2: *Well, one time I'm eating a candy bar at the beach, and a girl starts taking off her bathing suit.*
Skinner: *Get back to the candy bar.*

Creature Comforts:
Ralph: *Mister Army man? I can't sleep without my Reggie Rabbit.*
Skinner: *Is that some sort of plush novelty?*
Ralph: *Yes, ma'am.*
Skinner: *(reaching into the sack he's sleeping in) Well, here's a scouring pad. It's just as good.*
(Ralph rubs the scouring pad against his cheek.)
Ralph: *It's cold and hurty.*

Cheap Shot:
Skinner: *Defying orders, eh? Well, I see you Scotsmen are thrifty with courage, too.*
Groundskeeper Willie: *Okay, Skinner, that's the last time you'll slap yer Willie around! I quit!*

Caught in a Sack:
Bart: *That's it. Cinch it up around the neck.*
(Kearney tightens the rope in the opening of the dodgeball sack around Skinner's neck.)
Skinner: *Aaaggh. This is a gross misuse of school property! Where are the dodgeballs? (He is hit by several dodge balls.) Ow! Ow! Oh! All right, that's it! I'm writing all your names on the detention list in my mind.*
Bart: *Silence, Seymour! We're in charge now. Your reign of fussiness is over.*

I AIN'T NOT A DORKUS
I AIN'T NOT A DORKUS
I AIN'T NOT A DORKUS
I AIN'T NOT A DORKUS
I AIN'T NOT A DORK

OF SNOW

Episode CABF06
Original Airdate: 12/17/00
Writer: Tim Long
Director: Lance Kramer
Executive Producer: Mike Scully

SCIENCE CLASS SHOULD NOT
END IN TRAGEDY
SCIENCE CLASS SHOULD NO[T]
END IN TRAGEDY
SCIENCE CLASS SHOULD [NOT]
END IN TRAGEDY

RINGMASTER

Leader of:
Cirque de Purée

The price of "purée" entertainment:
Eighty dollars

Known for:
Hauntingly beautiful performances that nurture the child within

Performers include:
Fatalistic ushers that disappear into thin air; acrobats that join together to form the shapes of elephants and kites; clowns that carry jars of rainbows

Audience partici-"plants" are required to:
Have a pure heart and come with wires attached

> MESDAMES ET MESSIEURS, IT APPEARS THE CLOUD GODDESS IS RIPE WITH RAIN BABIES. WE MUST RUN FOR OUR TRUCKS.

THE STUFF YOU MAY HAVE MISSED

As Homer watches a football program, he holds a pennant that says "TV Sports." When his family forces him to go to Cirque de Purée, he puts that pennant in an umbrella stand next to the couch that holds many other pennants and pulls out one that reads "French Circus."

There's a Springfield Elementary My Dear Watson Detective School in town.

Apu and Manjula build an ice sculpture of the Hindu deity, Shiva, and one of their babies are perched in the hands of each of the statue's six arms.

Skinner shows the children an old, poorly produced black-and-white film called *The Christmas That Almost Wasn't but Then Was* (Consolidated Pictures ©1938).

Kearney fears that the snow will prevent him from being at his "kid's birthday." Kearney has been seen with a young son in "A Milhouse Divided" (4F04) and an infant in "Insane Clown Poppy" (BABF17).

Homer was Mr. Plow in "Mr. Plow" (9F07).

The elephant that eats Sergeant Skinner's soldier is wearing a coolie hat.

The children use flour and onion sacks as sleeping bags.

Nelson doles out relish to the other kids from a trophy that reads "Debate Meet—Last Place."

Milhouse's dad, Kirk Van Houten, was previously employed at the cracker factory, as mentioned in "Homie the Clown" (2F12), "Bart on the Road" (3F17), and "A Milhouse Divided" (4F04).

Lisa can recognize the sound of a silo falling over and Superintendent Chalmers can smell literature burning.

After the snow melts the ice outside of the school, it quickly begins to corrode and oxidize Flanders's car, destroying it in seconds.

Exhausting Their Options:
Homer: *Stupid ice! I always knew I would die caked in something.*
Ned: *Better turn off the engine before those fumes put us in tombs.*
Homer: *Wait. Let's just leave it on till we forget our troubles.*
Ned: *(dreamily) Sounds like a plan.*

Movie Moment:
Bart tortures Principal Skinner by poking him with a stick and shouting at him in Vietnamese, reminiscent of the way the soldiers were treated in Michael Cimino's *The Deer Hunter*.

On the Record:
Milhouse: *Hey, I got Skinner's key card. We can finally see our permanent records.*
Skinner: *No! You can't go in there!*
(Milhouse uses the card to open the walk-in safe.)
Kids: *Yay!*
Bart: *(reading) "Underachiever and proud of it." How old is this thing?*
Lisa: *(reading) "Lisa is an outstanding student, with a slight tendency toward know-it-all-ism." Gasp! That's not even a word!*

Fuzzy Math:
Nelson: *(reading from the "Payroll" binder) Hey! Look how much Skinner makes—twenty-five thousand dollars a year!*
Kids: *Wow!*
Bart: *Let's see...he's forty years old, times twenty-five grand...Whoa! He's a millionaire!*
Kids: *Wow!*
Skinner: *I wasn't a principal when I was one.*
Nelson: *Plus, in the summer, he paints houses.*
Milhouse: *He's a billionaire!*
Kids: *Wow!*
Skinner: *If I were a billionaire, why would I be living with my mother?*

Resorting to Bribery:
Skinner: *Nelson, if you get me out of this, there's a hall monitor position coming open in the spring.*
Nelson: *I spit on your monitors!*
Skinner: *I know. That's why the position's available.*

Homer's fume-induced harem fantasy: **"Marvelous! Marvelous! Enough! I grow weary of your sexually-suggestive dancing. Bring me my ranch dressing hose!"**

Crash Course in Miracles:
Flanders: *We're gonna crash!*
Homer: *Do you have airbags?*
Flanders: *No. The church opposes them for some reason.*

"You did it, Nibbles. Now chew through my ball sack."

Snow Job:
Superintendent Chalmers: *Skin-ner!*
(Chalmers dismounts from a snowmobile that reads "Springfield Public Schools.")
Skinner: *Superintendent Chalmers!*
Chalmers: *What are you doing in that ridiculous duffel, Seymour? And is that burning literature I smell?*
Skinner: *Uh, we...well, sir, I, uh...*
Chalmers: *There'd better be a good explanation for this.*
Bart: *There is, sir...*
Chalmers: *Ah, then I'm happy.*
(He gets back on the snowmobile and drives off.)

Clear Communication:
Skinner: *Bart, if there's one thing I'm good at, it's pretending things didn't happen. And I think this is one of those.*
Bart: *One of which?*
Skinner: *Exactly.*
Bart: *No, seriously, I wasn't listening.*
Skinner: *One of those situations where--*
Bart: *Gotcha!*

INTELLIGENT HOMER

HOMЯ

The result of:
A crayon being removed from his brain

Recognizable by:
His spiffy nerd ensemble

"Smart" things he likes to do:
Solve Rubik's Cubes by the basketful, listen to classical music, report safety violations to the Nuclear Regulatory Commission, and make codpieces for his friends

Thing he still does not like to do:
Walk

His message:
It's cool to be smart

Message he gets loud and clear:
Being a brain alienates him from all his friends

I'M DETECTING A DISTINCT STRAIN OF ANTI-INTELLECTUALISM IN THIS TAVERN.

T he Simpsons attend an animation festival, and Homer becomes excited by a new motion-capture animation process that he thinks will revolutionize the industry. He invests the family's life savings in the animation company's stock. At first, the stock does fine, but soon it plummets and the company has to file for bankruptcy. Homer loses everything.

Homer tries to think of a way to gain back the money. Barney tells him that he can earn cash by becoming a test subject at the local research facility. Homer is accepted as a subject and submits to several painful tests. While studying a head X ray, the researchers discover a crayon lodged in his brain. Once the crayon is removed, Homer's intelligence increases dramatically. He now enjoys going to the library with Lisa, helping his friends, and giving lectures. However, when he sends a report to the government on the substandard safety conditions at the power plant, everyone is laid off. Homer's friends and colleagues turn against him, and he cannot believe that he is being shunned by his intellectual inferiors.

Homer is burned in effigy at Moe's Tavern, and he gets tossed out of a movie theater for pointing out plot holes in the story. Although he has connected with Lisa in a meaningful way, he feels like he does not fit in anywhere. Desperate for a return to normalcy, Homer goes back to the research clinic and begs them to make him dumb again. The researchers refuse to help, but point Homer in the direction of an unlicensed surgeon who will—Moe Szyslak. Upon discovering a missing crayon in her crayon box, Lisa realizes too late that Homer intends to reverse the procedure. Moe performs the operation, and Homer returns home his old unintelligent, but blissfully ignorant self. Lisa finds solace in a letter that Homer wrote while still intelligent, telling her how much he appreciates her.

SHOW HIGHLIGHTS

Beauty in Animotion:
Homer: *That motion-capture suit is just what this country needs. Just think of all the hilarious motions that are going uncaptured. Like this...(He jumps up on the table and performs a horse-riding bit.) See? (He gets down from the table.) Now, wouldn't you love to see that move performed by a cartoon possum?*
Carl: *An opossum capering around like that would be a smash hit!*
Lenny: *It would be the world's funniest marsupial.*
Homer: *You're right! That suit gizmo could be worth billions! And I'm gonna get a piece of the action!* (He runs off, and we hear the sounds of his car door closing and him speeding away.)
Carl: *So, does he still work here or what?*

Taking Stock:
Computer Voice: *For automated stock prices, please state the company name.*
Homer: *Animotion.*
Computer Voice: *Animotion. Up one and one-half.*
Homer: *Yahoo!*
Computer Voice: *Yahoo. Up six and a quarter.*
Homer: *Huh? What is this crap?*
Computer Voice: *Fox Broadcasting. Down eight.*

Family Meeting:
Homer: *All right, first item: I lost our life savings in the stock market. Now, let's move on to the real issue: Lisa's hogging of the maple syrup!*
Lisa: *Well, maybe if Mom didn't make such dry waffles...there, I said it.*
Marge: *Well, maybe if you ate some meat, you'd have a natural lubricant...Gasp! You lost all our money?*
Homer: *Point of order. I didn't lose all the money. There was enough left for this cowbell. (He rings the cowbell, and it breaks into many pieces.) Damn you, eBay!*

An Indecent Proposal:
Homer: *I have a great way to solve our money woes! You rent your womb to a rich, childless couple. If you agree, signify by getting indignant.*
Marge: *Are you crazy? I'm not going to be a surrogate mother!*
Homer: *C'mon, Marge, we're a team. It's uter-us, not uter-you.*
Marge: *Hm. Forget it!*

The Crayon in Homer's Brain:
Male Researcher: *Mr. Simpson, this could be responsible for your subnormal intelligence.*
Homer: *Hey, I came here to be drugged, electrocuted, and probed, not insulted!*
Female Researcher: *We could remove the crayon for you. It could vastly improve your brainpower...or it could possibly kill you.*
Homer: *Increase my killing power, eh? Let's do it!*

Episode BABF22
Original Airdate: 01/07/01
Writer: Al Jean
Director: Mike B. Anderson
Executive Producer: Mike Scully

From Dull to Sharp:

Marge: *Do you feel smarter?*
Homer: *Is the capital of North Dakota Bismarck?*
(The family looks to Lisa for confirmation.)
Lisa: *It is!*
Bart: *I don't believe it! Say something else smart.*
Homer: *Dr. Joyce Brothers may be well-known, but her psychological credentials are highly suspect.*
(They look to Lisa again.)
Lisa: *It's true!*

God Is Dead:

Homer: *Hey, Flanders, headin' for church? Well, I thought I could save you a little time.*
Flanders: *Ooo...found a new shortcut?*
Homer: *Better. I was working on a flat-tax proposal, and I accidentally proved there's no God.*
(Homer hands Flanders a sheet of paper covered with equations and walks off.)
Flanders: (examining paper) *We'll just see about that...uh-oh. Well, maybe he made a mistake...Nope. It's airtight.* (He pulls out a lighter.) *Can't let this little doozy get out.*
(He lights the paper, but as it burns away, it reveals Homer whistling "The Battle Hymn of the Republic" as he puts copies on the windshield of every car on the street.)

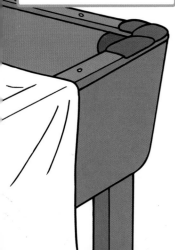

The newer, smarter Homer: **"Now, who's up for a trip to the library tomorrow? Notice I no longer say 'liberry' or 'tomorry.'"**

The Power of the Podium:

Principal Skinner: *Welcome to the third lecture in our series on "Not Putting Things Up Your Nose." Please welcome Homer Simpson.*
Homer: *I am here to give hope to the least of you, because we all have a crayon up our nose. Maybe it's not a crayon made of wax. Maybe it's a crayon made of prejudice.*

Turnabout Is Fair Play:

Nelson: *Question!*
Homer: *Yes, Nelson?*
Nelson: *A moron says, "What?"*
Homer: *Not being a moron, I wouldn't know. However...*(mumbling)
Nelson: *What?*
Homer: *Ladies and gentlemen, I give you your moron.*
(All the kids point at Nelson.)
Kids: *Ha, ha!*

Movie Moments:

The title of this episode and some of the plot comes from the 1968 movie *Charly*, a story about a mentally challenged man who gains incredible intelligence by taking a research drug, only to lose it all and become intellectually inferior again.

Itchy and Scratchy kiss on the beach as waves roll over them, just like Burt Lancaster and Deborah Kerr did in 1953's *From Here to Eternity*.

With the promise of riches in the Animotion venture, Homer imagines himself as part of a chorus line of gold diggers singing "We're in the Money" just before the big theatrical unveiling of King Kong. *The Gold Diggers of 1933* and *King Kong* were both released in 1933.

Churlish Chums:

Homer: *So you all hate me?*
Lenny: *That's right, Brainiac! You cost us our jobs, which we need for workin'!*
Carl: *Not to mention drivin' to!*
Moe: *And I was a lot happier before I knew Dame Edna was a man...a lot happier.*

"Dad, as intelligence goes up, happiness often goes down. In fact, I made a graph. I make a lot of graphs."

Homer's new perspective: **"I'm a Spalding Gray in a Rick Dees world! Change me back to the blissful boob I was!"**

That's Right...Moe's a Surgeon:

Moe: *So what do you want here? Ah, appendectomy, lipo, or the sampler? That's very popular.*
Homer: *I want you to stick this crayon into my brain.*
Moe: *No problem. The ol' "Crayola Oblongata"!*

A Delicate Procedure:

(Moe cautiously inserts the crayon up Homer's nose.)
Moe: *All right, tell me when I hit the sweet spot.*
Homer: *Deeper, you pusillanimous pilsner-pusher.*
Moe: *All right, all right.*
(He takes a small hammer and chisel and taps the crayon twice.)
Homer: *De-fense!* (grunting twice) *De-fense!* (grunting twice)
Moe: *That's pretty dumb...but, uh...*
(He taps the crayon again.)
Homer: *Extended warranty? How can I lose?*
Moe: *Perfect.*

Homer's letter to Lisa: **"Lisa, I'm taking the coward's way out. But before I do, I just want you to know: Being smart made me appreciate how amazing you really are."**

THE STUFF YOU MAY HAVE MISSED

The Simpsons attend the "Totally Sick, Twisted, F***ed-Up Animation Festival."

Booths seen at the animation festival include "Happy Little Elves," "Radioactive Man," "Veggie Tales," "Trek Toons," "Cel-Out," "History of Animation," "Itchy & Scratchy," "3D Training Videos," "Poochie!" and the "Lance Murdock Cartoon Show."

The Comic Book Guy is wearing a T-shirt that reads "Worst Convention Ever!"

"The New Adventures of Gravey and Jobriath" is based on the Christian-influenced, stop-motion series "Davey and Goliath" (1962–77). The sequence was produced by Chiodo Brothers Productions, Inc.

Louie the Butler in the Laramie Cigarette commercial is based on Eddie "Rochester" Anderson from the classic radio and TV show "The Jack Benny Program."

The logo for the First Bank of Springfield is BS.

The male and female researchers at the Screaming Monkey Medical Research Center bear a striking resemblance to the Pharm Team technicians who developed Focusyn in "Brother's Little Helper" (AABF22).

At the Old Springfield Library, there's a banner out front that reads "Home of Bookworms and Silverfish."

Cletus tries to crack a turtle open with a copy of *Trinity* by Leon Uris.

Mr. Burns leaves his employee meeting by means of a golf cart with the Springfield Country Club logo on it. The club was first mentioned in "Scenes from the Class Struggle in Springfield" (3F11).

Signs that Homer passes in search of a place for people with high IQs: "Smart People Not Welcome," "Dum-Dum Club," "Lunkheads—A Place for Drooling," and "Disney Store."

POKEY

O n their way back from an apron expo, the Simpsons stop to watch a prison rodeo. Homer injures his back while taunting a raging bull, and with Marge by his side, spends time in the prison infirmary. Marge spots some paintings on the infirmary wall created by one of the inmates and is very impressed with his artistic talent.

Marge cannot get the artist/convict, Jack Crowley, off her mind, so she decides to volunteer her time at the prison teaching an art class. After talking with Jack, she concludes that he is too sensitive and talented to be in prison and pleads his case at a parole hearing. The warden paroles Jack and places him in Marge's custody. To help him re-enter society, Marge gets Jack a job painting a mural intended to raise school spirit at Springfield Elementary, but she keeps his past a secret.

Meanwhile, Homer continues to have problems with his back. Visits to Dr. Hibbert and to Dr. Steve, a chiropractor, do not seem to help, but when Homer falls backwards over a garbage can, his pain goes away. Homer decides he can

become a chiropractor and cure other people with his garbage can method. The chiropractors in town resent Homer's amateur practice and flagrant disregard for their profession. First, they threaten him, and then they seize the garbage can he has built his practice on and destroy it.

At Springfield Elementary, Jack Crowley and Principal Skinner do not agree on how the school mural should be painted. Marge urges the convict to sacrifice his artistic vision for a chance at an honest life, and Jack agrees to paint the mural as Skinner originally conceived it, although he comes to despise the principal. When the mural is unveiled to a lackluster response, Skinner places the blame on the convict. Jack Crowley's anger gets the best of him, and he torches the mural. When Marge confronts him, he lies to her and plays on her sympathy, so that she will help him escape. He quickly loses Marge's trust when he takes his vengeance on Skinner by setting his car ablaze. Feeling burned herself, Marge tells Chief Wiggum to take Jack back to prison.

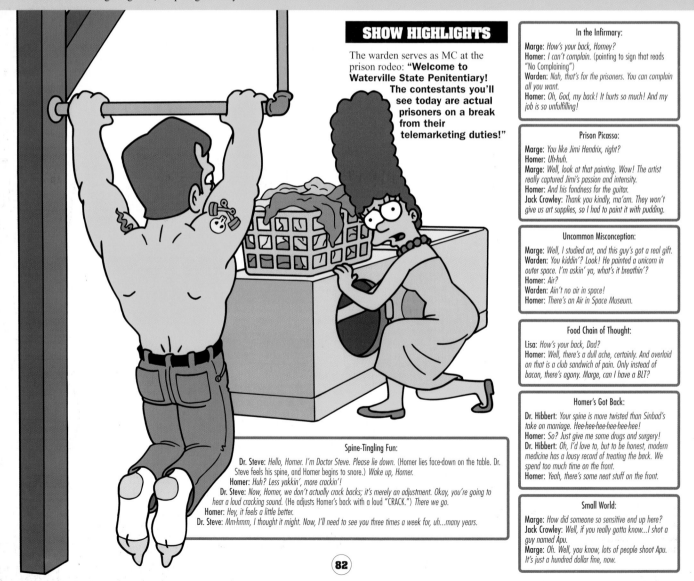

SHOW HIGHLIGHTS

The warden serves as MC at the prison rodeo: **"Welcome to Waterville State Penitentiary! The contestants you'll see today are actual prisoners on a break from their telemarketing duties!"**

Spine-Tingling Fun:
Dr. Steve: *Hello, Homer. I'm Doctor Steve. Please lie down.* (Homer lies face-down on the table. Dr. Steve feels his spine, and Homer begins to snore.) *Wake up, Homer.*
Homer: *Huh? Less yakkin', more crackin'!*
Dr. Steve: *Now, Homer, we don't actually crack backs; it's merely an adjustment. Okay, you're going to hear a loud cracking sound.* (He adjusts Homer's back with a loud "CRACK.") *There we go.*
Homer: *Hey, it feels a little better.*
Dr. Steve: *Mm-hmm, I thought it might. Now, I'll need to see you three times a week for, uh...many years.*

In the Infirmary:
Marge: *How's your back, Homey?*
Homer: *I can't complain.* (pointing to sign that reads "No Complaining")
Warden: *Nah, that's for the prisoners. You can complain all you want.*
Homer: *Oh, God, my back! It hurts so much! And my job is so unfulfilling!*

Prison Picasso:
Marge: *You like Jimi Hendrix, right?*
Homer: *Uh-huh.*
Marge: *Well, look at that painting. Wow! The artist really captured Jimi's passion and intensity.*
Homer: *And his fondness for the guitar.*
Jack Crowley: *Thank you kindly, ma'am. They won't give us art supplies, so I had to paint it with pudding.*

Uncommon Misconception:
Marge: *Well, I studied art, and this guy's got a real gift.*
Warden: *You kiddin'? Look! He painted a unicorn in outer space. I'm askin' ya, what's it breathin'?*
Homer: *Air?*
Warden: *Ain't no air in space!*
Homer: *There's an Air in Space Museum.*

Food Chain of Thought:
Lisa: *How's your back, Dad?*
Homer: *Well, there's a dull ache, certainly. And overlaid on that is a club sandwich of pain. Only instead of bacon, there's agony. Marge, can I have a BLT?*

Homer's Got Back:
Dr. Hibbert: *Your spine is more twisted than Sinbad's take on marriage. Hee-hee-hee-hee-hee-hee!*
Homer: *So? Just give me some drugs and surgery!*
Dr. Hibbert: *Oh, I'd love to, but to be honest, modern medicine has a lousy record of treating the back. We spend too much time on the front.*
Homer: *Yeah, there's some neat stuff on the front.*

Small World:
Marge: *How did someone so sensitive end up here?*
Jack Crowley: *Well, if you really gotta know...I shot a guy named Apu.*
Marge: *Oh. Well, you know, lots of people shoot Apu. It's just a hundred dollar fine, now.*

82

MOM

Episode CABF05
Original Airdate: 01/14/01
Writer: Tom Martin
Director: Bob Anderson
Executive Producer: Mike Scully

Guest Voices: Charles Napier as Warden, Robert Schimmel as Convict, and Bruce Vilanch as Himself

THE STUFF YOU MAY HAVE MISSED

The control settings on Marge and Homer's adjustable bed are "Max Power" and "Full Reverse." Max Power is the name Homer took for himself in "Homer to The Max" (AABF09).

The apron Lisa gets at the expo and plans to wear on the Fourth of July reads "Barbecue Is Murder."

At the prison rodeo, Homer holds a pennant that says "Criminals."

Sideshow Bob is in the prison infirmary in a cast from the neck up, along with Tornado the bull, who is having his horns bandaged.

Marge can see both the Waterville Prison and Springfield Elementary from her kitchen window.

When Marge's joke does not go over well with the prisoners in her art class, the sound of a shotgun being cocked can be heard off-screen. Later, when Principal Skinner's joke falls flat at the mural unveiling, the same sound is heard again.

A sign at Dr. Homer's Clinic says "Pay in Advance."

Homer takes out bus advertising for his clinic under the name "El Clinico Magnifico."

The chiropractors beat Homer's garbage can with spinal columns and pelvic bones.

Principal Skinner plans the lunch menu as if he were a TV executive scheduling programs. The lunch menu includes: Texas Hash and Corn on Wednesday and Mystery Fish and Goulash on Friday.

Marge's parole plea: **"This man is a gentle soul. I know he's made mistakes, but someone with his talent belongs on the boardwalk doing caricatures, not behind bars."**

Gentleman Bandit:

Warden: Lady, I know he charmed you with some "pleases" and "thank yous," but he wasn't so polite to the guy he shot.
Apu: Actually, he was. He waited with me until the ambulance came, then ran like a deer.

Like Father, Like Son:

Homer: Ow! Owww, my back! Dr. Steve didn't do anything.
Bart: Did you do those exercises he gave you?
Homer: Yeah, right. I did 'em while you were studying.

At Dr. Homer's Chiropractic Clinic:

Lenny: So, Homer, do you think you can fix my sciatica?
Homer: I don't know what that is, so I'm gonna say "yes." Now, go limp.

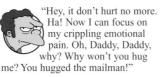

"Hey, it don't hurt no more. Ha! Now I can focus on my crippling emotional pain. Oh, Daddy, Daddy, why? Why won't you hug me? You hugged the mailman!"

Fibbing for a Future:

Jack: You told a lie for me.
Marge: I know, but the Lord will forgive me if it helps you get a second chance.
Jack: Actually, Marge, it's the third, if you count that farm couple.
Marge: Farm couple?
Jack: But I got a good feeling about this one, Marge! I really do!

Mural Misunderstanding:

Skinner: Dear Lord! What are you doing?
Jack: You don't like it?
Skinner: No, no, it's all wrong. The shapely female form has no place in art!

Art Isn't Easy:

Superintendent Chalmers: Skin-ner! How are we going to raise school spirit with this sappy hokum?
Skinner: I know, sir. It's an embarrassment. (He steps over to Jack and starts poking him with his finger.) This isn't what I wanted! Where's the edge?
Jack: (barely controlling anger) I followed your napkin...
(He holds up the napkin. Skinner angrily crumples it.)
Skinner: No napkin could wipe the crumbs of failure from your mouth.

Movie Moment:

The scene when Homer cries in the street over his destroyed trash can, and Moe says, "Forget it, Homer. It's Chirotown," echoes the closing moments of *Chinatown* (1974), starring Jack Nicholson.

Planning the Lunch Menu:

Skinner: Now, uh, pizza's working well on Thursday, but I think the kids'll follow it to Tuesday.
Groundskeeper Willie: That's what ya said about the stuffed peppers, and ya lost the young males!

As a Fire Rages:

Skinner: It's crystal-clear who did this—Jack Crowley!
Marge: Now, wait. You don't know that Jack did this. Just because he's an ex-con...oh.
Skinner: Crowley's an ex-con? Dear Lord! I peed in front of him!

Skinner on fire safety: **"That felon could have torched the whole school...were it not stuffed with asbestos."**

Liar, Liar, Car on Fire:

Marge: You crumb-bum! You looked me right in the eye and lied to me!
Jack: Marge, this is the God's truth—I burned the mural, but I did not burn Skinner's car.
Marge: I just saw you!

JACK CROWLEY

Who he is:
Passionate, sensitive painter/dangerous convict

How bad he is:
Bob Dylan wrote a song to keep him in prison

Prison amenities:
Basic cable, pudding to paint with, and the occasional rodeo

What he hates most about prison:
The foul language

Bad habit:
He's a liar, but not a very good liar

Other talents besides art:
Starting fires; making booze in a washing machine

ALL RIGHT. YOU'RE THE BOSSMAN, AIN'T YA?

Guest Voice:
Michael Keaton as Jack Crowley

RADIOACTIVE MAN

Who he is:
A comic book superhero

His alter-ego:
Millionaire playboy Claude Kane III

Origin:
Developed nuclear superpowers after getting his pants caught on barbed wire during an A-bomb test

Superhero drawback:
Lightning-shaped piece of shrapnel stuck in his head requires that he always wear a hat when not in costume

Sidekick:
His youthful ward, Rod Runtledge, a.k.a. Fallout Boy

Amazing Fact:
Radioactive Man #1000 in perma-mint condition sells for $25

UP AND ATOM!

art wins a $50 bet with Homer, so he and Milhouse go on a spending spree that eventually takes them to the Android's Dungeon. While there, they get the Comic Book Guy mad and are banned from the store for life. To make matters worse, Bart and Milhouse also do not get to see a presentation by special-effects guru Tom Savini taking place at the Android's Dungeon that evening. They are outside, however, trying to peek in, when Savini humiliates the Comic Book Guy in front of his patrons. The Comic Book Guy gets so irate that he has a heart attack.

Bart and Milhouse call 911, and the Comic Book Guy's life is saved. At the hospital, Dr. Hibbert tells him that he has got to take time off from work to recover. The Comic Book Guy is hard-pressed to think of anyone who can fill in for him, and Bart and Milhouse, who are visiting him in the hospital, volunteer. Without the stress and responsibility of work, The Comic Book Guy attempts to

make some friends, and that is when he meets and quickly falls for Agnes Skinner. Meanwhile, Bart and Milhouse are a success at the comic shop until Milhouse orders too many copies of a very unpopular comic entitled *Biclops*, featuring a superhero who wears glasses.

Bart and Milhouse come to blows over Milhouse's error. While wrestling around the comic shop, the boys discover the Comic Book Guy's huge collection of pirated videotapes. They decide to exhibit the tapes at a midnight showing for profit, but are busted by the Springfield Police Department. Unaware of what is happening at his store, the Comic Book Guy enjoys a romantic evening with Agnes, and the two sweethearts end up in bed together. In the midst of their lovemaking, the police break in and arrest Comic Book Guy for possession of the pirated tapes. Agnes tells the Comic Book Guy that she is too old to wait for him to get out of prison, and their relationship comes to an end.

SHOW HIGHLIGHTS

A Fridge Too Far:
Lisa: *Eww! How long has this baking soda been in here?*
Marge: *I don't know. It came with the house.*
Bart: *Hey, Dad! Bet you five bucks you can't eat the whole box.*
Homer: *Five? Why don't we make it fifty? Ho, ho! You're gonna regret this!*
Lisa: *I'll call poison control. (dialing the phone) Fran? It's me. Just a heads-up.*

Bart's Binge:
Bart: *Milhouse my friend, you and I are going on a spending spree.*
Milhouse: *My doctor says I'm not supposed to go on sprees.*
Bart: *What about jags?*
Milhouse: *Jags are fine.*

A Sticky Subject:
Apu: *Our wide variety of gum comes in both stick and ball.*
Bart: *I'm not really about gum, but I like the whole chewing thing.*
Apu: *Are you averse to crispy centers, sir?*
Bart: *Not at all.*
Apu: *Then we have much to discuss.*

"My mom doesn't believe in fabric softener—but she's not around! Ha-ha-ha-ha-ha-ha-ha!"

To Barter Smarter:
Mrs. Prince: *While my son's at Fat Camp, I cleaned out his room. How much will you give me for this?*
Comic Book Guy: *Probably nothing, but let us see...oh! A handwritten script for Star Wars by George Lucas? Princess Leia's anti-jiggle breast tape! Film reel labeled, "Alternate ending—Luke's father is Chewbacca"?! Oh! Oh!...I'll give you five dollars for the box.*
Mrs. Prince: *Sold!*

Comic Book Guy has a heart attack:
"Ooh! Ooh! Breath...short. Left arm...numb! Can't go on... describing symptoms much longer!"

Bemused Bedside Manner:
Dr. Hibbert: *Young man, you've had what we call a "cardiac episode."*
Comic Book Guy: *Worst episode ever!*
Dr. Hibbert: *Oh, not even close. If these boys hadn't called 911, I'd be wearing that watch right now. Ah-hee-hee-huh! Just kidding. But you would be dead.*

Comics of Death:
Dr. Hibbert: *My prognosis...or is it diagnosis? Whichever. You need to avoid stress. What kind of work do you do?*
Comic Book Guy: *I run a comic book store.*
Dr. Hibbert: *Oh dear Lord! We call that profession "The Widowmaker"—or we would, if any of the proprietors were married.*

Frankly Friendless:
Dr. Hibbert: *You should close down the store for awhile.*
Comic Book Guy: *But I'd lose all my business to "Frodo's of Shelbyville"!*
Dr. Hibbert: *Then get a friend to run it for you. You do have friends, don't you?*
Comic Book Guy: *Well, the Super Friends.*
Dr. Hibbert: *You should get some friends who aren't printed on paper.*
Comic Book Guy: *What? You mean action figures?*

Calorie-Filled Communique:
Milhouse: *Okay, here's Comic Book Guy's instructions. (reading) "A carton of malted-milk balls, one box confectioners' sugar, a can of chocolate frosting--"*
Bart: *That's just his shopping list.*
Milhouse: *No, it's his instructions.*

THE STUFF YOU MAY HAVE MISSED

Homer's "antacid trip" takes him through food eaten over forty years of historical moments, including: Johnny Cochran's "glove" speech from the O.J. Simpson trial, Richard M. Nixon's resignation, and Neil Armstrong's walk on the moon.

Milhouse is seen wearing "My Little Pony" underwear. Bart and Homer find his "My Little Pony" blanket in the trash in "Days of Wine and D'oh'ses" (BABF14).

When Comic Book Guy demonstrates how liquid flies off the cover of *Radioactive Man #1000* and onto "lesser comics," the comic shown is titled *Bongo*. Bongo is the name of a character in Matt Groening's *Life in Hell* comic strip, and the name of the company that publishes *Simpsons* comics.

Others "Banned for Life" at the Android's Dungeon include: Sideshow Bob, Nelson, and Matt Groening.

Lisa reads about Tom Savini's comic store appearance in a paper called *The Daily Set-Up*.

The Death of Sad Sack comic cover parodies a "classic" comic entitled *Crisis on Infinite Earths.* The seventh issue of the maxi-series chronicled the death of Supergirl.

The cover of the *Biclops* comic shows Biclops slugging a football player and saying, "That's for making me cry!" The comic is produced by Lenscrafters, a popular optical chain.

Restaurants seen at the Springfield Squidport include: "Have it Uruguay," "What They Eat in Iceland," "The Karachi Hibachi," "A Taste of Serbia," "Mussolini and Frank's" (a parody of the famous Hollywood haunt "Musso and Frank's"), and "The London Broil."

In this episode, Ned Flanders is tormented by a radioactive ape. Ned Flanders had an earlier encounter with dangerous primates in "In Marge We Trust" (4F18).

EPISODE EVER

Episode CABF08
Original Airdate: 02/04/01
Writer: Larry Doyle
Director: Matthew Nastuk
Executive Producer: Mike Scully
Guest Voice: Tom Savini as Himself

Bart chats up his customers: **"Ah, nice to see ya. Hey, how about that 'Bloodzilla'? Bwa-ha-ha-ha-ha! Vampire dinosaur! Ah, you can't make that stuff up."**

"Get out! And take your Sacajawea dollars with you!"

Fish out of Water:
Moe: *Hey, Homer, who's the manatee?*
Homer: *Aw, now be nice, Moe. This guy just got out of the hospital.*
Moe: *Oh, sorry. Lemme buy ya a drink.*
Comic Book Guy: *Very well. I will have a shot of cranberry schnapps.*
Moe: (referring to the "bottles" on the shelf and patting the wall) *Ha, ha! These, they're just painted on there. Your choices are beer and (pointing to the pickled eggs) egg soakings.*
Comic Book Guy: *I'll pass. Beer is the nectar of the nitwit.*

Credit Where It's Due:
Lisa: *Milhouse, I'm impressed! The store is so busy. You and Bart are really great businessmen.*
Milhouse: *Well, I'm really the brains. Bart's just the eye-candy.*

There's Somebody for Everyone:
(The door outside of a classroom reads "How to Make Friends.")
Comic Book Guy: (reaching for the doorknob) *Human contact: the final frontier.*
Agnes: *Out of the way, tubby!*
Comic Book Guy: *Pardon me, Oldie Hawn.*
Agnes: *Wha...hah! Why you ill-mannered sack of crap!*
Comic Book Guy: *Oh, goody! Now I know whatever happened to Baby Jane.*
Agnes: *You are the rudest man who ever... (seductively) bought me dinner.*
Comic Book Guy: *Correction. I do not believe I have ever bought you...oh.*

Mama Mia!
Agnes: *Here I come! (She slides down the bannister dressed in a flapper outfit.)*
Seymour: *Gasp! Good Lord, Mother! I can see your... (disgusted) figure.*
Agnes: *Oh, you see a lot more when you do my daily mole check.*
Seymour: *What I do for my allowance money is nobody's business.*

Music Moment:
The Comic Book Guy and Agnes Skinner's romance is played out to the musical strains of Paul Anka's "Puppy Love" and "Baby I'm-a Want You" by Bread.

Out of the Mouths of Babes:
Milhouse: *Okay, so I made one bad decision.*
Bart: *Oh, it's my fault for leaving you in charge. Sometimes I forget how young you are.*
Milhouse: *I'm only three months younger than you!*
Bart: *Oh, look, you're getting cranky. You haven't had your juice.*
Milhouse: *Well, my straw broke off in the carton...that's not the point! We're supposed to be partners, and you're pushing me around like a Playskool corn-popper!*
Bart: (snickers) *It's a vacuum cleaner, Milhouse.*
Milhouse: (screaming) *Whatever! I demand respect! I have feelings! I'm a human boy, just like you!*
Bart: *Shh! Use your "indoor" voice.*

A Match Made in Hell:
Marge: *Oh, look at you two. You look so "couple-y."*
Comic Book Guy: *Yes, we're a perfect match. Her sneer just lights up my day.*
Mrs. Skinner: *And we're always finishing each other's insults.*

Filling in the Blanks:
Chief Wiggum: *Well, well, well! This place has got more pirated tapes than a...*
Lou: *A Chinese K-Mart?*
Wiggum: *Eh, that'll have to do. Are these yours, son?*
Milhouse: *No, sir. We're just exhibiting them for profit without permission.*
Wiggum: *Fair enough, but the owner is in more hot water than...*
Lou: *A Japanese tea bag?*
Wiggum: *Why don't you lay off the Asians, Lou?*

The End of an Affair:
Chief Wiggum: *Comic Book Guy, you're under arrest for the possession of illegal videos, but we'll reduce the sentence if you put your pants on—fast! God!*
Lou: *Come on, Romeo.*
Comic Book Guy: *They can't lock me up for long, Agnes! Will you wait for me?*
Agnes: *Are you crazy? My bones are half dust.*

AIEEEE!

SIGH...

Abe Simpson wins a free autopsy during the Springfield Retirement Castle's Talent Show, so he, Homer, and Bart go to the funeral home to pre-register. While there, the funeral home salesman shows them the many luxurious services they provide, but Homer feels it is all too costly. When the salesman mentions that the price of a mausoleum is about what you would pay for a tennis court, Homer decides to have a tennis court built in his backyard instead.

Their new tennis court is quite a hit, and Marge and Homer have a fine time entertaining guests. Homer spends more time clowning around on the court than playing competitive tennis, which upsets Marge because they never win. When Marge overhears others talking about how lousy she and Homer are, Marge demands he take his playing more seriously. To Marge's horror, Homer responds by signing them up for a doubles tournament, but he does not show much interest in practicing for the event. Bart practices with Marge in Homer's place and eventually replaces him as her tennis partner.

Being dumped as a partner upsets Homer. He gets even more perturbed when Bart and Marge win trophies and are invited to enter a charity tennis competition. Homer talks Lisa into being his new partner, and a family rivalry begins. Later, desperate to win the competition, Homer replaces Lisa with professional tennis player Venus Williams. Marge is forced to counter by replacing Bart with Serena Williams. Marge is then switched with Pete Sampras, and, finally, Homer is replaced by Andre Agassi. In the end, the Simpsons all make up with each other after being so competitive and watch the four superstars play tennis.

SHOW HIGHLIGHTS

Classic Humor:

Old Comedian: *Ever notice after dialysis, you always get...the munchies?!*
(The old folks laugh.)
Jasper: *He's sayin' the stuff we all forgot.*
Old Comedian: *And you know what I can't open? Cabinets!*
(The old folks laugh some more.)
Grampa: *Can he say that?*
Old Comedian: *You know what else scares me? Everything!*
(The old folks laugh again.)

"Wasn't he great, folks? Now, all the contestants are gonna receive extra servings of honey mush. But there can only be one winner, and, uh, since Abe's already standing here, what the heck?"

Planning Ahead:

Funeral Home Salesman: *What other funerary services may we provide for the pre-deceased?*
Homer: *Oh, the whole deal! Coffin, tombstone, anti-stink spray.*
Funeral Home Salesman: *Sir, we prefer the term "casket" to coffin, and "monument" to tombstone. We have all the leading brands of anti-stink spray.*

Decisions, Decisions:

Funeral Home Salesman: *O-kay, with mole insurance, your total comes to...$17,000.*
Homer: *What?! Ohhh!*
Funeral Home Salesman: *Or you could just toss him in the woods and let the wolves carry him off. It's really up to you.*
Homer: *Mr. Salesman?*
Funeral Home Salesman: *Yeesss?*
Homer: *We're gonna go with the wolves.*

Pointing Fingers:

Grampa: *Oh, I can't believe we went through all that, just to wind up with a tennis court.*
Homer: *I'll bet you didn't see that comin'.*
Abe: *You don't care what happens to me when I die!*
Homer: *Of course, I do, Dad. Aw, and if it were up to me, you wouldn't die at all. But try telling that to (pointing heavenwards) Killy McGee up there!*

Marge, impressed by the royal treatment: **"You know, a tennis court can really make your house look classy. I hear Mel Brooks has one. I mean, Sir Mel Brooks!"**

Another Snub:

Homer: *It'd be nice to entertain friends and have people over.*
Ned: *Hey! You got a tennis court?*
Homer: *Keep walkin', Flanders!*
Ned: *Will do.*
Homer: *Faaaster!*

Flubbed Line:

Kent Brockman: *H-ha, ha! That's game, set, and match to us! But the real winners here are Marge's hors d'oeuvres.*
Homer: *Wow! How do you come up with such witty remarks?*
Brockman: *Ha, ha! Well...*
(Camera moves in to reveal Kent Brockman is wearing an earpiece. Cut to two men in a van nearby. One is furiously typing something. The other has a microphone)
Man with Microphone: *Come on! Come on! Hurry up!* (He takes the paper from the typist and reads it into the mike.) *I guess you could say it's my racket.*
(Cut back to Kent receiving the transmission.)
Brockman: *I guess you could say I'm Iraqi.*
Homer: *Gasp! Get off my property!*

MENACE

Episode CABF07
Original Airdate: 02/11/01
Writer: Ian Maxtone-Graham
Director: Jen Kamerman
Executive Producer: Mike Scully

Guest Voices: Andre Agassi, Pete Sampras, Serena Williams, and Venus Williams as Themselves

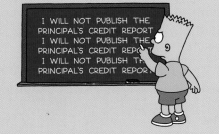

I WILL NOT PUBLISH THE PRINCIPAL'S CREDIT REPORT
I WILL NOT PUBLISH THE PRINCIPAL'S CREDIT REPORT
I WILL NOT PUBLISH THE PRINCIPAL'S CREDIT REPORT
I WILL NOT PUBLISH THE PRINCIPAL'S CREDIT REPORT

THE FUNERAL HOME SALESMAN

Unsure of:
What lies beyond this life

Tells customers that:
God prefers people who travel in style

Deluxe items he offers:
Unused virgin graves, self-cleaning monuments, and an optional weeping-widow service

Top of the line:
The "Mauso-Palooza" brand mausoleum, which can be seen from outer space

SIR, IF I MAY, THINK OF IT AS AN INVESTMENT IN EXTRAVAGANCE.

Social Graces:
Lenny: *We win again!*
Homer: *Hey, this was a lot of fun, guys.*
Lenny: *Yeah, we never knew nobody with their own tennis rink.*
Carl: *So what happens now? Is the food free, or do we pay someone?*
Lenny: *(kicks Carl) Of course not! They send ya a bill.*
Carl: *Well, that's why I asked! (kicks Lenny back) That's how you learn, by asking, ya dumbass!*

Desperately Seeking Segue:
Bart: *...so from now on, all hats are banned from the school.*
Marge: *Even bonnets?*
Lisa: *Especially bonnets.*
Homer: *I've had it with that school! (The doorbell rings.) Door!*

"I don't know what's sadder about the Simpsons: the fact that we mock them, or that they shall never know. Never ever ever...ever!"

THE STUFF YOU MAY HAVE MISSED

By turning on the hot and cold water downstairs, Bart gets Homer to scream in the shower the tunes to "Mary Had a Little Lamb" and Beethoven's 5th Symphony.

Jasper's plate-spinning act consists of him spinning fellow retirement-home occupants' dental plates on their fingers.

At the funeral home there's a banner that reads "Sales from the Crypt."

Names of anti-stink spray sold at the funeral home: "Country Mourn," "Mrs. Rotwell's," and "Stank Off!"

The two wolves seen at the cemetery first appeared in "Skinner's Sense of Snow" (CABF06) as they waited for victims outside of the snowed-in elementary school.

One of the two men feeding lines to Kent Brockman from the Channel 6 News van is Brockman's nephew, last seen in "Faith Off" (BABF06).

When Marge hears others mocking her at the grocery store, she's in the area where they sell Tennis Cookies.

Marge uses a vacuum cleaner to spiff-up the tennis court.

The little cotton balls Homer tears off of Marge's socks have enough weight to break a car window when he throws them.

While waiting for Marge and Bart to return after dumping him, Homer has angrily whittled the end of his tennis racket into a sharp point.

Homer mistakes Andre Agassi for the late wrestler Andre the Giant.

Musical Moment:
Grampa wins the Springfield Retirement Castle talent show by singing Burt Bacharach's "What's New Pussycat?" His "painful" gyrations suggest that he is attempting an impression of Tom Jones, the singer that made the tune famous.

Homer, citing precedent to justify his tennis buffoonery: **"All sports have their lovable clowns: John Rocker, O.J. Simpson, Dorf..."**

Springfield's Tax Dollars at Work:
Lou: *Hey, Chief, we're gonna bust-up that crack house tonight.*
Chief Wiggum: *We did that last night.*
Lou: *Yeah, but this time we got the right address.*

Out of Bounds:
Marge: *I found out we're the laughingstock of the town.*
Homer: *Oh. Well, that's bad news for Dingbat Charlie. He's gonna be crushed.*
Marge: *I thought our tennis court was bringing us a little respectability. Instead, people make fun of our lousiness.*
Homer: *Okay. Now, some of that is me.*
Marge: *All of that is you!*

Making It Worse:
Marge: *Oh, Homey, I'm sorry I hurt your feelings. (She tries to hug him.) Ohhh.*
Homer: *Don't touch me. Your hands feel like salad tongs.*
Marge: *I just wanted to win for once. Please don't take it as a threat to your manhood.*
Homer: *Gasp! My manhood? I never thought of that!*

Kharity Kase:
Bart: *We were good, Dad. They asked us to play in the Krusty Klassic!*
Marge: *It's for charity—it benefits victims of balcony collapse.*
Bart: *We can wipe out B.C. in our lifetime.*
Homer: *I don't care about B.C., I care about M.E.—my enjoyment.*
(He runs up the stairs sobbing.)

Literary Lesson:
Homer: *It's obvious what's happening. I'm being replaced with a younger, more in-your-face version of me.*
Lisa: *Dad, you're just going through a classic Oedipal anxiety. You remember the story of Oedipus, don't you?*
Homer: *Hmnh...maybe five bucks would refresh my memory.*
Lisa: *Uh! Oedipus killed his father and married his mother.*
Homer: *Icch! Who pays for that wedding?*

"You know, there's a lesson here for all of us: it's better to watch stuff than to do stuff."

Trash Talk:
Homer: *Well, look who's here. You two are going down.*
Marge: *No we're not. You're going down.*
Homer: *Did you hear that? She said we're going down!*
Lisa: *All we can do is play our very best.*
Homer: *Oh, that's loser talk!*
(He runs off sobbing.)

Say What?
Lisa: *You're replacing me?*
Homer: *Now, Lisa, "dumping" is such a harsh word. Let's just say I'm replacing you.*

DAY OF THE

THE NETWORK EXECUTIVES

Primary goal:
To get their stars to open it up, run wild, shatter boundaries, slash-and-burn—without alienating anyone

Their sage advice:
Be dangerous, but warm, and edgy-cute

Their favorite pastime:
Giving notes

The terrifying truth about them:
If you kill one, two more will take their place

The network executives in charge of Krusty's show become so demanding and annoying that the clown announces his impending retirement. Sideshow Bob is released from prison again, and immediately plots his next act of revenge—against both Bart and Krusty. Bob is especially mad at Krusty, who erased all the videotapes of the shows with Bob in them. Bob's first step is getting a job at Springfield Elementary, which he manages to do despite his history of crime.

One of Bob's new duties at Springfield Elementary is making the morning bulletin announcements over the P.A. system. He uses this position to lure Bart out to a deserted shack behind the school. Once Bart is in his clutches, Bob ties him up and hypnotizes him. Under Bob's complete control, Bart is ordered to kill Krusty during his final show.

The Simpsons are invited to attend Krusty's last broadcast,

and while Krusty shows his favorite clips from years past, Sideshow Bob arms Bart with plastic explosives. Bart, still in a hypnotic trance, is instructed to approach and hug Krusty when he hears Krusty say, "I've never had such a great audience," thereby setting off a deadly explosion. As the show draws to a close, Krusty takes a moment to pay a special tribute to Sideshow Bob. Bob is touched and, then, horrified to see Bart approaching Krusty. At the last moment, Sideshow Bob shouts a warning, and Mr. Teeny the chimp, spotting the life-threatening explosives, swings into action. He snatches the explosives off of Bart and flings them into the network executives' office. After the explosion, the network executives are revealed to be liquid metal androids bent on destruction. Sideshow Bob and Krusty the Clown reconcile briefly, just before Chief Wiggum subjects Bob to an impromptu and highly questionable execution.

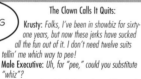

> WE'RE LOSING MALE TEENS. CAN YOU GET JIGGY WITH SOMETHING?

> I WAS JUST THINKING THAT!

SHOW HIGHLIGHTS

Fancy Passing:
Krusty: *Eh, this quiz show crap is just a fad.*
Male Executive: *Well, fad or not, it's here to stay.*

The Clown Calls It Quits:
Krusty: *Folks, I've been in showbiz for sixty-one years, but now these jerks have sucked all the fun out of it. I don't need twelve suits tellin' me which way to pee!*
Male Executive: *Uh, for "pee," could you substitute "whiz"?*
Female Executive: *I don't know, that could upset the Cheez Whiz people.*
Male Executive: *I was just thinking that.*
Krusty: *I can't take it anymore!*

Fun Factoid:
The Female Network Executive first appeared in "The Itchy & Scratchy & Poochie Show" (4F12) and later in "Girly Edition" (5F15). She later evolved into Lindsey Naegle in "They Saved Lisa's Brain" (AABF18) and has appeared regularly ever since.

Speak for Yourself:
Marge: *I think it's good for a show to go off the air before it becomes stale and repetitive.*
Smithers: *(bursting in) Maggie shot Mr. Burns again!*

Lost to the Ages:
Kent Brockman: *Ever watch the old episodes?*
Krusty: *Oh, Kent, that's a sad story. I taped over all my old episodes. Well, ya know, I had a thing for Judge Judy and blank tape was $3.99! What would you do?*
Sideshow Bob: *(watching TV, aghast) Those are my shows!*
Krusty: *Frankly, Kent, those episodes were no big loss. The show didn't really get funny until we fired Sideshow Bob and hired Who's-Its.*

Sideshow Bob's parole plea: **"Your honor, my incarceration is cruel and unusual punishment. First, my prison-issued shower sandals are grossly undersized. Secondly, the prison book club consists mainly of prisoners who club me with books!** *(He pulls up his shirt to reveal book-sized bruises.)* **These are from the new Tom Clancy. Although it's less painful than reading him. Am I right, folks?"**

> **Revealed this episode:**
> Wiseguy's name is Rafael.

Mutual Disdain:
Principal Skinner: *Now Bob, your graduate degrees more than qualify you to be assistant janitor.*
Sideshow Bob: *Heh, heh. My blushes.*
Principal Skinner: *But I am troubled by your constant attempts to murder people.*
Sideshow Bob: *To be fair, most of those people were Bart Simpson.*
Principal Skinner: *Ho, ho, ho! Good luck! That kid's like the Roadrunner—he won't go down!*
Sideshow Bob: *Tell me about it!*
(They both laugh.)

Foes Reunited:
Sideshow Bob: *Hello, Bart.*
Bart: *Gasp! Oh, it's you, Bob. How ya doin'?*
Sideshow Bob: *No screams? Not even an "eep"?*
Bart: *Hey, I'm not afraid of you. Every time we tangle, you wind up in jail. I'm 6 and 0.*
Sideshow Bob: *I'll admit the record is a little one-sided, but this time I cannot fail. (He steps on a rake; it hits him in the face, and he shudders.) Rakes! My old arch-enemy.*
Bart: *I thought I was your arch-enemy.*
Sideshow Bob: *I have a life outside of you, Bart.*

THE STUFF YOU MAY HAVE MISSED

On the "Me Wantee" game show (a parody of "Who Wants to Be a Millionaire?"), Moe says he was born in Indiana, and Homer informs everyone that Moe has a bowel obstruction.

Homer holds a pennant that reads "Game Shows" when Moe calls him as a lifeline.

One of the guests on Krusty's show is Madame Mimi and Her Cheese-Seeking Poodles.

Chief Wiggum disperses the kids staging a sob-filled sit-in in front of Krustylu Studios with "Time-Out Gas."

Sideshow Bob is reading *Prison Bride* as he sits in his cell.

Sideshow Bob stays at Broken Dreams Storage Lockers, "The Most Depressing Place on Earth." Fellow residents include Gil and several people planning revenge in varying degrees.

The Krusty statue that Bart destroys resembles the Big Boy statues that stood outside of Bob's (and Elias Brothers' and Frische's) Big Boy restaurants.

Krustyburger sells "Laffy Meals," similar to McDonald's "Happy Meals."

At Krusty's final show, Ron Howard walks down the red carpet, drinking a martini and dressed as he was in "When You Dish upon a Star" (5F19) and "Hello Gutter, Hello Fadder" (BABF02). Gary Coleman makes an appearance, showing off the same martial arts moves he displayed in "Grift of the Magi" (BABF07).

Apparently, Krusty has retired four times before this episode.

Sideshow Bob tastes his plastic explosive concoction to make sure it's good and does a Jackie Gleason impression in the process.

JACKANAPES

Episode CABF10
Original Airdate: 02/18/01
Writer: Al Jean
Director: Michael Marcantel
Executive Producer: Mike Scully

Guest Voices: Gary Coleman as Himself and Kelsey Grammer as Sideshow Bob

Fun Factoid:

Bart's 6-0 record against Sideshow Bob is chronicled in: "Krusty Gets Busted" (7G12), "Black Widower" (8F20), "Cape Feare" (9F22), "Sideshow Bob Roberts" (2F02), "Sideshow Bob's Last Gleaming" (3F08), and "Brother from Another Series" (4F14).

Hypnotic Performance:

Sideshow Bob: *Watch the spiral, Bart. Let it entrance you with its twirliness...twirliness...You are in my power!*
Bart: *I am at your command.*
Sideshow Bob: *I didn't say anything about "command." If you're in my power, say so.*
Bart: *I am in your power.*
Sideshow Bob: *Excellent...actually, go back to "command." No, "power." "Power!"*

Lame Excuses:

Bart: (hypnotized) *Hello, family.*
Marge: *Where have you been, young man? It's nearly bedtime.*
Bart: *I was...I was...*
Sideshow Bob (in Bart's mind): *If anyone asks, you were at the flower shop.*
Bart: *I was at the flower shop.*
Homer: *Oh yeah, uh, I was at the flower shop, too. Yep! Gettin' drunk at the ol' flower shop!*

Fallen Star:

Kent: *Kent Brockman here, at Krusty the Clown's final show. And here comes out-of-work actor Rainier Wolfcastle!*
Rainier: (disheveled) *Someone please give me a job! I've lowered my quote to eight million.*
Kent: *Ha, ha! Hear that, Hollywood? The boy wants to work.*
Rainier: *I do nude scene, I play nerd...don't make me punch your throat!*
Kent: *Ha, ha! Always a delight!*

"Ah, the catwalk! The perfect vantage point...for revenge! Hmm-ha-ha-ha! Ah, kettle chips! The perfect side dish...for revenge!"

Showstopper:

Dr. Hibbert: *Can I embarrass this guy for a moment? Three years ago, Krusty pledged over a million dollars to start Krusty's Kare Center.*
(The audience applauds.)
Krusty: *Please! Stop, already.*
Dr. Hibbert: *To this day, Krusty has not given us a dime...Has he, Francis?*
Francis, a crippled boy: *I'm cold all the time.*
Krusty: *Aw, look—it was all a bookkeeping snafu.*
Dr. Hibbert: *Can I have the check now?*
Krusty: *Now?! Eh, ah, sure.*
Francis: *God bless you, Krusty.*
Audience: *Awww!*
Krusty: *And if my banker's watching, let nothing STOP you from PAYMENT of this check.*

Everybody's a Critic:

Sideshow Bob: *Well, Krusty, this is your Waterloo. Soon you'll be Napoleon Blown-apart!*
Spotlight Guy: *Ugh. Terrible.*
Sideshow Bob: *Oh, hush-up, Leo!*

Krusty's Song to Sideshow Bob:

(to the tune "Mandy")
Oh Bo-ob!
You repaid my abuse with raw hatred,
But I need you today.
Oh Bo-ob!
Well, you went to Apu's and you framed me,
So they locked you away...

"You know, I'd like to thank God for all my success, even though I never worshipped or believed in him in any way."

Movie Moments:

The title of this episode comes from the thriller, *Day of the Jackal*, but the plot owes more to *The Manchurian Candidate*, where captured American soldiers are brainwashed into attempting a presidential assassination at a political convention.

Bart crossing the deserted schoolyard and the children's voices reciting a creepy poem, is a parody of the *Nightmare on Elm Street* films.

During Krusty's final show, Mr. Teeny does a striptease to "You Sexy Thing" by Hot Chocolate in a tip of the G-string to the film *The Full Monty*.

When the network executives are blown up, they congeal out of a puddle of liquid metal and reform just like the T1000 terminator played by Robert Patrick in *Terminator II: Judgment Day*. This "surprise" ending is foreshadowed when the male executive is dragged behind Krusty's studio cart at the beginning of the episode, again like the T1000.

All's Well That Ends:

Sideshow Bob: *Krusty, I'm so sorry about the attempted murder.*
Krusty: *Will ya stop with the "sorry"? Every time ya try to kill me, my ratings go through the roof, ya nut!*
Sideshow Bob: *We are good together, Krusty.*
Krusty: *It makes me sad that you're getting the death penalty.*

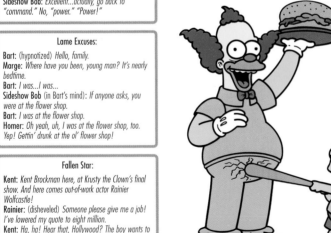

NEW KIDS ON THE

Bart wins the Springfield Marathon by disguising himself as an Italian runner and joining the competition near the finish line. At the award ceremony, Bart's deception is revealed and an angry mob of racers threatens him. Luckily, a stranger comes along and helps Bart make a getaway, protecting him from harm. The stranger turns out to be L. T. Smash, a record producer who is starting a new boy band called Party Posse, and he wants Bart to join because of his bad-boy attitude.

The other members of Party Posse are Milhouse, Nelson, and Ralph. None of the boys can sing very well, but L. T. Smash uses "Studio Magic," a voice-enhancing sound machine created by NASA, to make their voices sound smooth and harmonious. Party Posse is an instant success. They receive encouragement from fellow boy band 'N Sync, and they debut their first music video on TV. Something about the video disturbs Lisa, and after some detective work, she realizes that it has subliminal messages convincing viewers to join the Navy.

Lisa runs to L. T. Smash with this information, but she discovers that he is, in reality, a Navy lieutenant and that he is responsible for the recruitment scheme. Soon after, at a Party Posse concert aboard a Navy aircraft carrier, Lt. L. T. Smash is told to close down his boy-band operation by a superior officer. It seems *MAD Magazine* is planning to do a parody of Party Posse, ruining the band's image and the Navy's recruitment program. Lt. Smash disobeys orders, goes berserk, and uses the battleship to attack the *MAD Magazine* building. The Party Posse determines that the only way to stop the crazed lieutenant's plan is to sing the ultimate "chill out" song. 'N Sync comes to the rescue with the perfect tune, but while the two boy bands disagree on the appropriate choreography for the song, Lt. Smash launches a missile strike on the *MAD Magazine* building, destroying it. As the lieutenant is led away by police, Bart and the rest of the Party Posse are disappointed that they will not get to appear on the cover of *MAD Magazine*.

SHOW HIGHLIGHTS

On Your Mark, Get Set-Up, and Go:
Homer: *Marge, after a lot of thought, I've decided to run the Springfield Marathon.*
Marge: *Oh, please! You get exhausted watching the "Twilight Zone" marathon. Ha, ha! I'm a regular Billy Crystal!*
Bart: (sarcastic) *You got that right.*
Lisa: *Well, Dad, I think running's good exercise. It adds years to your life.*
Homer: *Stay out of this, Lisa. Marge, I've made up my mind: I'll do your job for a day, and you do mine. Then we'll see who has it tougher!*
(He struts out of the room, leaving the rest of the family confused.)

Anatomically Incorrect:
Lisa: *You got all your equipment, Dad?*
Homer: *Let's see—sweatbands? Check! Anti-chafing nipple tape? Check, check, and check!*

"Well, hold the phone, Dora! A new challenger has emerged out of nowhere! He's running on sheer pluck, moxie, and grit—all of which he'll be tested for after the race."

Unnecessary Introductions:
Bart: *Who are you?*
L. T. Smash: *Oh, you'll find out in due time.*
Bart: (pointing to a tag hanging from the rearview mirror) *Well, it says your name is L. T. Smash.*
L. T. Smash: *Time has come. I'm L. T. Smash.*

Thanks All Around:
Marge: *Thank you so much for saving our son from that murderous mob.*
L. T. Smash: *Well, thank you for letting me chill in your crib.*
Homer: *And thank you for assuming we're hip.*

Homer sticks to his guns: **"Now listen to me, Smash! We're not signing anything...unless it's a contract!"**

Marge's Choice:
Marge: *Now, hold on! I have some concerns.*
Bart: *Please, Mom! My dream is to be a rock star!*
Homer: *And my dream is to get rid of Bart!*
Marge: *But...*
Homer: *How many lives must you ruin?!*

Making the Band:
L. T. Smash: *Bart, I want you to meet 'n' greet the other members of the "Party Posse." He's smart...He's soulful...He's Milhouse!*
Milhouse: *What up, G-money?*
L. T. Smash: *Next, he'll break your nose, your glasses, and your heart...Nelson!*
Bart: *Wait, these are just guys from school. Who's next? Ralph Wiggum?*
Ralph: *Wheee! I'm a pop sensation.*

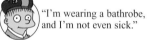
"I'm wearing a bathrobe, and I'm not even sick."

Party Posse Premiere:
Principal Skinner: *...so from now on anything caught in your zipper will be handled by the school nurse, and not me. And now...are you adequately prepared to rock?*
Kids: *Yeah!*
Skinner: *Silence! Here they are...the Party Posse!*
(Skinner walks off as the curtain rises, revealing Bart, Milhouse, Nelson, and Ralph standing in sulky poses. The kids cheer.)
Bart: *Hello, Springfield! Now, here's a song that your Principal Skinner doesn't want us to play.*
(The kids boo. Skinner steps back onto the stage.)
Skinner: *That's not true! This assembly was my idea. I like your brand of inoffensive pop rock.*
Bart: (ignoring him) *Screw you, man! We're gonna play it anyway!*

Mack Daddy vs. Mama's Boy:
L. T. Smash: *Man, they're gonna be big. And you stood in their way.*
Skinner: *No, I didn't! I even came in early and made orange drink.*
L. T. Smash: *Orange drink? What, do you live with your mama?*
Principal Skinner: *She lives with me!*

"Yvan Eht Nioj":
Party Posse: *Oh, say can you rock!*
Milhouse: *There's trouble in a far-off nation.*
Ralph: *Time to get in love formation.*
Bart: *Your love's more deadly than Saddam.*
Nelson: *That's why I've got to drop da bomb.*
Arab Women: *Yvan eht nioj.*
(pronounced: eevan et knee-oj)
Yvan eht nioj.
Yvan eht nioj...nioj!
Nelson: *This party's happenin'. It's no mirage.*
Bart: *So sing it again.*
Milhouse: *y (eee)...*
Ralph: *...van...*
Nelson: *...eht...*
Party Posse: *...nioj.*
Arab Women: *Yvan eht nioj. Yvan eht nioj.*

Catchy Lyrics:
Homer: *"Yvan eht nioj!" Ya gotta love that crazy chorus!*
Lisa: *What does it mean?*
Homer: *It doesn't mean anything. It's like "Rama-lama-ding-dong" or "Give peace a chance."*

BLECCH

Episode CABF12
Original Airdate: 02/25/01
Writer: Tim Long
Director: Steven Dean Moore
Executive Producer: Mike Scully

Guest Voices: 'N Sync (Lance Bass, J. C. Chasez, Joey Fatone, Chris Kirkpatrick, and Justin Timberlake) as Themselves

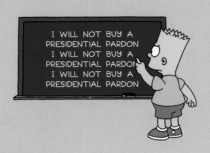

THE STUFF YOU MAY HAVE MISSED

The tag-line for the 97th Springfield Marathon is "Ruin Your Knees for Charity."

El Barto graffiti can be seen under the "No Parking" sign by the marathon starting line.

Party Posse lays down their musical tracks at Classified Recordings.

The Classified Recordings sign has the music notation to the beginning of "The Star Spangled Banner."

Written on Smash's studio clipboard: "Moves: Fresh," "'Tudes: Fly," and "Boogaloo: Electric."

Cienega, the MTV-style VJ, introduces Party Posse's video. She first appeared in "Kill the Alligator and Run" (BABF16).

Party Posse's music video, "Drop Da Bomb," was directed by Ang Lee.

The "bouncing ball" in the music video is Ralph's head.

Party Posse putting up the tetherball pole resembles the historic photo of WWII soldiers raising the flag on the island of Iwo Jima.

After the admiral cuts the power during Party Posse's concert, it is revealed they cannot really sing. A similar thing happened to Grammy-winning duo Milli Vanilli, who were exposed as frauds when they experienced technical difficulties during a "live" performance.

Smash starts the aircraft carrier by flipping a switch from "De-commission" to "Commission."

This is the first episode where we see live performers (in this case, 'N Sync) recording voice-overs for "The Simpsons" over the final credits.

Sex, Lies, and Music Videos:

Lisa: *There's something weird about this video.*
Marge: *None of those girls has had three kids, I can tell you that!*
Lisa: *No, something else.*

The Awful Truth:

Lisa: *But you have recruiting ads on TV! Why do you need subliminal messages?*
L. T. Smash: *It's a three-pronged attack. Subliminal, liminal, and super-liminal.*
Lisa: *Super-liminal?*
L. T. Smash: *I'll show you.* (He opens a window and yells down to Lenny and Carl.) *Hey, you! Join the Navy!*
Carl: *Uh, yeah, all right.*
Lenny: *I'm in!*

Parents Are People, Too:

Homer: *Wait a minute. Bart's band is brainwashing kids with subliminal messages? That's pretty far-fetched, Lisa.*
Marge: *Are you sure someone hasn't been bitten by the "jealousy bug"?*
Homer: *Heh, heh, heh! Here comes the "jealousy bug"! Gonna getcha! Gonna getcha!* (He pinches Lisa.)
Lisa: *Hey! Cut it out! You're a grown man!*
Homer: *Gasp!* (sulking) *I wanna go home now.*
Marge: *Nobody's going home. We're going to see Bart's concert.*

"Let's Re-Up Tonight":

Milhouse: *Had a girl in every port*
From here to Barcelona.
Nelson: *But now I'm docked in Springfield,*
And, girl, I'm gonna phone ya.
Ralph: *Stormed a lot of beaches,*
But you're the one that I missed.
Bart: *Let's get back together, girl!*
Let's re-enlist!
Party Posse: *So sign me up for a hitch of love.*
Recruit my heart.
Four sweet years of love...
Let's march all day
And clean latrines all night.
Don't bust me down.
Let's re-up tonight!
Let's re-up tonight!

Takes One to Know One:

Bart: *Dad! L. T.'s gone crazy!*
L. T. Smash: *Ha-huh-huh! Ah-ha-ha!*
Homer: *Yeah, that's the look. Heh, heh, heh.*

Milhouse, oblivious in the Big Apple: **"The Statue of Liberty? Where are we?"**

A Sneak-Peek Inside MAD Magazine:

Writer #1: *Why don't we call it "Everybody Hates Raymond"?*
(All the writers laugh.)
Writer #2: *Well, we stayed up all night, but it was worth it.*

LIEUTENANT L. T. SMASH

The 411 on his duties:
Record producer and Navy recruitment officer

His fly résumé:
The mack-daddy behind such groups as "New Kids in the Ditch" and "Boynudo"

His ol'-school attitude:
Militarily dope

His bogus drawbacks:
Subject to hippie-attack fantasy hallucinations; prone to insane violence

PERMISSION TO SAY THAT'S CRAZY, SIR!

HOWARD K. DUFF VIII

His legacy:
Heir to the vast Duff Brewery empire; ownership of the Springfield Isotopes

His plan:
To move the Isotopes to Albuquerque, New Mexico

His modus operandi:
Bribe, slander, lie, and drug people so they forget

His company's most recent development:
An additive that makes Duff Beer taste super, super malty

> THE ONLY STORY HERE IS THE RICH, SMOOTH TASTE OF DUFF.

HUNGRY,

T he Simpsons spend a day at Blockoland, an amusement park made entirely out of blocks. On the way home, Homer learns that Lisa's Blockoland Eiffel Tower souvenir is missing a piece. He turns the car around, goes back to Blockoland, and demands that the missing piece be replaced. Lisa is very grateful, and Homer likes the way it feels to "stick up for the little guy." He decides to continue helping others, so he goes around righting wrongs whenever he comes across a person in need.

Lenny is disappointed by the performance of the Springfield Isotopes baseball team, but he cannot get a refund on his season ticket. Homer volunteers to help, and he has words with the team's owner Howard K. Duff VIII. Duff refuses to refund the price of the ticket and asks Homer to leave. As he is leaving, Homer walks through the wrong door and discovers a room full of Albuquerque Isotopes merchandise. He realizes that Duff plans to relocate the team. Homer is outraged and holds a press conference, but Duff tricks the media into thinking Homer is crazy. Homer vows to go on a hunger strike

until Duff comes clean and admits he plans to move the team to Albuquerque.

Homer chains himself to a pole in front of Duff Stadium, but he attracts so much attention that Duff has him moved to a spot inside the ballpark to draw bigger crowds. The stadium announcer explains to the fans that Homer is on a hunger strike until the Isotopes win the pennant. Homer's message is not being heard. Desperately hungry and delirious, Homer is visited by the ghost of labor activist Cesar Chavez, who encourages him to fight on. The team owner believes that Homer has gone crazy and that he has become a pathetic eyesore, so he decides to remove him from the ballpark by getting him to break his fast. In front of the baseball crowd, Duff offers him a special hot dog, but Homer realizes that it has Southwestern toppings. In the bleachers, Moe notices that Lenny's hot dog wrapper says, "Albuquerque Isotopes," and Howard K. Duff VIII's plan to move the team is confirmed. Springfield's team spirit is reawakened, Duff's relocation scheme comes undone, and Homer is vindicated.

SHOW HIGHLIGHTS

Underwhelming Reaction:
Homer: Kids? How would you...like to go to...Blockoland?!
Bart and Lisa: Meh.
Homer: But the TV gave me the impression that--
Bart: We said, "Meh."
Lisa: M-E-H. Meh.

The different sections of Blockoland: Rectangle Land, Cube Country, and Squaresville.

"Squaresville sounds pretty cool."

Whoops!
Bart: Oh! Why did I get this "Lego" shirt?
Marge: Don't you mean "Blocko" shirt?
Bart: Right, right. "Blocko" shirt.

Civil Unrest:
Homer: Welcome to real life, Lisa. You can't fight City Hall...a.k.a. Blockoland. So don't even try.
Marge: What kind of a thing is that to tell your children?
Homer: That's what I always tell them. I told them that twice yesterday. And then again as they were going to sleep.

Homer comes to Lisa's aid: **"Any friend of Marge is a friend of mine."**

Going to Bat for Bart:
Homer: Come on! Why won't you go out with Bart?
Sherri: He's a smelly, ugly dork.
Homer: Please. Ugly is such a smelly word. Who would you rather go out with?
Sherri: (pointing at a handsome boy) Tommy.
Homer: Well, duh! He's breathtaking. But Bart has inner beauty...like you'd find in a rodent.

Checking the Books:
Homer: Boy, you weren't kidding! Your profit margins are razor thin.
Male Hairdresser: You see? Zees is what I'm--
Homer: Wait a minute! Four hundred a month for loafer lightener?
Male Hairdresser: But we must have it. It is ze lifeblood of ze industry.
Homer: You get the same results with a mincing gel.

"The satisfaction of helping another human being is all the thanks I et cetera!"

Homer gets self-referential: **"And I gave that man directions, even though I didn't know the way, 'cause that's the kind of guy I am this week."**

Family Outing:
Carl: Wait a minute. Duff owns the Springfield Isotopes? Since when?
Moe: They bought 'em a year ago from the Mafia. It was the last of the family-owned teams.

Looking for Duff in All the Wrong Places:
Homer: I'm trying to get a refund for this ticket. Is this the executive office of the ball club?
Equipment Manager: No. This is the equipment shed.
Homer: Oh. Well, is that it?
(He points to a small shack.)
Equipment Manager: That's where we keep the water heater.
Homer: (pointing) Is...?
Equipment Manager: That's a tractor.
Homer: I see.

Hard Evidence:
Kent Brockman: Sooo, let me get this straight, Mr. Duff. The Isotopes are not moving to Albuquerque?
H. K. Duff VIII: Absolutely not.
Kent Brockman: So, are you calling Homer Simpson a liar?
H. K. Duff VIII: Well, we have obtained this footage of him with his pants on fire.

"I don't mind being called a liar when I'm lying, or about to lie, or just finished lying, but NOT WHEN I'M TELLING THE TRUTH!"

Movie Moment:
Duffman's moment of doubt and decision to lift Howard K. Duff VIII over his head and throw him over a fence recalls Darth Vader's victory over Emperor Palpatine during the climactic moments of *Star Wars: Return of the Jedi.*

HUNGRY HOMER

Episode CABF09
Original Airdate: 03/04/01
Writer: John Swartzwelder
Director: Nancy Kruse
Executive Producer: Mike Scully

"TEMPTATION ISLAND" WAS NOT A SLEAZY PIECE OF CRAP

Doubting Spouse:

Homer: *That's it! I'll go on a hunger strike.*
Marge: *Oh, Homey, you couldn't keep up a hunger strike. You eat while you brush your teeth.*

Consider the Source:

Milhouse: *What a great ball game. Thanks, Weekend Dad.*
Kirk: *Stop calling me that.*
Homer: *Hey, kid and man! Don't support a team run by liars.*
Milhouse: *Liars?*
Homer: *They're secretly planning to move to Albuquerque.*
Kirk: *That's crazy. It would have been on a talk-radio show like "Sports Chat" or "Sportzilla and the Jabber Jocks."*

"Homer's Hungry Song":

*Dancin' away my hunger pangs.
Movin' my feet so my stomach won't hurt.
I'm kinda like Jesus,
        But not in a sacrilegious way...*

Tummy Trouble:

Ralph: *His tummy sounds angry, Daddy.*
Chief Wiggum: *Yeah, that's his stomach eating itself.*

Corporate Evil:

Duff VIII: *Hmm, people seem to be drawn to that kook. Maybe we can exploit him.*
Duffman: *It's too dangerous, sir. He knows about Albuquerque. Duffman is a cautious cat.*
Duff VIII: *No, listen. Fans love wackos. Remember that busty woman who ran out on the field and farted at the ballplayers?* (looking out the window) *I think we've got our newest attraction.*
Duffman: *Duffman has a bad feelin' about this.*

Revealed this episode:

Duffman goes by the name Sid. In "Pygmoelian" (BABF12) his name was revealed to be Larry.

Appetite Apparition:

Homer: *Who are you?*
Cesar: *The spirit of Cesar Chavez.*
Homer: *Why do you look like Cesar Romero?*
Cesar: *Because jou don't know what Cesar Chavez looks like.*

Duffman has an attack of conscience:
"New feelings brewing in Duffman! What...would Jesus do?"

The Truth:

Duff VIII: *Well, Homer, your hunger strike lasted twelve amazing days.*
Homer: *Me so hungee.*
Duff VIII: *Of course, you are, Hungry, Hungry Homer. So why not break your fast with our brand-new Isotope Dog Supreme?*
Homer: (sniffing) *Oh! So hard to resist. Mesquite-grilled onions, jalapeño relish...wait a minute! Those are Southwestern ingredients!*
Audience: *Gasp!*
Homer: *Mango-lime salsa? That's the kind of bold flavor they enjoy in...Albuquerque!*

THE STUFF YOU MAY HAVE MISSED

At Blockoland, Bart and Nelson play "Rock 'Em, Block 'Em Blockbots," a parody of the classic game "Rock 'Em, Sock 'Em Robots."

The sign at the Blockoland buffet reads "Build Your Own Meal."

The man at the souvenir kiosk is smoking an oversized novelty Blockoland cigar, and he takes the missing Blocko piece out of a box labeled "Missing Eiffel Tower Pieces."

Hairy Shearers, the salon that will not honor Marge's coupon for hair streaks, is named after Simpsons voice actor Harry Shearer and appeared previously in "The Two Mrs. Nahasapeemapetilons" (5F04).

The neon sign at Duff Stadium shows a baseball player about to pitch a ball, then drinking a Duff Beer instead.

When Bart finds Homer asleep on top of Santa's Little Helper's doghouse just like Snoopy in the *Peanuts* comic strip, he utters Charlie Brown's famous catchphrase, "Good Grief!"

Duffman, posing as a reporter, claims that Homer was once in a loony bin. Homer was institutionalized in "Stark Raving Dad" (7F24) for wearing a pink shirt to work.

The sign next to the skeleton of the previous person who went on a hunger strike at Duff Stadium says "Clean the Ladies Room!"

The fountains at Duff Stadium are two giant beer cans.

Homer's line "Me so hungee" is echoed in the Season 12 finale, "Simpsons Tall Tales" (CABF17), when Homer appears as Paul Bunyan.

B art and Lisa are late for school, so Marge tries to catch the bus, but she soon finds herself in a race with Otto. Marge beats Otto to the school, and she insists that Bart and Lisa get on the bus as part of her small victory. Otto realizes that he has forgotten a new student on his route, and so he goes back to pick her up. Her name is Francine and she is a big, imposing, quiet loner. Lisa feels sorry for her because she does not know anybody. She decides to be the first to welcome Francine, but when Lisa approaches her on the playground, the big girl punches Lisa in the eye.

At the same time, Homer and Marge get a visit from a home baby-proofing saleswoman, who points out many dangers to Maggie around the house. This proves to be a real eye-opener for Homer. He declines to pay the saleswoman, but goes on a baby-proofing crusade. He is so inspired by his home safety improvements that he starts his own baby-proofing service. Homer does a terrific job of protecting the babies of Springfield by using some dubious methods.

Back at school, Lisa tries again to make friends with Francine, but with no success. She does some research and comes to the conclusion that Francine beats on her and the other nerds at school because of the way they smell.

Meanwhile, Springfield's child injury–related services are in crisis thanks to Homer's baby-proofing efforts. Many providers are losing money and some companies are forced to close down. Horrified, Homer quits his baby-proofing ways and begs the town's wee ones to go back to getting hurt like they did before. Lisa's efforts prove successful as well. By distilling the sweat of nerds into a concentrated form, she is able to prove her nerd-scent theory. At a local science convention, Lisa demonstrates her findings using Francine as a test subject. She also unveils an anti-bully spray made of salad dressing that effectively blocks the "nerd" scent. Lisa wins the science award, but, unfortunately, she does not bring enough bully repellent, and Francine goes on a rampage, beating up all the scientists in attendance.

SHOW HIGHLIGHTS

Milhouse gets into the thrill of the chase: **"It's like *Speed II*, only with a bus instead of a boat!"**

Inexcusable Absence:
Marge: *Ah! Homer, you're still here? You should have left for work an hour ago.*
Homer: *They said if I come in late again, I'm fired. I can't take that chance.*

Mixed Messages:
Marge: *Stop! Stooop!*
Otto: *Oh, you wanna drag?*
Marge: *Gasp! Hrmmm. I'm not racing! It's me, Marge Simpson!*
Otto: *No, you eat my dust!*

The New Girl:
Terri: *Red hair?*
Sherri: *What's she trying to pull?*
Janey: *Those shoes look Canadian.*
Boy with Orthodontic Headgear: *She'll never fit in.*
Lisa: *Oh, it's tough being the new kid. Someone should go talk to her.*
Bart: *Yeah, somebody should. (looking out window) One Hour Dry Cleaner? Man, that's fast!*

Stunning Sales Pitch:
Lady: *Your baby is dead!*
Marge and Homer: *Gasp!*
Lady: *That's what you'd hear if your baby fell victim to the thousands of death-traps lurking in the average American home.*
(She hands Marge a business card.)
Marge: *"Springfield Baby-Proofing"?*
Homer: *You— you really scared us!*
Lady: *Sorry about that. But the truth is, your baby, Maggie Simpson, is dead!*
Marge and Homer: *Gasp!*
Lady: *Dead tired of baby-proofers who don't provide a free estimate.*

Hello Dolly:
Marge: *Why don't you try reaching out to this new girl? See if you two have a common interest.*
Lisa: *Hmm. Well, lots of people like jazz fusion.*
(Lisa pulls out her sax and demonstrates.)
Marge: *Okay, that's in the maybe file. What if you two bond over your Malibu Stacy dolls?*
Lisa: *They're not dolls, they're aspiration figures.*

Thoughtful Father:
Homer: *That baby-proofing crook wanted to sell us safety covers for the electrical outlets. But I'll just draw bunny faces on them to scare Maggie away.*
(He begins to draw.)
Marge: *She's not afraid of bunnies.*
Homer: (ominously) *She will be.*

Safety First:
Homer: *Now do you realize how unsafe the American home is? Baby accidents occur every three minutes.*
Marge: *I'm the one who told you that!*
Homer: *Yeah, but this is me talkin'. Look! I already encased the phone in concrete.*
Marge: *How are you supposed to dial?*
Homer: *Reach into these holes. I use a carrot.*

Taking Out Insurance:
Lisa: *Would you bullies be interested in some bodyguard work?*
Nelson: *This is so funny. We were just talking about moving into protection.*
Dolph: *We're offering a recess and lunch package that's very affordable.*

Consulting the Experts:
Nelson: *Sorry, we don't do girls. They bite and kick and scratch.*
Dolph: *And sometimes we fall in love.*
All bullies: *Sigh!*
Lisa: *Wow, there's so much I don't understand about bullying.*
Nelson: *Yeah, there's a lot of history there. Did you know it predates agriculture?*

Big Brother Is Watchin' Ye:
Lisa: *Willie, I need to see the school security tapes.*
Groundskeeper Willie: *Security tapes? There's no security tapes!*
Lisa: *It's hard to miss the cameras. (pointing at a camera)*
Willie: *Aye. Willie's a stinkin' liar.*
Lisa: *Why does the school need to watch us all the time?*
Willie: *School?*

No Sweat:
(Milhouse, Martin, and Database, all shirtless, are exercising on StairMasters.)
Lisa: *Come on, people! Move it! I want to see some sweat!*
Martin: *I'm not mastering another stair until you explain the purpose of this monstrous experiment.*
Lisa: *I believe the key to bully-nerd antagonism lies in your drippings.*
Martin: *Then I shall drip like a pot roast.*
Lisa: *Excellent. Now don't mind the squeegee.*
(She scrapes sweat off of Martin's body.)

Fair Warning:
Principal Skinner: *Thank you, Drederick Tatum. That was truly a K.O.—Knockout Oration.*
Mrs. Krabappel: (flirting) *Need a ride home?*
Drederick Tatum: *You really don't want that. Trust me.*

NERDIE

Episode CABF11
Original Airdate: 03/11/01
Writers: John Frink and Don Payne
Director: Lauren MacMullan
Executive Producer: Mike Scully
Guest Voice: Jan Hooks as Manjula

I WILL NOT SCARE THE VICE PRESIDENT
I WILL NOT SCARE THE VICE PRESIDENT
I WILL NOT SCARE THE VICE PRESIDENT

FRANCINE

Description:
New kid in school; active addition to the bully pool

Favorite pastimes:
Hogging teeter-totters; biting the heads off dolls; shoving kids into lockers

Special Skill:
Administering Indian burns with a triple twist

Has been compared to:
A big ape

Easily repelled by:
Salad dressing

Her reward for a day of nerd-beating:
A good night's sleep

> SUCK FIST, DR. DORK!

Guest Voice:
Kathy Griffin as Francine

THE STUFF YOU MAY HAVE MISSED

Otto has an eight-ball stick-shift and surfer-footprint gas pedal on the school bus.

The undercarriage of the school bus looks like the bottom of a skateboard, and it says "World Industries Flameboy." The Flameboy character is also pictured. World Industries is a skateboard, snowboard, and clothing manufacturer in El Segundo, California.

The nerd on the school bus with the orthodontic headgear is wearing a T-shirt that reads "Frankie Says: Relax." This is a term made popular by music group Frankie Goes to Hollywood, whose biggest hit was the song "Relax."

Items offered by Springfield Baby-Proofing: window bars, toilet latches, dingo alarms, and grapefruit-squirt shields.

After Homer throws the baby-proofing lady out of the house, she catches Maggie, who falls out of a second-story window.

Milhouse takes a drug called Repressitol to help him forget traumatic episodes from his past.

The Malibu Stacy "Grad-School Glamour Pack" comes with miniature surfboard, coffee cup and binder that says "Pepperdine," which is an university in Malibu, California.

Homer calls his baby-proofing service "Wee Care." He paints the name on the side of his car and affixes a statue of a baby wearing an armor helmet to the roof.

Homer tells Apu and Manjula that he is Hindu.

The driver who is thrown through the windshield after nearly running over Ralph Wiggum appears to have been on his cell phone.

The door to Groundskeeper Willie's security room has a sign that says "Keep Oot."

Lisa conducts her research at the Marvin Monroe Memorial Gymnasium.

The science convention is called the "12th Annual Big Science Thing."

The illustration of Sir Isaac Newton depicts a bully throwing apples at him from up in a tree.

Dr. C. Everett Koop, a former surgeon general of the United States, is among the scientific minds present at the convention.

Lisa names her distillation of nerd sweat "Poindextrose," perhaps referring to the character of the super-brainy kid, Poindexter, who appeared in *Felix the Cat* cartoons.

Movie Moment:
Marge and Otto race through a dry aqueduct, an action-sequence used in many films, most notably *Terminator II: Judgment Day* and *Grease*.

Homer's impassioned plea for a return to normalcy: **"Babies of Springfield! We need your help! Please, skin your knees, put dice up your nose, let cats sleep on your face!"**

Meeting of the Minds:
Marge: *That's quite an act to follow, Lisa.*
Lisa: *I know, and the crowd is so distinguished. The inventor of the walkie-talkie is out there.*
Marge: *Where?*
Lisa: *Third row, near the aisle.*
Marge: *Oh, you're right! And that's not his wife.*

"Airborne Pheromones and Aggression in Bullies":
Lisa: *But why do the brawny prey on the brainy? Is it jealousy?* (The scientists murmur assent.) *No! The reason is chemicals.*
(The scientist murmur disagreement.)
Male Researcher: *Tha— that's impossible! Chemicals are our friends.*
Dr. C. Everett Koop: *She's a witch!*

Music Moment:
A high school–aged Homer beats up a young Waylon Smithers while singing "Kung-Fu Fighting." Barney accompanies him on the kazoo.

NRBQ's "Always Safety First" plays during Homer's child-safety montage and over the end credits.

 "I have isolated the chemical which is emitted by every geek, dork, and four-eyes. I call it 'Poindextrose.'"

Cracking the Bully Code:
Scientist: *The little girl's invented some sort of bully repellent!*
Lisa: *(holding up an atomizer) Actually, it's just ordinary salad dressing.*
Marge: *So that's where that went.*
Lisa: *The pungent vinegar and tangy Roquefort blocked the smell receptors, rendering the bully harmless.*

The Summing Up of All Fears:
Homer: *So all her bullying was just to get some attention.*
Lisa: *No, Dad! Didn't you listen to anything I said?*
Homer: *Just to get some attention.*

KITENGE

Occupation:
Formerly, an African tour guide; currently, president of a small African nation

Turn-offs:
Bush babies climbing on his new shirt; poachers

Turn-ons:
Eavesdropping in the dark; dancing into a frenzy

Special talents:
Mosquito-net reversing; hippo wrangling

Drink of choice:
Cow's blood

Favorite pastime:
Sitting quietly and waiting for nature to unveil herself

> GOOD NIGHT, AND DON'T LET THE BEDBUGS PARALYZE!

When Homer does the grocery shopping for Marge, he manages to incite a bag boy walkout and a subsequent strike. Soon there is no food to be had anywhere in town. Santa's Little Helper discovers a forty-year-old box of animal crackers in the attic that just happens to contain a prize. The prize, a solid-gold giraffe, indicates that they have won a free trip to Africa, but the company who made the crackers does not want to honor the terms of the contest decades after it has ended. When Homer is injured by the "defective" animal cracker box, the company lawyers avoid a lawsuit by sending them on the trip.

Once in Africa, the Simpsons are met by a friendly guide named Kitenge, who shows them the beautiful wonders of his homeland. A native tribe allows them to join in a ritual dance, but Homer ruins things by accidentally slapping a hippopotamus on the butt. The furious hippo breaks up the dance and chases the Simpsons into a nearby river. Using a tribal shield as a canoe, the family floats downriver, which sends them over Victoria Falls.

The family survives the drop and an encounter with a man-eating plant. They meet a chimpanzee who leads them to a refuge run by Dr. Joan Bushwell. The Simpsons enjoy the doctor's hospitality until the refuge is attacked by poachers who want to take away the monkeys. At first, the Simpsons help Dr. Bushwell fight back, but they soon discover that the attackers are not poachers at all; they are from Greenpeace. Dr. Bushwell has been using the chimps to dig diamonds out of a mine, and she has gone mad with greed. She begs not to be put away and promises the Simpsons diamonds if they help her. The Simpsons leave Africa with a fortune in gems.

SHOW HIGHLIGHTS

Homer goes grocery shopping: **"Olive oil? Asparagus? If your mother wasn't so fancy, we could shop at the gas station like normal people."**

Impulse Shopping:
Bart: *I need this candy for school. Candy class.*
Homer: *Well, okay. But get five bags, in case we eat four on the way home.*
Lisa: *My teacher said I need cupcakes...cupcakes to learn.*
Homer: *(pointing at the cart) In the cart.*
Bart: *I'm out of wine.*
Homer: *Cart.*

License to Annoy:
Homer: *Wait, I've changed my mind. Stack it in the order I'll eat it driving home.*
Bag Boy: *Sir, please! I've already bagged it by color, and in order of each item's discovery by man.*
Homer: *The customer is always right. That's what everybody likes about us. Now, mush!*

Unrealistic Expectations:
Agnes: *I want everything in one bag.*
Bag Boy: *Yes, ma'am.*
Agnes: *But I don't want the bag to be heavy.*
Bag Boy: *I don't think that's possible.*
Agnes: *What are you, the "Possible Police"? Just do it!*

Pokey Man:
Homer: *(poking bag boy with a baguette) Hurry up! I can't stand here jabbing you all day!*
Bag Boy: *Ow, stop! Bag boys have feelings, too, you know.*
Homer: *No you don't.*

Digging Through the Cupboards:
Homer: *So hungry! There's gotta be some food left! Sulfur Jerky? Cream of Toast? Where did we get all this crap?*
Marge: *Most of it was sent by relatives who couldn't see very well.*

On-the-Spot Coverage:
Kent Brockman: *Pledging to honor the bag boy strike are "The Brotherhood of Fruit Packers and Unpackers," "The Shelf Dusters Union," and "The Unattractive Waitresses of America."*
Unattractive Waitress: *(leaning in from off-camera) Kiss my grits!*
Kent Brockman: *Indeed!*

Nibbling at History:
Homer: *Gasp! Very old animal crackers!*
(He blows the dust off of one and eats it.)
Marge: *Homer, no! Those were made in the '60s!*
Homer: *Mmm...turbulent.*

Things Are Looking Up:
Bart: *Whoa! A solid-gold animal cracker.*
Lisa: *(reading box) "Find the golden giraffe, and we'll send you and your family to Africa."*
Homer: *Africa!? They're bound to have food there!*

Homer makes demands: **"And on my free African safari I want to do everything on this box: I want to shoot a lion in the face, fight Muhammad Ali, and ride in a convertible with two happy zebras."**

Prepare for Landing:
Flight Attendant: *Attention, passengers. Please prepare for our landing in Tanzania. (Another flight attendant hands her a note.) I'm sorry, it is now called New Zanzibar. (She is handed another note.) Excuse me. It is now called Pepsi Presents New Zanzibar.*

Political Intrigue:
Marge: *Who's Muntu?*
Kitenge: *He is our leader. He seized power in a bloodless coup. All smothering. (He makes a pillow-smothering gesture.)*
Homer: *Just like Jimmy Carter.*

Homer on poaching: **"Poachers are nature's way of keeping the balance. Whenever there are so many species that people get confused and angry, a poacher is born."**

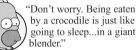
"Don't worry. Being eaten by a crocodile is just like going to sleep...in a giant blender."

Lofty Goal:
Bart and Lisa: *Are we insane yet? Are we insane yet? Are we insane yet?*
Homer: *I told you, yes! Now, Bart, go to the top of that hill and see if you can spot our hotel.*
Bart: *Mt. Kilimanjaro?*
Homer: *Go!*

Fine Dining:
Marge: *A chimp!*
Lisa: *Hello, little fella.*
Bart: *Hey! Maybe he'll lead us to bananas.*
Homer: *Or more mouth-watering monkeys!*

SAFARI

Episode CABF13
Original Airdate: 04/01/01
Writer: John Swartzwelder
Director: Mark Kirkland
Executive Producer: Mike Scully

A Day with the Doctor:

Dr. Bushwell: *Everyday I get up at 5:30, watch the chimps, eat a quick lunch of roots and water, then more chimp watching. After dark, I come home and think about chimps until it's time for bed.*
Homer: *You must be the most boring woman on Earth.*
Dr. Bushwell: *Possibly, but...*
Homer: *I mean, I knew scientists wasted their lives, but geez!*

Movie Moment:

The beauty of an African sunrise, silhouettes of animals, and the rhythmic music playing across the veldt are reminiscent of the opening moments of the Disney animated film *The Lion King*.

Tea Time:

Homer: *So, I noticed your home smells of feces.*
Dr. Bushwell: *Yes.*
Homer: *And not just monkey feces, either.*
Dr. Bushwell: *Could we talk about something else?*

Dr. Bushwell comes unglued: **"All right! So I snapped! You don't understand the crushing loneliness and greed!"**

Bart Weighs In:

Lisa: *How could you exploit your beloved chimps like this?*
Bart: *I think we should look at her research before we condemn her entirely.* (Everyone looks at him, stunned.) *I haven't said anything for a while.*

Dedicated to the hardworking bag boys of America...

...whose ineptness and greed were the inspiration for this episode.

THE STUFF YOU MAY HAVE MISSED

Homer, Bart, and Lisa go shopping at Costmo Foods.

The *Springfield Shopper* newspaper with the headline "Food Supply Cut Off" has the sub-headline "Even Pies."

The sign for Kitchen-Maid Inc. has a picture of a housewife slicing the Earth like it is a ham.

On the plane, Marge peruses an *Unnecessaries* in-flight catalog.

Billboards the Simpsons pass on the way from the airport read "Hail President Muntu," "Muntu Means Progress," and "Muntu Builds Stadiums."

The Simpsons visit the "Ngorongoro Wildlife Preserve."

Before it charges them, the hippo scratches the ground with one foot like a bull.

At Joan Bushwell's Chimp Refuge, there's a chimpanzee-shaped, doggie door–style entrance for the chimps to use.

Dr. Joan Bushwell is modeled after world-renowned anthropologist Jane Goodall, who has devoted her life to the study of apes in their natural habitat.

The chimpanzee that points out the coming danger is named Pointy. The one that disapproves of Dr. Bushwell's hairstyle is named Jojo.

Dr. Bushwell hides diamonds on the soles of her shoes. "Diamonds on the Soles of Her Shoes" is a song from Paul Simon's African-inspired album *Graceland*.

In the folder labeled "Serious Research" are pictures of monkeys from *The Planet of the Apes*, *The Wizard of Oz*, and *King Kong*.

Music Moment:

When Homer sings along with the African song on the radio, he's singing "Good Morning Starshine," from the rock musical *Hair*.

A day in the life of the Simpsons is told from three different perspectives. All three versions combined make for one complete story:

Homer's Day: Lisa shows Homer her science fair project, a grammar robot of her own invention named Linguo. Homer proceeds to poor beer in its mouth, causing it to short-circuit. He then harasses Marge as she tries to cut a fresh batch of brownies, and she accidentally cuts off his thumb as he reaches for a brownie. Santa's Little Helper runs off with the thumb, and when Homer finally retrieves it, Marge rushes him to the hospital. On the way to the hospital they crash into Rainier Wolfcastle in his Ferrari. While Wolfcastle assaults their car with golf clubs, Marge and Homer use his car to get to the hospital. Once there, Dr. Hibbert informs them that Homer's HMO will not pay for a thumb reattachment. They decide to go to Dr. Nick Riviera instead, but on the way, Homer makes Marge stop by Moe's to get more ice to preserve the thumb. Homer stays and gets drunk, and when he finally comes out of the bar, Marge is gone. Homer hitches a ride with Cletus, and when they get to Dr. Nick's, his office is on fire. While they are not looking, Cletus's truck is stolen. Homer attempts to walk to the hospital in Shelbyville, but as his thumb starts to

wither, he gives up hope of having it attached again. Suddenly, there is an explosion, and Linguo's severed head lands at Homer's feet.

Lisa's Day: After Homer wrecks her robot, she quickly repairs it, but she misses the school bus. She decides to ride her bike, but it has been stolen. Her parents are off to the hospital, so Lisa is forced to run to school and is almost hit by Krusty's limousine. Krusty offers her a ride to school, but inadvertently drops her off at West Springfield Elementary, which looks just like her school. After spending too much time with a boy she meets there, she is once more forced to run. She tries to find Homer at Moe's, but instead she finds Chief Wiggum, who is monitoring the progress of his new informant on short-wave radio. Lisa goes out the rear entrance moments before Homer enters the bar. Out on the street Lisa finds Marge waiting for Homer. Marge agrees to take Lisa to school, but the car runs out of gas in front of Dr. Nick's, and Marge borrows Cletus's truck. Just as they near the school, Bart emerges from a manhole directly in their path.

Bart's Day: Milhouse comes to the Simpsons house to tell Bart that he has discovered a huge cache of fireworks in a nearby cave. To get there, Bart

Ned Flanders prepares for a book burning: **"And Harry Potter...and all his wizard friends...went straight to Hell for practicing witchcraft."**

ERROR

Episode CABF14
Original Airdate: 04/29/01
Writer: Matt Selman
Director: Mike B. Anderson
Executive Producer: Mike Scully
Guest Voice: Joe Mantegna as Fat Tony

unlocks the chain on Lisa's bike so that Milhouse can ride it. When they get to the cave, they take a sack full of the fireworks and spend the day blowing things up. One wayward spinning rocket wheel accidentally burns down Dr. Nick's clinic. The police nab Bart and Milhouse, and Chief Wiggum forces them to help catch whoever is smuggling the fireworks by wearing a wire. Bart and Milhouse discover that the illegal fireworks belong to Fat Tony, but Chief Wiggum blows their cover. They flee from Fat Tony and his henchmen, and Bart is almost run over by Marge. When the mobsters trap Bart and Milhouse in a dead-end alley, Marge throws Lisa's science project at the gangsters to distract them. The gangsters' poor grammar causes Linguo to self-destruct, setting off a fireworks explosion. The police arrive at the scene the same time as Homer, and Fat Tony offers a solution to both Lisa and Homer's dilemmas. Legs, one of his henchmen, sews on Homer's thumb in Lisa's classroom, and the operation becomes Lisa's entry in the school's science fair.

This plot made no sense!

"If anyone ever tells you a hog won't eat a finger, they's lyin'."

Homer's drunken diatribe: **"Did you ever see that Blue Man Group? Total rip-off of "The Smurfs"! And the Smurfs...they suck!"**

Grammar Duel:
Lisa: *Almost done. Just lay still.*
Linguo: *Lie still.*
Lisa: *I knew that. Just testing.*
Linguo: *Sentence fragment.*
Lisa: *"Sentence fragment" is also a sentence fragment.*
Linguo: (eyes darting back and forth) *Must conserve battery power.*
(Linguo shuts himself down.)

"Inflammable means flammable? What a country!"

Outside Moe's:
Lisa: *Mom, where'd you get that car?*
Marge: *I stole it from McBain after I cut off your father's thumb.*
Lisa: *Can you take me to school? Please?*
Marge: *Not right now! Your father's in there and...*
Homer: (from inside Moe's) *Did you ever see that Blue Man Group? Total rip-off of...*
Marge: *He's on the Blue Man Group again. Come on, we've got lots of time.*

FIRE IS NOT THE CLEANSER
FIRE IS NOT THE CLEANSER
FIRE IS NOT THE CLEANSER
FIRE IS NOT THE CLEANSER
FIRE IS NOT THE CLEANSER
FIRE IS NOT THE CLEANSER

Practically Magic:
Homer: (pretending he's magically removing his severed thumb) *Abra-ca-thumb-ra!*
Cletus: *Ha! Ha-ha! Dang! You could be one of them TV magic queers!*

Movie Moment:
Like the title character in the cult-favorite German film *Run, Lola, Run*, Lisa is seen running as fast as she can through town, while pulsing electronic music underscores the action. The episode also borrows the three-part structure from the film, but instead of the same story being told from three different perspectives, *Run, Lola, Run* shows the same story with three different outcomes.

Satisfying Ride:
Bart: *What's it like riding a girl's bike?*
Milhouse: *It's disturbingly comfortable.*

Salty Operation:
Dr. Nick Riviera: *So, what are we doing? A lengthening or a widening?*
Capt. McCallister: *Yarrr. Uh...let's make it both!*

Gangsta-Style Gunplay:
Officer Lou: *Hey, Chief, can I hold my gun sideways? It looks so cool.*
Chief Wiggum: *Ha-ha-ha-ha! Ahhh, sure. Whatever you want...birthday boy.*

Music Moment:
Lisa and Thelonious join hands and spin in circles to The Turtles' "Happy Together."

Fireworks Bust:
Wiggum: *Great Grucci's ghost! We've uncovered a hard-core 'cracker house'!*
Lou: *There's enough Chinese sky-candy here to put you boys away for a long time.*
Milhouse: *I can't go to juvie! They use guys like me as currency!*
Wiggum: *Yeah, they'll pass you around like...like currency. Like you said.*

Let's Make a Deal:
Wiggum: *Your mission is to find the fireworks smugglers and get them to say something incriminating on this tape.*
Bart: *Hootie and the Blowfish?*
Wiggum: *Yeah. It's cheaper than blank tape.*

Mob Mentality:
Legs: *Great idea to smuggle fireworks, boss.*
Louie: *Yeah, I was gettin' sick of runnin' those unions.*
Legs: *So much paperwork.*

Not Programmed to Respond in This Area:
Louie: *Hey, they's throwin' robots!*
Linguo: *They are throwing robots.*
Legs: *It's disrespecting us.* (to robot) *Shutuppayouface!*
Linguo: *Shut up your face.*
Legs: *Whatsamattayou?*
Linguo: *You ain't so big!*
Legs: *Me and him are gonna whack you inna labonza.*
Linguo: *Bad grammar overload. Error! Error!*

Handy Henchman:
Legs: *There you go! Enjoy your thumb.*
Lisa: *As the circulation returns, the subject prepares for a long and painful recovery.* (The class applauds.) *It's lucky for me that Legs is an experienced Mob doctor.*
Fat Tony: *He once pulled a slug out of my arm and inserted it into a stoolie's brain.*

99

THELONIOUS

School:
West Springfield Elementary

Perspective on his name:
Its esoteric appeal is worth the beatings

Common ground with Lisa:
Knows the work of architect leoh Ming Pei; does not have any friends, either

Idea of romance:
Spinning in circles with a girl for hours

YOU CAN'T SACRIFICE GRADES FOR ROMANCE.

Guest Voice:
Frankie Muniz as Thelonious

THE RICH TEXAN

Who he is:
Greedy philanthropist

Proud owner of:
Omni-Pave Construction, portions of the Springfield Forest, and the lucky hat he wore the day Kennedy was shot

His fondest dream:
To build the world's first drive-through humidor

Strange Behavior:
Breaks into a giddy dance while shouting, "Yee-Haw!" and "Yipee-ki-yi-yay, little doggies!"

Surest indication of character:
The license plate on his limo reads "NO SHAME"

> MAY THE LORD HAVE MERCY ON YOUR GAS-SNIFFIN', ORPHAN-BEATIN' SOUL.

A t a church ice cream social, Ned Flanders runs into Rachel Jordan, the Christian rock singer he met just after Maude's death. Determined to move on with his life, Ned invites Rachel to stay at his house while she is in town. Rachel is slightly taken aback by all the memorials to Maude around Ned's house, but she is truly appalled when she wakes up to find that Ned has given her a haircut just like Maude's. She leaves in a huff, and Ned realizes he is far from being over his dead wife.

The Simpsons volunteer to help remove Maude's possessions from the house, since Ned cannot bear to part with any of them. Before all of them are disposed of, however, Bart finds a sketchbook of Maude's drawings. Inside are the designs for a Christian-themed amusement park. Ned vows to make Maude's dream a reality, and with the Simpsons' help, he creates Praiseland. On opening day, customers find Praiseland tedious and overtly religious, and they begin leaving en masse. When a discarded Maude mask floats into the air and hovers eerily in front of Maude's statue, the park patrons believe they have witnessed a miracle.

The drawing power of the "Miracle Maude" statue grows when people standing before it start to have vivid "visions." Patrons are willing to pay ten dollars each and wait in a long line to experience this marvel. Ned plans to give the money to orphans, but is conflicted when he discovers that a leaky gas line is causing the "visions." Just before two orphans place a lit candle next to the gas leak, Ned and Homer tackle them, knocking them out of harm's way. Their act of heroism is taken for an act of child abuse, and Ned is forced to close Praiseland. Ned encounters Rachel Jordan outside of the gates of the amusement park, and together they are able to put the past behind them and to look forward to a possible future.

SHOW HIGHLIGHTS

> "Ice cream at church? I'm intrigued, yet suspicious."

Professor Frink's newest invention: **"Mm-hoy-mm. I've created the first intra-bovine ice cream maker. It makes use of all four stomachs, the first being filled with rock salt, then sugar, cream, and, of course, freon, so cold it burns me."**

Face the Music:
Ned: *So, where's your band?*
Rachel Jordan: *They switched from Christian music to regular pop. All you do is change "Jesus" to "Baby."*
Ned: *Oh, how horrible!*
Rachel Jordan: *Eh. They'll all go to Hell.*

Neighborhood Watch:
Homer: *Why don't you just stay at Ned's place?*
Ned: *My place? What would the neighbors think?*
Lisa: *We're the neighbors, and we don't think.*

Remedy for Neddy:
Ned: *I sure appreciate you folks offering to go through Maude's things. If it were up to me, I wouldn't throw anything away.*
Marge: *Don't you worry. We'll make all the hard decisions so you won't have to.*
Bart: *We can take whatever we want, right?*
Ned: *Ye- what?!*
Lisa: *Don't listen to him. You just have a good time at the eye doctor.*
Ned: *Always do!*

Potion Notion:
Lisa: *Don't throw this away! It's Rod's first tooth.*
Bart: *You're right. We can use this for witchcraft.*

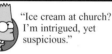

> "Wow! Three pairs of shoes. Someone had a fetish."

Bart suggests a location for Praiseland: **"You could fix up the old Storytime Village. They've been out of business ever since that kid got his head cut off."**

Passive/Aggressive Philanthropy:
Rich Texan: *Tell ya what. Maybe I could donate the park as a tax write-off.*
Ned: *Oh, if you could do that, I'd make this place a shining beacon for the Lord.*
Rich Texan: *Aw, you are so full of it! God's grace, that is. It's really sickening...there aren't more people like you. Now, get out...your pen, and we'll make it official.*

Happy Helper:
Lisa: *How about asking the community for donations?*
Ned: *Oh, ho! I'm not very good at begging people for stuff.*
Homer: *I am! I'd be glad to spearhead the entire begging initiative.*
Ned: *Well, thanks, Homer.*
Homer: *No problem. I'll need a sack and something sharp.*

A Scottish Secret:
Groundskeeper Willie: *This sawdust'll soak up the puke from the rooller-coaster! It's Willie's special blend!*
Homer: *Sniff! Sniff! Do I detect a hint of cinnamon?*
Willie: *Ooh, I'll never tell.*

THE STUFF YOU MAY HAVE MISSED

The banner at church reads "Ice Cream Social—'A Sundae Service You Can Swallow.'"

Cruci-Fixin's ice cream toppings offered by Reverend Lovejoy: "Blessed Virgin Berry," "Command-mint," and "Bible Gum."

When Mootilda the cow kicks Professor Frink, he exclaims, "Ivan Reitman!" Ivan Reitman directed such comedies as *Stripes*, *Ghostbusters*, and *Kindergarten Cop*.

Dr. Hibbert injects hot fudge into Nelson's mouth with a caulking gun.

Reverend Lovejoy introduces Rachel Jordan as "the Christian Madonna."

While removing Maude memorabilia from the Flanders' house, Homer and Bart get rid of some of Ned's furniture, too.

Storytime Village first appeared in "Lisa the Vegetarian" (3F03), but in that episode it was referred to as "Storytown Village."

The inscription on Maude's statue reads "She Taught Us the Joy of Shame and the Shame of Joy."

In Disco Stu's vision, among those standing in line to get into Heaven are John Travolta, Liza Minnelli, Andy Warhol, and the Very Tall Man.

Saint Peter was last seen in the "G-G-Ghost D-D-Dad" segment of "Treehouse of Horror XI" (BABF21).

The orphans, Patches and Poor Violet, first appeared in "Miracle on Evergreen Terrace" (5F07).

> "It is with, uh, great pride that I dedicate this new school, sports arena, or attraction."

PRAISELAND

Episode CABF15
Original Airdate: 05/06/01
Writer: Julie Thacker
Director: Chuck Sheetz
Executive Producer: Mike Scully
Guest Voice: Shawn Colvin as Rachel Jordan

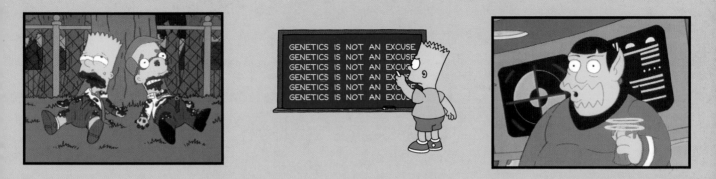

Revealed this episode:
Ned Flanders's first name is
really Nedward.

At the Souvenir Stand:

Ned: Oo...what can I get you, little Christian? How about a Noah's Ark of jellies?
Chief Wiggum: Oh, are there two of every flavor?
Ned: No, they're all the same. Plain.
Wiggum: Oh.
Ned: How about a Maude mask? (putting one on and imitating Maude) I'm Maude. God is super!
Ralph: Can I sit in the car?
Wiggum: Let's both sit in the car.

An Educational Vision:

Principal Skinner: It was incredible! I saw Heaven! But it wasn't clouds and angels playing harps like at the end of so many "Three Stooges" shorts. It was a golden elementary school with a teacher's lounge that stretched as far as the eye could see. And no one was ever tardy.
Bart: Was I there?
Principal Skinner: No! It was Heaven! My vision of Heaven.

The Highly Suggestible Type:

Homer: Stupid grill! Why won't you light? The gas is on full-blast!
Bart: You better stick your head in and see what's going on.
Homer: Good idea!

At the Whack-A-Satan Game:

Nelson: What do you hit him with? There's no mallet.
Ned: You can stop Satan with your faith.
Nelson: My face? Are you callin' me ugly?
Ned: No-no-no-no! I think you're beautiful!
Nelson: Oh, that's it! (punching his fist)
Ned: (running away) Aaah!

At the Refreshments Stand:

Lenny: A bible park without beer? Now I've seen everything.
Carl: And this candy is sub-par. Any religion that embraces carob is, uhh, not for Carl Carlson.

Homer passes the collection plate:
"I'm sorry, the ticket price doesn't cover visions, miracles, or other godly hoo-hah."

The Mysteries of Life:

Rod Flanders: How come everybody's having visions, Daddy?
Ned: Oh, there's no explaining God's will, Roddy. That's like explaining how an airplane flies.

Homer delivers the message:
"Praiseland has touched an entire town with its inspiring message and toxic super freakouts. Look at those smiling faces—rich laughing with poor, bullies breaking bread with nerds, orphans lighting candles over a leaking gas line..."

Music Moment:

Disco Stu's vision and the ending credits are accompanied by "Get Dancin' " by Disco Tex & His Sex-o-lettes. The same song played during the "Hooray for Everything" halftime show in "Bart vs. Thanksgiving" (7F07).

When the Simpsons attend an open house at the Springfield YMCA, Homer injures his leg badly during a basketball game. A successful operation repairs the damaged leg, but Homer is told he has to stay off the leg completely for two weeks and cannot go back to work.

At home, a wheelchair-bound Homer is as bored as can be. The only thing that cheers him up is when he baby-sits the Flanders boys. Rod and Todd have a great time with Homer, and Homer really enjoys spending time with other people's children. He likes it so much, he decides to open his own daycare center, which becomes wildly popular. Homer keeps the daycare open even after he is back on his feet. All the constant attention he lavishes on his daycare kids causes Bart and Lisa to become jealous. They try to win back their father's attention with no success.

Homer is nominated for a Good Guy Award for his daycare work. A film crew takes up residence in the house to profile Homer and his "Homer Cares" daycare program. At the ceremony, all is going well until the documentary about Homer is shown. Bart and Lisa have spliced in home-movie footage that does not show Homer in a positive light. The audience is appalled, and many parents refuse to allow their kids to be around Homer any longer. Upset, Homer kidnaps some of his daycare kids and flees in a police van. He does not get far and is arrested. After three mistrials, life returns to normal at the Simpson home. Homer admits to learning his lesson, and promises to lavish attention only on his own three kids from now on.

SHOW HIGHLIGHTS

No Illusions:

YMCA Man: Welcome to the Springfield YMCA. Tonight you can sample all of our classes for free. And if you find one you like, you can pay the membership fee and enroll.
Townspeople: (laugh uproariously)
YMCA Man: Ah-ha-ha-heh. I know. We'll never see any of you again.
Homer: You got that right.

Past Her Prime:

Coach Lugash: What a little angel! How old are you?
Lisa: Eight.
Lugash: Eight? Too old! Go home, grandma!

"I have purchased the Springfield YMCA. I plan to tear it down and turn the land into a nature preserve, where I'll hunt the deadliest game of all...man! Now, let's play ball!"

Take It to the Hoop:

Homer: Woo! You da man, Carl. I believe you can fly.
Carl: Boy, I am so sick of everyone assuming I'm good at basketball because I'm African American. (He suddenly leaps into the air and completes an incredible 360° dunk, shattering the backboard. He begins to chant.) Go Carl. Go Carl. It's my birthday. It's my birthday. Three-peat! You've got mail, baby!

Movie Moment:
Professor Frink's flubber-enhanced basketball shoes allow him to perform gravity-defying moves on the court, just like in the Fred MacMurray film *The Absent-Minded Professor*.

In the Operating Theater:
Lisa: So many times we've seen our father go under the knife.
Marge: One more, and I get a free hysterectomy!

General Hospitality:

Dr. Hibbert: Now, Homer, you'll have a full recovery from your spinal cord injury.
Marge: What spinal cord injury?
Dr. Hibbert: Oh, he fell off the gurney. But it will take plenty of time and rehab before you can go back to work.
Homer: Miss work? But my life would be nothing without the nucleon plant!
Dr. Hibbert: Oh! You're also responsible for this hefty hospital bill. You shouldn't have ordered all those hospital haircuts and porno films.
Homer: But Dr. Screwlittle sounded like a delightful romp!

Doctor's Orders:

Dr. Hibbert: Now, Homer, I want you to stay off that leg for two weeks.
Homer: Two weeks!? What am I suppose to do, just sit on my ass and watch TV? That ain't my style, man!
Dr. Hibbert: Now, Homer, there are people right through that door that have it much worse than you.
Homer: Sniff! No they don't.

On the Loose:

Homer: I'm so bored!
Abe: Oh, come on, there's lots of ways to pass the time: hitch up your pants, air-whittle, make friends with a Chinese man.
Orderly: Uh, Mr. Simpson, you weren't supposed to leave the home.
Abe: Thank you, Ping-Pong.
Orderly: My name is Craig.
Abe: Sure it is.

Neighborly Help:

Ned: Would you mind watching the kids? I'm kind of in a pickle here.
Homer: Well, they would keep me company. And this pickle you're offering only sweetens the deal.

Chris Rock in Concert:

Homer: How was the concert?
Flanders: Well, sir, I never heard a preacher use the "m-f" word so many times.

Homer Makes Up His Mind

Flanders: So you are running a daycare center?
Homer: Oh, you'd like that, wouldn't you?
Flanders: Well, I sure would. It would give the boys a place to go after school.
Homer: Then I'll do it, just to see the look on your face. (Ned smiles.) That's the one.

The Great Escape:

(Apu holds on to his octuplets, each on a baby leash.)
Apu: Hello. I would like to take advantage of your baby prison.
Marge: Oh, we're calling it daycare.
Apu: Yes, whatever, just take them!
(Homer walks up with a cane and takes the octuplets' leashes.)
Homer: Aw, aren't they sweet. Any medical things I should know about?
Apu: (off-screen) Yes, probably!
(Homer looks out the window and sees Apu running off.)

TV Moment:
During Homer's morphine-induced space fantasy, George Jetson of "The Jetsons" crashes his space car into Homer's leg. Homer reacts as if he were George Jetson's boss, Mr. Spacely.

Uncle Homer's Daycare Center:
Marge: Why did you put my name on the sign?
Homer: It's just a legal thing...to protect me.

Homer's Hooked:
Dr. Hibbert: Why, Homer, your surgical incision is completely healed.
Homer: I owe it all to my rewarding work with children...and not picking at it.
Dr. Hibbert: Ah, yes. How is your daycare center doing?
Homer: Wonderful! Being with those kids gives me a high that only morphine can top. You got any?!

THE STUFF YOU MAY HAVE MISSED

The Springfield YMCA marquee reads "Now 30 Percent Less Stank!"

Abe and Mr. Burns are the only two players in the Over-85 Basketball League. They use a peach basket instead of a hoop, like the first players did when the game was invented by Dr. James Naismith, a teacher at a YMCA.

Rainier Wolfcastle's plan to build a preserve and hunt humans for sport, and his subsequent chasing of Lenny with a rifle, is a reference to Richard Connell's famous short story "The Most Dangerous Game."

Comic Book Guy wears a T-shirt with Hanna-Barbera character Muttley on it from the cartoon show "The Wacky Racers."

Ned Flanders's pet names for his sons are Rowdy Roddy and Typhoon Todd.

What Ned thinks is a Christian Rock concert is really comedian Chris Rock in concert.

Homer takes off his shirt at the hospital to have his leg examined.

While talking with Bart and Milhouse on the playground, Ralph gets distracted by a butterfly and wanders away.

When the Teamsters take over Bart's room, they put a sign on the door that says "Quiet—Teamsters Need Their Sleep" and pictures a big man sleeping on some boxes with a wad of cash in his hand.

At the ceremony, the marquee reads "The Good Guy Awards. 'Pointless.' —N.Y. Times."

Feeling Left-Out:
Bart: Hey, Homer, I thought you were only going to do this daycare thing until your knee was better.
Homer: Yes, but then I discovered the joys of raising children.
Lisa: What about us?
Homer: Don't worry, honey, you'll have children of your own some day. Then you'll know my joy.

LESSER CLOD

Episode CABF16
Original Airdate: 05/13/01
Writer: Al Jean
Director: Mike Polcino
Executive Producer: Mike Scully

"You haven't seen the real Homer; it's all burping and neglect."

Music Moments:

Homer plays Marvin Gaye's "Let's Get It On" for Snowball II and Santa's Little Helper while they are tied in a sack.

The music of NRBQ is heard once again, as their song "Encyclopedia" plays in the background at Homer's daycare.

When Rod and Todd ask Homer to sing their favorite song, he launches into an emotional rendition of the Peggy Lee torch song "Is That All There Is?"

Fun with Dirty Words:

Homer: (singing) *"If you're happy and you know it, say a swear!"*
Nelson: *Boobs!*
Milhouse: *Hiney!*
Ralph: *Mitten!*

Krusty the Clown announces the Good Guy Awards: **"Every year we find one Good Samaritan, so deserving that not recognizing him would make Santa Claus himself vomit with rage."**

Homer, after winning the Saint Who Walks Among Us Award: **"All my love has come back in trophy form!"**

On-the-Air Meltdown:

Kent Brockman: *An awards ceremony erupted in kidnapping tonight, as alleged "Good Guy" Homer Simpson absconded with several children in a stolen paddy wagon. Now, let's go to Arnie Pie in the sky.*
Arnie Pie: (in helicopter) *I can see them right below me! I'm going to try to nail the driver with one of my shoes.*
Kent: *Arnie, please, leave this to the police.*
Arnie: *I'm sick of being a reporter! I want to make the news!*
Kent: *Arnie, this is not the time!*
Arnie: *You're not the time, Kent! You're not the time!*

Honesty Is the Best Policy:

Homer: *Why did you rat me out, kids? Was it because I showered love on those other children while ignoring you?*
Bart: *Yep.*
Lisa: *Pretty much.*

COACH LUGASH

Occupation:
YMCA Gymnastics Instructor

Formerly from:
East Germany

Escaped by:
Cartwheeling over the Berlin Wall in '83

Distinguishing Characteristics:
Handlebar mustache; a sweet disposition that turns into uncontrollable rage

Further education:
Anger management class

Gymnastic enrollment:
Limited to children under 8

NO GIGGLING! IT WEAKENS THE HAUNCHES!

SINGING RAILROAD HOBO

Way of life:
Riding the rails, swapping stories for sponge-baths

Limited worldview:
You are either a hobo or a nobo

Special talents:
Singing, telling tall tales, playing banjo, and doing impressions of other hobos

Creature comforts:
Anything with alcohol or pills in it

Bad grooming habit:
Lets glass build up between his toes

> HERE'S A BALLAD THAT'LL SET FIRE TO YOUR TRASH CAN.

The Simpsons win a free trip to Delaware, but because Homer threatens the ticket agent at the airport, they are forced to hop a freight train to reach their destination. On the train they meet a hobo who regales them with stories. His first tall tale is about Paul Bunyan (Homer), a giant idiot who is always making life difficult for the local settlers by accidentally stepping on them or crushing their homes. Sick of Paul's destructive behavior, the townspeople slip him a knock-out drug and drag him out of town. On his own and feeling lonely, Paul carves a giant blue ox out of stone, and it comes to life in a lightning storm. Paul wanders the countryside with Babe the Blue Ox, and he later falls in love with a young pioneer woman (Marge). When the townspeople discover that a meteor is headed right for their town, they ask Paul to come back and save them. Paul obliges, and in doing so, causes The Great Chicago Fire. The Simpsons enjoy this tall tale, but it comes with a price: Homer must give the hobo a sponge-bath as compensation.

The hobo's second tale is about Connie Appleseed (Lisa), and how she brought apples to the Wild West. Connie is fed up with her wagon train's shortsighted habit of killing every buffalo they come across, and she believes that the supply of buffalo will run out. Looking for an alternate source of food, she happens upon an apple tree. Her father, like many of the settlers, is not interested in Connie's apples, and does not believe all the buffalo can be killed. Connie leaves in frustration, to spread apple seeds wherever she goes. Meanwhile, the wagon train does run out of buffalo, and the pioneers are about to eat each other. Connie returns to save the day with her delicious apples, but not before Moe takes a few bites out of Homer.

The final tale concerns Tom Sawyer (Bart) and Huck Finn (Nelson). When Becky Thatcher (Lisa) is caught holding hands with Huck, Judge Thatcher (Homer), Becky's father, forces them into a shotgun wedding. Huck is an unwilling groom, so he and Tom flee and are chased by the town's posse. After several adventures on the Mississippi River, Huck and Tom are unceremoniously caught and hung. By the end of this tale, the train has reached Delaware, and the hobo reminds them that they owe him two more sponge-baths. Homer stays behind to do the dirty duty.

SHOW HIGHLIGHTS

Ridin' the Rails:
Hobo: *Mornin', folks.*
Homer: (scared) *What are you gonna do to us?*
Hobo: *Now, don't worry, I'm not a stabbin' hobo. I'm a singin' hobo.*
(The Simpsons sigh with relief.)
Hobo: (sings) *Nothin' beats the hobo life, Stabbin' folks with my hobo knife! I gouge them...*

"A King-Sized Woodsman":
Won't you listen to my tale that's ten stories tall, 'Bout a king-sized woodsman name-a Bunyan comma Paul.
Born mighty big he continued to expand, Thanks to a hopped-up pituitary gland.
His body grew big, but his brain stayed small.
He was tree-choppin', friend-stompin', house-crushin' Paul!
Paul was just as lonely as a man could get, So he took out his ax, and he carved himself a pet. Now, Paul and Babe were a mighty fine match, But the man had an itch that an ox couldn't scratch.

 "Me hungee!"

A Giant Problem:
Moe: *Look, we gotta do something about Bunyan. We're goin' bankrupt just feedin' and clothin' the guy! Not to mention the crushings.*
Carl: *Hey! I say we get him drunk and drag him out of town, the same way we got rid of Laura Ingalls Wilder.*

Destroy All Non Sequiturs:
Lisa: *Excuse me! Paul Bunyan never fought Rodan, and his size seems to be really inconsistent. I mean, one minute he's ten feet tall, the next his feet are as big as a lake.*
Hobo: *Hey, hey, hey! Who's the hobo here?*

A Growing Need:
Paul Bunyan: *We've been together a long time now. When are we gonna...you know.*
Marge: *Soon. I just need a few more yoga classes.*

Wanting to Be Wanted:
Paul: *Oh, I get it! When I'm crushing and killing you, you don't like me, but when I can save your lives, suddenly, I'm Mr. Popular.*
Lenny: *Yeah, that's pretty much it.*
Paul: *Woo-hoo! I'm Mr. Popular!*

Let's Eat:
Connie Appleseed (Lisa): *Dad! You just killed a poor, defenseless buffalo!*
Homer: *A poor delicious buffalo! He'll be dinner for the whole wagon train.* (He shoots another buffalo.)
Connie: *Why'd you kill another one?*
Homer: *Dessert.*

Apples of Her Eye:
Connie: *Mom! Dad! Look what I found!*
Homer: *Oh, boy! Buffalo testicles!*
(He bites into a pair.)
Connie: *No, Dad. They're apples.*
Homer: *Yuh! Blaah! Yuck!*

A hungry, hungry Homer:
"**I haven't had buffalo in six hours. Marge, how about whipping up some buffalo sausage, huevos buffaleros, and some fresh-squeezed buffal-OJ?**"

Remorsefully Remorseless:
Marge: *The buffalo are gone. I think you shot them all.*
Homer: *Ohhh! Connie was right! We wiped out the entire species! What have I done? What have I done?!*
Bart: *Calm down, Pa. There's two left.*
(Homer shoots the last two buffalo.)
Homer: *What have I done? What have I done?!*

An Alternative to Cannibalism:
Connie: *Stop! I've got apples. Delicious, nutritious apples! And there's enough for everyone!*
Sideshow Mel: *Sweet! It's like a hootenanny in my mouth!*
Skinner: *We're saved!*
Ned: *It's a miracle!*
Carl: *Hooray for Connie Buffalkill!*
Moe: (emerging from inside Homer's coat) *What? So now we're not eating Homer?*

Apple of My Addiction:
Hobo: *And thanks to that little girl, today you can find apples in everything that's good—apple wine, apple whiskey, apple schnapps, apple martinis, Snapple with vodka in it, apple nail polish remover...*
Lisa: *Don't forget applesauce.*
Hobo: *Yeah. I suppose you could grind some pills into it.*

Huck Finn's Wedding:
Abe: *Hey! They done switched the groom with a pig!*
Judge Thatcher (Homer): *No wonder he was poopin' so much!*

TALL TALES

Episode CABF17
Original Airdate: 05/20/01
Writers: John Frink & Don Payne (Pt. 1),
Bob Bendetson (Pt. 2), and Matt Selman (Pt. 3)
Director: Bob Anderson
Executive Producer: Mike Scully

Movie Moments:

Paul Bunyan and Babe the Blue Ox battle the giant monster Rodan, crushing buildings in their wake, in a parody of countless *Godzilla* movies.

Dr. Hibbert sings "Ol' Man River" atop the riverboat, in an homage to the classic stage and movie musical *Showboat*.

Music Moment:

The song "Love Is a Many-Splendored Thing," from the film of the same name, plays as Paul Bunyan and Marge run toward each other.

Victual Reality:

Huck Finn (Nelson): *I'm considerable hungry. We got any food left?*
Tom Sawyer (Bart): *Hmm. Looks like we're out of cornpone, fatback, hardtack, fatpone, corntack...*
Huck: *Any tackback?*
Tom: *Tackback?*
Huck: *I mean, backtack.*
Tom: *Plum out.*

Compare and Save:

Apu: *One jug of whiskey, three plugs of tobacky, and some extra-strength opium. That will be two cents, boys.*
Tom: *Gasp!*
Huck: *Two cents!*
Apu: *Hey, if you think my prices are high, go across the street!*
(He points at a 99¢ Store.)

Judge Thatcher (Homer) loses Tom and Huck: **"Well, dog my cats! They's dis-separated!"**

Sponge-Bath Chat:

Homer: *Raise your arm. Okay, the other one.*
Hobo: *You know, I do 400 sit-ups a day.*
Homer: *Oh, it shows! I was gonna say something, but I thought it might sound, you know...queer.*
Hobo: *Oh, not at all. I like when people say nice things about my body.*
Homer: *And it's important to feel good about yourself. Okay, spread your toes...*

THE STUFF YOU MAY HAVE MISSED

At the airport, Fat Tony has a body in his luggage.

The Simpsons were planning to fly on Air Delaware.

Bart is seen wearing his lucky red hat.

The hobo calls the Simpsons "nobos," which is apparently hobo vernacular for non-hobos.

Places Paul Bunyan (Homer) and Babe the Blue Ox created by leaving their mark: Great Smoky Mountains, Death Valley, and Big Holes with Beer National Park.

Paul showers Marge with items from the Museum of Stuffed Animals, including a Happy Little Elf plush and a security guard.

On the pioneer trail, Sideshow Mel sports a pair of buffalo horns in his hair, instead of his usual bone.

The top of Huck (Nelson) and Becky's (Lisa's) wedding cake has a bride figure, a groom figure, and a father figure holding a shotgun aimed at the groom.

When Huck and Tom (Bart) raft over the state line, they leave Missouri and enter Missoura.

Apu's country store is called "Pone, Pelts and Beyond."

Tom's "Wanted" poster says he's wanted for "Moonshining" and pictures him with his pants down, mooning.

Two of the freeze-frame pictures shown during the end credits are not in this episode: Babe the Blue Ox kicking Paul in the groin and Kang and Kodos in their spaceship.

POT

"THE SOWER"
(Apologies to Millet)

ROUGH

CABF17 Act 11
JOHNNY POTHEAD
— Joe

cut from show.

DIRECTORS
APPROVAL   OCT 12 2000
C.U. 10·28·0

COLOR NOTE:

LUNG
HEART
LUNG
STOMACH
INTESTINES
LIVER

EPISODE: CABF08 /ACT 2
"MARGE IN HIPPIE GARB" (60'S CLOTHES)
KEVIN N.
FINAL 6·30·00

Self-ink
Hairline

ROUGH

6/12

CABF07 Act III
Marge in Homer's
Oedipal Dream
— Joe

HOMER

JUN 29 2000

EPISODE: CABF08 / ACT III
" MRS. SKINNER IN FLAPPERS OUTFIT "
KEVIN N.

DIRECTORS
APPROVAL

8"X10" FORMAT

REVISED FINAL 10/12/00
EPISODE CABF12 / ACT 3
PHOTO OF BEATLES Banqueting Dummy
KEVIN MOORE

BOX 6 - 130

OCT - 9 2000

Alternative
Spatula-shaped
Antenna

Note: Edge of
Teletubbies' "Sun" is
indistinct, lost in a
bright glow. See
reference video.

CABF01 Couch Gag
The Simpsons as Teletubbies
FINAL 5.11.0   -Joe

HOMER

OSTRICH
FEATHERS

HOMER'S SHORTS
CHEATED A LITTLE
SHORTER IN THIS
GET-UP.

CABF13 Act 11
Simpsons with Borrowed
Masai Items
        - Joe
FINAL 9·7·0

Severed Head

• ACTUAL PROP DESIGN OF
  SUITCASE WILL FOLLOW
  SEPARATELY. SUITCASE SHOWN
  HERE FOR COSTUME PURPOSES
  ONLY.

EPISODE: CABF04 / ACT III
"SMITHERS IN ALBUQUERQUEN CLOTHES"
        KEVIN N.

DIRECTORS
APPROVAL

CHURCH MARQUEES

BINGO!

First Church of Springfield

BINGO 7 PM

"Missionary Impossible" (BABF11)

EVERY SUNDAY IS SUPER SUNDAY

"Lisa the Greek" (8F12)

PRIVATE WEDDING, PLEASE WORSHIP ELSEWHERE

"Lady Bouvier's Lover" (1F21)

TODAY'S TOPIC: "WHEN HOMER MET SATAN"

"Homer the Heretic" (9F01)

GOD, THE ORIGINAL LOVE CONNECTION

"Homer vs. Lisa and the 8th Commandment" (7F13)

TODAY: "WHAT A F IEND WE HAVE IN GOD" ALSO: THE BE SHARPS

"Homer's Barbershop Quartet" (9F21)

TODAY'S TOPIC: "BE LIKE UNTO THE BOY"

"Bart's Inner Child" (1F05)

LOOSEST BINGO CARDS IN TOWN

"Homer Loves Flanders" (1F14)

2:00 PETERSON WEDDING, 8:00 HAYRIDE TO HEAVEN

"Principal Charming" (7F15)

EVIL WOMEN IN HISTORY: FROM JEZEBEL TO JANET RENO

"Bart's Girlfriend" (2F04)

NO SYNAGOGUE PARKING

"My Sister, My Sitter" (4F13)

THE LISTEN LADY IS IN

"In Marge We Trust" (4F18)

GOD WELCOMES
HIS VICTIMS

"Hurricane Neddy" (4F07)

TODAY'S SERMON:
HOMER ROCKS!

"Treehouse of Horror VIII" (5F02)

NED FLANDERS:
HUSBAND, FATHER,
WACKY NEIGHBOR

"Treehouse of Horror X" (BABF01)

TODAY'S SERMON:
CONQUEST OF
THE COUNTY OF
THE APES

"In Marge We Trust" (4F18)

TODAY'S TOPIC: HE
KNOWS WHAT YOU
DID LAST SUMMER

"Viva Ned Flanders" (AABF06)

TODAYS TOPIC:
LIFE IN HELL

"Faith Off" (BABF06)

TODAYS TOPIC:
THERE'S
SOMETHING ABOUT
THE VIRGIN MARY

"Take My Wife, Sleaze" (BABF05)

NO SHOES,
NO SHIRT,
NO SALVATION

"Bart Sells His Soul" (3F02)

CAN YOU
BELIEVE IT? THEY
GIVE YOU FIVE Q'S AND
ONLY TWO U'S! WHAT
A WORLD.

First Church
of Springfield

NEXT SUNDAY

THE MIRACLE
OF SHAME

"In Marge We Trust" (4F18)

111

HOMER SAYS, "D'OH..."

AABF21 - After realizing that he has taken Bart, Lisa, Milhouse, and Nelson to the zoo and not the *Springfield Shopper* newspaper. His annoyed grunt echoes through the zoo, causing all the animals to panic: flamingos take flight, elephants stampede, alligators go into the water, and a polar bear mounts a moose and together they hurtle a wall.

BABF01 - After he prays to God to save himself and the family, who are being pursued by the Werewolf Ned Flanders, and the car runs out of gas.

AABF19 - After the general-store owner points out he is scooping up Gummi Bears instead of seeds.

AABF19 - After he innocently returns home from the farm and sees the Southern Colonel sitting in a lawn chair, polishing his dueling pistol.

BABF02 - After Mr. Burns starts kicking him, using the leg protectors, while Homer tries to escape him in the power plant core.

BABF05 - After realizing that the Hell's Satans have left and taken Marge with them.

BABF09 - After reading the NFL rulebook and discovering that horses cannot play professional football.

BABF11 - After thinking that Bart has jumped out the window to get help but discovers that he is swinging on the swing set in the backyard instead.

BABF11 - After the shell crab, which substitutes for a ball, moves from number 6 to 31 on the roulette wheel at The Lucky Savage Casino.

BABF12 - After discovering that Moe had plans to sell his bar to Hooters before his face changed back.

BABF16 - After crossing the railroad tracks in their car safely, only to be hit by an oncoming train going in the other direction.

BABF19 - After he decides to drive to Hollywood to "shake things up" and realizes, after traveling 410 miles, that he has been going in the wrong direction.

BABF19 - After being pinched on the nose by a lobster in a "supposed" episode of "The Simpsons."

BABF20 - After Lisa tells him that The Who concert is scheduled to take place in Olde Springfield instead of New Springfield.

BABF17 - After discovering that one of several violin cases on Fat Tony's bed contains a machine gun.

CABF04 - After being run over by a cyclist while gathering up money that Mr. Burns has thrown into the street.

CABF03 - After he walks into the gift shop addition at Magic Palace, having already successfully navigated his way out of buying Bart a magic set in the main gift shop.

BABF22 - After being beaten to a lighted button by a white lab rat as part of an experiment (twice).

CABF14 - After he unsuccessfully tries to tackle Santa's Little Helper to get his severed thumb back.

HOMER SAYS, "MMM..."

"Mmm...ovulicious."
After eating one of the strawberry-flavored fertility pills he gave to Manjula. (BABF03)

"Mmm...danish."
After Moe recommends Tuborg, the beer of Danish kings, to Homer. (BABF08)

"Mmm...sugar walls."
While eating through one of the walls of the gingerbread house in the Deep Dark Forest. (BABF21)

"Mmm...donuts."
While making "donuts" by driving his car in circles and laying down rubber outside of the Dirt First meeting. (CABF01)

"Mmm...hug."
While receiving a hug from Lisa and eating a sandwich at the same time. (BABF22)

"Mmm...turbulent."
After eating an animal cracker dating back to the '60s that he finds in the attic. (CABF13)

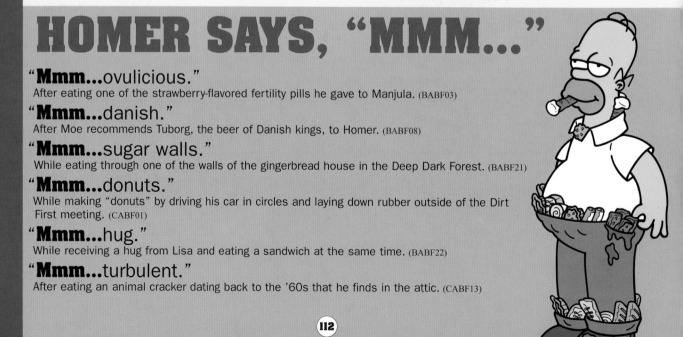

The Tears of a Clone

(BABF04: "Little Big Mom")

At a funeral for Scratchy, Itchy grieves over his lost adversary. Later in his home, Itchy, dressed in a robe and drinking whiskey from a bottle, reminisces through a photo album that features Scratchy being killed in many gruesome ways. He notices a newspaper on the floor with the headline "Scientist Clones Sheep" and gets an idea. He goes to the closet and rummages through a pile of weapons until he pulls out a bloody cleaver. Inside a laboratory, Itchy uses an eyedropper, extracts a drop of blood from the cleaver, and drops it into a large machine with the words "Cloning Machine" on the side. At the other end, several living Scratchys emerge on a conveyor belt. Itchy happily kills them as they come out by various means: shooting, chain-sawing, decapitating with a sword, swinging a mace into one's face, and dropping an anvil on another. But Itchy soon grows tired. He has a better idea. He builds a machine labeled "Killing Machine" and slides it next to the cloning machine. The freshly minted Scratchys are swiftly shredded by the killing machine as they emerge from the cloning machine. The killing machine sprays blood out of a large vent. The blood splatters against a wall and spells out "THE END."

Classic Cartoon Commercials

(BABF22: "НОМЯ")

Itchy and Scratchy (in a blonde wig), both in swimwear, are making out on a beach amidst crashing waves à la *From Here to Eternity*. Scratchy has his eyes closed. Itchy reaches into the ocean, pulls out a large shark, deftly replaces himself with it in Scratchy's arms, and runs off. Scratchy makes out with the shark for a little longer until he reaches around and feels its dorsal fin and its sharp teeth. Scratchy's eyes open wide with fear and the shark grabs him by the upper torso, shaking him violently. Scratchy begins to scream as he is ripped to shreds. A clapboard reading "Itchy & Scratchy 'From Here to Infirmity'" signals the end of the take, and the director (off-screen) cuts the scene. Itchy jumps into a director's chair, as Scratchy's

mangled and bloody body, as well as the shark, are hauled off screen by the crew.

Announcer: After a tough day on the set, how do Itchy and Scratchy relax?
Itchy: With Laramie extra-tar cigarettes!
(An Eddie "Rochester" Anderson–type butler walks up carrying cigarettes on a tray.)
Butler: Here's your smokes, Mister Itchy.
Itchy: Thank you, Louie.
(He lights up and puffs on a cigarette. A dismembered Scratchy bounds onto the tray, flipping a pack of cigarettes into the air and one into his mouth. Itchy lights the cigarette for him, and, with his one remaining arm, Scratchy begins to smoke a cigarette. Smoke seeps out of him through the stump of his left arm.)
Scratchy: Mmm-hmm. And now there's more nico-glycerol.
(Scratchy's cigarette sparkles, and we hear a magical twinkle.)
Butler: I don't know what's in 'em. I just know I can't stop smokin' 'em.
(Itchy and Scratchy and the butler all have a long laugh that leads to a smoker's cough. All three begin to cough up parts of their lungs.)

The Itchy & Scratchy "Stabby-Oh's" Commercial

(CABF11: "Bye, Bye, Nerdie")

(It is morning, and a boy and girl walk into their kitchen and rub their eyes. A figure in a bathrobe and curlers is preparing the food with its back to us.)
Commercial Announcer: Hey, kids! Look who's making breakfast!
(The figure turns around and we see that inside the bathrobe is Scratchy standing on Itchy's shoulders.)
Boy and Girl: Itchy and Scratchy?!

(Scratchy doffs the bathrobe and hops off Itchy's shoulders.)
Scratchy: That's right, kids!
Itchy: Never start the day on an empty stomach.
(Itchy grabs a box of cereal labeled "Stabby-Oh's." He jams a funnel into Scratchy's mouth and pours the entire contents of the box down his throat. Scratchy's stomach quickly begins to bulge.)
Scratchy: It's delicious! Wanna try?
Boy and Girl: Yay!
(Scratchy flings himself onto the kitchen table in front of the two children and lies down face-up, as Itchy slices his stomach open like a mini cereal box, revealing the cereal inside. Scratchy screams in pain. Then Itchy pours a carton of milk into Scratchy's stomach.)
Scratchy: (shivering) Ooo...so cold!
(The kids pick up spoons and hungrily dig in. Colored marshmallows in the shapes of weapons fly up out of his stomach and float in the air above them.)
Boy: Wow, pink daggers!
Girl: Green hatchets!
Boy: Yellow ice picks!
Scratchy: (getting woozy) And Stabby-Oh's are part of this nutritious breakfast...
(We see that he is holding up a plate of eggs and bacon, a plate of toast and jam, and a large plate of broccoli. He is holding them with his hands and one of his feet. He passes out, and his skin color goes from gray to green.)
Girl: Hey, if you guys made breakfast, where's Mom?
Mom: (off-screen) Here I am!
(Itchy quickly pulls the silver dome off a serving platter, revealing the mother's bloodied severed head.)
Mom: (cheerfully) But thanks to "Stabby-Oh's," most of me is still in bed!

COUCH GAGS

AABF23 Beyond Blunderdome, BABF14 Days of Wine and D'oh'ses—The Simpsons, drawn in their "original" style, are sitting on the couch when the "present-day" Simpsons run in. Both versions of the family stop and look at each other. Horrified, they all scream and run away. *AABF22 Brother's Little Helper, BABF18 It's a Mad, Mad, Mad, Mad Marge*—The Simpsons run in and take their places on the couch. They are completely white with "paint by numbers" on their bodies. Five artists rush in with palettes, paint in the colors, and run off. *AABF21 Guess Who's Coming to Criticize Dinner, BABF12 Pygmoelian*—The Simpsons run in and take their places on the couch. Marge notices Matt Groening's signature written on the floor next to her. She grumbles and quickly rubs the signature off with a rag. Then, to her surprise, Matt comes in and signs his name again. *BABF01 Treehouse of Horror X*—The Simpsons watch Kang and Kodos's television

appearance from their couch in the living room. Each family appears in the form of a previous Halloween Special incarnation: Homer is the Jack-in-the-box from "Treehouse of Horror II" (8F02), Marge is the Wicked Witch and Bart is the Fly-Headed Bart from "Treehouse of Horror VIII" (5F02), and Maggie is Kodos's alien baby from "Treehouse of Horror IX" (AABF01). Lisa appears with an ax imbedded in her skull, which is not from a previous special. She criticizes the television

show and Maggie orders her to be silent and disintegrates her with a ray gun. Maggie pops her pacifier back in her mouth and resumes watching the show. *AABF19 E-I-E-I-(Annoyed Grunt), BABF13 Bart to the Future*—The living room looks like a makeshift nightclub with a mirrored disco ball hanging over the couch and several trendy people hanging around. The Simpsons run up to a velvet rope, and a bouncer allows all of them inside, except for Homer, who is turned away. *BABF02 Hello Gutter, Hello Fadder, CABF15 I'm Goin' to Praiseland*—A cement truck backs into the living room and pours out cement statues of the Simpson family one by one: first, Marge with Maggie in her lap, then Bart, Lisa, and Homer, who holds a remote control in his hand. All the statues are staring at the television. As the truck pulls away, the top of the Homer statue breaks off and falls to the floor. *BABF03 Eight Misbehavin', CABF05 Pokey Mom*—The Simpsons run in and sit on the couch. The wall behind them rotates around, and they are replaced by a maniacally laughing Vincent Price in his torture chamber. His victim is a fearful Ned Flanders, who hangs upside down, strapped to the wall. *AABF20 30 Minutes over Tokyo, BABF05 Take My Wife, Sleaze*—The family rushes to the couch. After sitting down, they are sucked into the cushions like paper into a shredder. Their shredded image slides out from under the cushions. *BABF07 Grift of the Magi*—The Simpsons slide down a fire pole that comes through a hole in their ceiling and bounce into place on the couch, except for Homer. He gets stuck in the hole, and the family looks up at him. Homer's legs dangle crazily from the ceiling above, and he calls for help. *BABF04 Little Big Mom, CABF16 Children of a Lesser Clod*—Crash test dummy versions of the Simpsons run in and sit on the couch. Like an automobile crash test, the couch slams forward into the TV and then reverses back into place. The jerking motion causes the Homer dummy's head to fall off. *BABF06 Faith Off, CABF10 Day of the Jackanapes*—Sigmund Freud sits in a chair next to the couch. The family runs in, and Homer, getting there first, frantically flops on the couch. He exclaims, "Oh, doctor! I'm crazy!" and begins to weep. Marge, Bart, Lisa, and Maggie watch him, look at each other, and then back at Homer. *AABF13 Maximum Homerdrive, BABF08 The Mansion Family*—The family rushes in and takes their places on the couch. Bart and Lisa are adult-sized, while Homer and Marge are like children. Homer, with a full head of hair and a Maggie doll, takes the remote from Lisa. Lisa takes it back, maternally slapping his hand. *BABF09 Saddlesore Galactica, CABF09 Hungry, Hungry Homer*—Wearing ghis with black belts, the Simpsons run into the living room. While Marge, Bart, Lisa, and Maggie obliterate the couch with their karate chops, Homer chops at and kicks the lamp and end table out of the way before joining the rest of the family. Then with an impressive spinning kick, Homer, making an intimidating sound, reaches into his ghi, pulls out the remote control, thrusts out a fist holding the remote, and activates the TV. *BABF10 Alone Again, Natura-diddily, CABF11 Bye, Bye, Nerdie*—The family drives into the living room in electric carnival bumper cars. The couch has been removed and everyone attacks Homer's car. Homer is bumped against the wall, causing cracks to form in the plaster and the sailboat picture to fall from its place on the wall. *BABF11 Missionary: Impossible, CABF17 Simpsons Tall Tales*—The Simpsons run in and sit on the couch in the living room, which has been transformed into the Evergreen Terrace subway station. A subway train comes along, stops, then leaves with the family

onboard. *BABF16 Kill the Alligator and Run*—The Simpsons run barefoot across hot coals to get to the couch. When Homer sits down, he lifts up his charred feet and sighs with relief. *BABF15 Last Tap Dance in Springfield*—Dressed in skins like jungle dwellers, the Simpsons swing in on vines and land on the couch one by one. Homer comes in last, starts to make a Tarzan yell, and swings off-camera, crashing into something. *BABF19 Behind the Laughter*—The Simpsons run in and take their places on the couch. Attached to the armrest next to Bart is a "Magic Fingers" box with a coin slot. Bart puts in a coin; the couch starts vibrating wildly and moves out of view. *BABF20 A Tale of Two Springfields*—Before the rest of the family runs in, Bart puts a whoopee cushion under the couch cushion where Homer sits. When Homer plops down on it, a rude noise is heard. Bart laughs, Homer looks embarrassed, and the girls look aghast. *BABF17 Insane Clown Poppy*—The Simpsons run into their living room, but we see them enter from a different perspective. They are in front of the television with the living room window behind them. As they enter, they leap up with arched backs and freeze in mid-air à la *The Matrix*. In a "bullet time" swivel shot, the camera rotates 180° around their airborne bodies so that we see them in front of the couch. They become unfrozen, land on the ground, jump into place on the couch, and Homer turns on the TV with the remote control. *CABF01 Lisa the Tree Hugger*—Maggie is sitting on the couch alone until the rest of the Simpsons come in dressed and acting like Teletubbies. Maggie claps with amusement. *CABF04 Homer vs. Dignity, CABF14 Trilogy of Error*—The Simpsons enter the living room one by one, doing acrobatic tricks off a skateboard ramp and landing on the couch. However, when Homer comes in, he falls off the ramp, crashes to the floor, and the skateboard he is riding lands on his head. *CABF02 The Computer Wore Menace Shoes*—Santa's Little Helper is dancing in front of the couch on his hind legs like Snoopy to "Peanuts"-style music. The Simpsons run in, stop, and stare at him. He keeps dancing until he notices them, and then, embarrassed, he sits and barks sheepishly. *CABF03 The Great Money Caper*—The couch is underwater. The Simpsons swim in wearing scuba outfits

and sit on the couch. The camera pulls back to reveal that they are inside a giant fishbowl. Outside the fishbowl is a large container of fish food. *CABF06 Skinner's Sense of Snow*—A loose football bounces into the living room. The Simpsons, all dressed in football uniforms, dog-pile on the ball. Maggie emerges from the pile with the football, spikes it, and performs a victory dance. *BABF22 НОМЯ*—The family is deposited onto the couch by futuristic air tubes—all except Bart. In Bart's place is Philip J. Fry from "Futurama." After Fry and the Simpsons briefly look at each other, Fry is sucked back out and replaced with Bart. *CABF08 Worst Episode Ever*—The Pimple-Faced Kid stands in the middle of the empty living room next to a sign that says "Valet." The family runs in, and Homer gives the kid a parking stub. The Pimple-Faced Kid exits and quickly re-enters pushing the couch. When the couch is in place, the Simpsons jump onto it. The Pimple-Faced Kid holds out his hand for a tip, but everyone ignores him, and he walks off disappointed. *CABF07 Tennis the Menace*—The floor in the living room is made of ice. The Simpsons stylishly skate in and take their places on the couch. Homer comes in last, a little unsure of himself on skates. He turns around and sits on the couch. Suddenly, he and the portion of the couch he is sitting on crash through the ice as the family looks on. *CABF12 New Kids on the Blecch*—The Simpsons' couch and TV are inside the walls of a prison yard. A siren wails, and a searchlight passes over the prison yard as the family attempts to escape by burrowing in separate tunnels underground. But instead of escaping, they all emerge from their tunnels, dressed in black and white prisoner's garb, and hop onto the couch. Homer clicks on the TV with the remote as the searchlight illuminates them. *9F08 Lisa's First Word, 9F13 I Love Lisa, 9F16 The Front, 9F22 Cape Feare, 2F08 Fear of Flying, 3F31 The Simpsons 138th Episode Spectacular, AABF17 Monty Can't Buy Me Love, CABF13 Simpson Safari*—The family rushes in. They dance in a chorus line. Soon, they are joined by high-kicking Rockettes, a variety of circus animals (including trained elephants), jugglers, trapeze artists, fire breathers, magicians, and Santa's Little Helper, who jumps through a hoop as circus music plays.

WHO DOES WHAT VOICE

DAN CASTELLANETA

Homer Simpson
Grampa Abraham Simpson
Barney Gumble
Krusty the Clown
Groundskeeper Willie
Mayor Quimby
Hans Moleman
Sideshow Mel
Arnie Pye
Louie
Bill
Gary
Gil
Squeaky-Voiced Teen (Pimple-Faced Kid)
Burns's Lawyer
Rich Texan
Kodos
Itchy
Mr. Teeny
Poochie
Senator Payne (AABF23)
Showgirls Choreographer (AABF22)
Complaining Soldier (AABF22)
Salvatore (AABF22)
French Chef (AABF21)
Musketeer (AABF19)
Man in the Iron Mask (AABF19)
Scarlet Pimpernel (AABF19)
King Arthur (AABF19)
Smiley the Elf (BABF02)
Sound Bite Reporter (BABF03)
Flamboyant Theater-Type (BABF03)
Cop (BABF05)
Goodwill Truck Driver (BABF04)
Anton Lubchenko (BABF06)
Kent Brockman's Nephew (BABF06)
Cornelius Chapman (BABF08)
Asian Pirate (BABF08)
Rat-Pack Kid (BABF09)
Giant Pearl (BABF09)
Jockey #2 (BABF09)
"Do Shut Up" Father (BABF11)
Rupert Murdoch (BABF11, BABF19)
Michael Finn (BABF12)
Gay Republican #2 (BABF12)
Casting Director (BABF12)
"Original" Dr. Tad Winslow (BABF12)
French Ambassador (BABF13)
British Ambassador (BABF13)
Gay Barfly (BABF14)
Stan the Organ Salesman (BABF15)
The Admiral (Otto's Father) (BABF18)
Phoney McRing-Ring (BABF20)
Wild Dolphin (BABF21)
George Cauldron (BABF21)

"For Dummies" Author (BABF17)
Frankie the Squealer (BABF17)
Frank Nelson–Type Salesman (CABF04)
Questo (CABF03)
Radio Weatherman (CABF06)
Singing Hobgoblin (CABF06)
Ozmodiar (BABF22)
Jobriath (BABF22)
A. D. R. Sessions (BABF22)
Delbert (CABF05)
Black Pawn (CABF07)
Hitler (CABF12)
Australian Runner (CABF12)
Dance Instructor (CABF12)
Admiral (CABF12)
MAD Writer #3 (CABF12)
Irish Cop (CABF12)
Villager (CABF13)
Bantu #2 (CABF13)
French Teacher (CABF14)
Mootilda (CABF15)
Coach Lugash (CABF16)

JULIE KAVNER

Marge Simpson
Patty Bouvier
Selma Bouvier

NANCY CARTWRIGHT

Bart Simpson
Nelson Muntz
Todd Flanders
Ralph Wiggum
Kearney
Database
Shelbyville Nine Mother (BABF03)
Woman Jockey (BABF09)
Snorky (BABF21)
Octoparrot (BABF22)

YEARDLEY SMITH

Lisa Simpson
Lisa, Jr. (BABF11)
Lisabella (BABF15)

HANK AZARIA

Apu Nahasapeemapetilon
Moe Szyslak
Chief Clancy Wiggum
Comic Book Guy
Lou
Carl
Dr. Nick Riviera
Snake (Jailbird)
Kirk Van Houten
Captain McCallister (Sea Captain)
Bumblebee Man

Superintendent Chalmers
Professor John Frink
Cletus Del Roy
Legs
Drederick Tatum
Doug
Old Jewish Man
Duffman
Wiseguy
Disco Stu
Luigi
Elec-Taurus Computer (AABF23)
William Milo (AABF23)
President of the United States (AABF23)
Batman (AABF23)
Pharm Team Male Researcher (AABF22)
Electronic Organizer (AABF22)
Level-Headed Soldier (AABF22)
Sir Widebottom (AABF22)
Üter's Father (AABF21)
Jamie Kilday, Farm Critic (AABF21)
Akira (AABF21)
Izzy's Deli Owner (AABF21)
Exodus Rocket Guard (BABF01)
Zorro (AABF19)
Rap Singer (AABF19)
Southern Colonel (AABF19)
La-Dee-Da Farmer (AABF19)
Laramie Executive/Sandy (AABF19)
Springfield Squares Announcer (BABF02)
Giggly the Elf (BABF02)
Allen Wrench (BABF03)
Shelbyville Nine Father (BABF03)
Wolfguy Jack (BABF05)
Johnny Bobby (BABF05)
Rebel (BABF05)
Funzo (BABF07)
Ski Instructor (BABF04)
Park Ranger (BABF04)
Mr. Sakamoto (BABF04)
Leprosy Orderly (BABF04)
Doug (BABF06)
Dean Peterson (BABF06)
Seat Filler (BABF08)
Mayo Clinic Doctor (BABF08)
Coast Guard Guy (BABF08)
Pirate Captain (BABF08)
Omnigogs Salesman (BABF09)
State Comptroller Atkins (BABF09)
Barker (BABF09)
Jockey #1 (BABF09)
Mr. Vanderbilt (BABF09)
Clay Babcock (BABF10)
"Do Shut Up" Son (BABF11)
PBS Host (BABF11)
Bank Teller (BABF11)
Craig (BABF11)

Ak (BABF11)
Croupier (BABF11)
Duff Days Greeter (BABF12)
Phil Angelides (BABF12)
Dr. Velimirovic (BABF12)
Park Ranger (BABF13)
Arthur Crandall (BABF13)
Casino Manager (BABF13)
Billy Carter's Ghost (BABF13)
Chinese Ambassador (BABF13)
Flight Instructor (BABF14)
Power Plant Inspector (BABF16)
Palm Corners Tour Guide (BABF16)
Cyborganizer (BABF15)
Robobaby (BABF15)
Eduardo (BABF15)
Latin Milhouse (BABF15)
Mall Security Guard (BABF15)
Dr. Foster (BABF18)
Huckleberry Hound (BABF19)
Paramedic (BABF21)
Saint Peter (BABF21, CABF15)
Satan (BABF21)
NFL Franchise Representative (BABF20)
The Who's Security Guard (BABF20)
Johnny Tightlips (BABF17)
Mr. Thai (CABF01)
Caleb (CABF01)
Singing Sirloin Owner (CABF04)
Panda Zookeeper (CABF04)
Mr. Costington (CABF04)
Computer Salesman (CABF02)
Number 2 (CABF02)
Fake Homer (CABF02)
Diablo the Magician (CABF03)
Cirque de Purée Usher (CABF06)
French Man in Crowd (CABF06)
Cirque de Purée Ringmaster (CABF06)
Santa (CABF06)
Cracker Factory Security Guard (CABF06)
Meganaut (BABF22)
I.P.O. Friday's Stockbroker (BABF22)
Screaming Monkey Male
    Researcher (BABF22)
Sardonicus (CABF05)
Chiropractor #2 (CABF05)
Nuclear Defense Officer (CABF08)
Funeral Home Salesman (CABF07)
Channel 6 Assistant Director (CABF07)
Black Rook (CABF07)
Male Network Executive (CABF10)
Leo the Spotlight Guy (CABF10)
Djiboutian Runner (CABF12)
Lt. L. T. Smash (CABF12)
MAD Writer #2 (CABF12)
Blockoland Souvenir Salesman (CABF09)
Henri the Hair Stylist (CABF09)

Cesar Chavez's Ghost (CABF09)
Mayor of Albuquerque (CABF09)
Francine's Dad (CABF11)
Bag Boy (CABF13)
Kitchen-Maid Executive (CABF13)
Ngongo (CABF13)
Kitenge (CABF13)
"Poacher" / Animal Activist (CABF13)
Linguo (CABF14)
Rapper (CABF16)
Craig the Chinese Orderly (CABF16)
Singing Railroad Hobo (CABF17)

HARRY SHEARER
C. Montgomery Burns
Waylon Smithers
Ned Flanders
Principal Seymour Skinner
Otto the Bus Driver
Reverend Timothy Lovejoy
Dr. Julius Hibbert
Kent Brockman
Jasper
Lenny
Eddie
Rainier Wolfcastle/McBain
Herman
Marty
Judge Snyder
Benjamin
Kang
Scratchy
Bus Tour Guide (AABF23)
Senate Leader (AABF23)
Hosey the Bear (AABF22)
MLB Satellite (Vin Scully) (AABF22)
Garth Trelawny, TV Critic (AABF21)
Dinner Theatre Owner (AABF21)
"Stretch Dude & Clobber Girl"
 Announcer (BABF01)
Sneed's Feed Storekeeper (AABF19)
Laramie Executive/J. P. (AABF19)
Happy the Elf (BABF02)
Guinness Book Announcer (BABF05)
Greaser's Cafe Commercial
 Announcer (BABF05)
Tuesday Morning Movie
 Announcer (BABF05)
Grim Father (BABF05)
Funzo Commercial Announcer (BABF07)
Chair Lift Operator (BABF04)
Benjamin (BABF06)
Football Announcer (BABF06)
President Clinton (BABF09)
Toadstool Jockey (BABF09)
Track Announcer (BABF10)
PBS Announcer (BABF11)
Qtoktok (BABF11)
Surly (BABF12)
Duff Days Announcer (BABF12)
Gay Republican #1 (BABF12)
Soap Opera Announcer (BABF12)
German Ambassador (BABF13)

Phone Book Contest Announcer (BABF14)
Psychiatrist (BABF16)
Southern Judge (BABF16)
Chain Gang Foreman (BABF16)
Dance Coach (BABF15)
Mall Announcer (BABF15)
Mall Manager (BABF15)
Bojangles (BABF15)
Snorky (Male Voice) (BABF21)
Man with Jeweler's Loupe (BABF17)
Old Barber (CABF01)
Albuquerquean Man (CABF04)
Cirque de Purée Clown (CABF06)
Radio Announcer (CABF06)
Itchy & Scratchy Butler (BABF22)
Animotion Spokesman (BABF22)
Bank Teller (BABF22)
Dr. Steve (CABF05)
Chiropractor #1 (CABF05)
Biclops Salesman (CABF08)
Old Comedian (CABF07)
Black King (CABF07)
Virgil Sinclair (CABF10)
Olympic Announcer (CABF12)
MAD Writer #1 (CABF12)
Isotopes Trainer (CABF09)
Duff Stadium Announcer (CABF09)
"Stabby-Oh's" Commercial
 Announcer (CABF11)
Store Manager (CABF13)
Kitchen-Maid Male Lawyer (CABF13)
Doorman (CABF13)
Masai Chief (CABF13)
Bantu #1 (CABF13)
King David Robot (CABF15)
YMCA Representative (CABF16)
"Good Guy" Interviewer (CABF16)

MARCIA WALLACE
Edna Krabappel

JIM CUMMINGS
Duncan/Furious D (BABF09)

PAMELA HAYDEN
Milhouse Van Houten
Rod Flanders
Janey Powell
Jimbo Jones
Malibu Stacy
Patches
Sarah Wiggum
Elec-Taurus Salesperson (AABF23)
Showgirls Dancer (AABF22)
Funzo Commercial Girl (BABF07)
Fan-Demonium Cheerleader (BABF10)
Titania (BABF12)
High School Crush (BABF12)
Cleo (BABF12)
Animotion Technician (BABF22)
Stephanie the Weather Lady (CABF07)
"Stabby-Oh's" Commercial Girl (CABF11)

TRESS MACNEILLE
Dolph
Brandine Del Roy
Agnes Skinner
Poor Violet
Lindsey Naegle/Female Network Executive
Bernice Hibbert
Robyn Hannah (AABF23)
Pharm Team Female Researcher (AABF22)
Navajo Boy (AABF22)
Springfield Shopper Tour Guide (AABF21)
Mimi the Food Critic (AABF21)
Üter's Mother (AABF21)
Princess (AABF19)
Laramie Executive/Mindy (AABF19)
Swimming Instructor (BABF02)
Fretful Mother (BABF05)
Kids First "Teacher" (BABF07)
Funzo Commercial Boy (BABF07)
Nurse (BABF04)
Lucy McGillicuddy Ricardo
 Carmichael (BABF04)
Mrs. Vanderbilt/Wealthy
 Dowager (BABF09)
Tree Jockey (BABF09)
Mrs. Babcock (BABF10)
Video Dating Manager (BABF10)
"Do Shut Up" Mother (BABF11)
Amy (BABF11)
Duff Days Hostess (BABF12)
Plastic Surgery Nurse (BABF12)
Snake's Son (BABF12)
Helen Morehouse (BABF12)
Contessa (BABF12)
Presidential Aide (BABF13)
Sepulveda (BABF16)
Cienega (BABF16, CABF12)
Velma the Diner Owner (BABF16)
Southern Dowager (BABF16)
Optometrist (BABF15)
Little Vicki Valentine (BABF15)
Richie Rich (BABF19)
Dolphin Trainer (BABF21)
Rapunzel (BABF21)
Suzanne the Witch (BABF21)
Goldilocks (BABF21)
Erin (Female Soldier) (BABF17)
Poor Kid (CABF04)
Pulitzer Prize Committee
 Woman (CABF02)
Female Island Scientist (CABF02)
Willie's Lawyer (CABF03)
Little Bo Peep (CABF06)
Princess Tempura (BABF22)
Gravey (BABF22)
Screaming Monkey Female
 Researcher (BABF22)
Weeping Widow (CABF07)
Francis the Crippled Boy (CABF10)
Arab Woman (CABF12)
"Stabby-Oh's" Commercial Boy (CABF11)
"Stabby-Oh's" Commercial Mom (CABF11)

Boy in Orthodontic Headgear (CABF11)
Baby-Proofing Saleswoman (CABF11)
Francine's Mom (CABF11)
Unattractive Waitress (CABF13)
Kitchen-Maid Female Lawyer (CABF13)
African Flight Attendant (CABF13)
Dr. Joan Bushwell (CABF13)
Society Matron (CABF16)
Airline Ticket Agent (CABF17)
Mrs. Abe Bunyan (CABF17)

MARCIA MITZMAN-GAVEN
Maude Flanders (AABF22, BABF01,
 BABF04, BABF10)
Helen Lovejoy (CABF07)
Miss Hoover (CABF14)

MAGGIE ROSWELL
Jimmy Stewart's Granddaughter (AABF23)
Maude Flanders (AABF21)
Daphne Beaumont, Theater Critic (AABF21)

RUSSI TAYLOR
Martin Prince
Üter
Sherri/Terri
Lewis
Wendell
Mrs. Prince (CABF08)

FRANK WELKER
Santa's Little Helper
Barnyard Animals (AABF19)
Werewolf (BABF01)
Nature Preserve Animals (BABF10)
Mountain Lion (BABF15)
Badger (BABF20)
African Animals (CABF13)
Babe the Blue Ox (CABF17)
Pioneer Animals (CABF17)
Various Animals (8F06, 8F13, 1F18,
 2F18, 3F01, 4F16, 4F18, 4F19)

KARL WIEDERGOTT
Robin (AABF23)
Showgirls Stage Manager (AABF22)
King Lear's Herald (AABF21)
Jimmy Carter (AABF19, BABF19)
Laramie Executive/Emile (AABF19)
Gas Station Attendant (BABF05)
Soap Opera Director (BABF12)
Boisterous Student (BABF16)
John Wayne (BABF21)
Singing Sirloin Waiter (CABF04)
Muntu (CABF13)

MARC WILMORE
Dr. Wilmore (BABF18)

Songs Sung Simpson!

Included here are song lyrics and musical-number descriptions from Seasons 11 and 12 of "The Simpsons."

Bart's Ritalin Song:
(to the closing tune of "Popeye, the Sailor Man")

When I can't stop fiddlin',
I just takes me Ritalin.
I'm poppin' and sailin', man!

(From AABF22, "Brother's Little Helper")

"Mental House Rock":

Doctors threw a party at the looney bin.
You gotta be crazy if you wanna get in.
Napoleon is playin' his imaginary sax.
The dance floor's fillin' up with maniacs.
Let's rock. Do the Mental House Rock.
(chorus)
Let's rock. Do the Mental House Rock.
If you won't dance with the Doc,
He'll give you electroshock.
If you won't dance with the Doc,
He'll give you electroshock.
Zap! Zap! Zap!

(From BABF05, "Take My Wife, Sleaze")

Homer's Food Song:

I like pizza.
I like bagels.
I like hot dogs, with mustard and beer...
I'll eat eggplant.
I could even eat a baby deer...
La-la-la-la-la-la, la, la, la-la...
Who's that baby deer on the lawn there...

(From AABF21, "Guess Who's Coming to Criticize Dinner")

Homer & Bart's Song:

You showed me everything, you took me by the hand.
Puppy dogs and Lincoln Logs and castles made of sand.
You gave me the courage to spread my newborn wings,
Like mayonnaise and marmalade and other spreadable things.
So I guess you are my hero, and there's something you should know,
I want to make it clear, so I'm gonna sing it slow.
If you weren't a man and my father, too,
I'd buy you a diamond ring, and then I'd marry you.

(From BABF05, "Take My Wife, Sleaze")

"On the Spaceship Lollipop":
(to the tune of "On the Good Ship Lollipop")

On the Spaceship Lollipop
Gingerbread men like to do hip-hop,
And chocolate chips
Make a rockin' fuel for rocket ships.
We just love to dance on Mars
Where everything's made from candy bars...

(From BABF15, "Last Tap Dance in Springfield")

Rachel Jordan's Song:

In a motel room in Delacroix,
I was drinkin' like a Dartmouth boy,
And thinkin' 'bout the wrong turns that I took.
Well, I woke up on the puke-green floor,
And opened up a dresser drawer,
Lookin' for a bottle, but instead I found a book.
A book about a man!
A book about the Dude who lives above!
A book about a man who drives a pick-up
Full of sweet, sweet love.
Now if you think he doesn't care,
Or maybe that he isn't there,
It's not too late to see how wrong you are.
So when your soul has gone astray,
Just let God be your Triple-A.
He'll tow you to salvation, and He'll overhaul your heart.

(From BABF10, "Alone Again, Natura-diddily")

Rachel Jordan's Reprise:

It's a show about Ned,
About him losing his sweet wife.
She landed on her head,
But now it's time for him to get on with his life.

(From BABF10, "Alone Again, Natura-diddily")

"Simpsons (Christmas) Boogie":

We're gonna groove tonight.
We'll make you feel all right.
Simpsons (Christmas) Boogie!
We're dancing to the beat.
We'll make you move your feet.
Simpsons (Christmas) Boogie!
Simpsons (Christmas) Boogie!
Simpsons (Christmas) Boogie!

(From BABF19, "Behind the Laughter")

Brother Faith's Song:

Now let's hear it
For the Holy Spirit.
No need to fear it.
Just revere it!
He works in Heaven.
That's 24/ 7. (That's right.)
Check the Bible. (Yeah.)
John 2:11! (Jump back!)

(From BABF06, "Faith Off")

"Testify" (Brother Bart's Revival Song):

Bart: *Satan, eat my shorts!*
I was a sinner, a real bad kid.
What thou shalt not, I shalt did.
Neighbor's cat I tried to neuter,
Took a whiz on the school's computer.
Sherri and Terri: *He took a whiz, oh, yes he did.*
Bart: *But now I changed, you can't deny.*
Come on up, and testify.
Sherri and Terri: *Testify, testify, come on up and testify!*
Abe: *My hip's misbehavin'.*
(Bart kicks his cane away.)
Sherri and Terri: *Testify!*
Patty: *Got a nicotine cravin'.*
(Bart slaps the cigarette out of her mouth.)
Sherri and Terri: *Testify!*
Frink: *There's a cramp in my glavin.*
(Bart kicks Frink in the back side.)
Bart: *Testify!*
Crowd: *Testify! Testify!*
Milhouse: *My glasses make me look like a geek!*
(Bart tosses Milhouse's glasses away.)
Bart: *Now you'll get the girls you seek!*
Sherri and Terri: *We'll see you at Makeout Creek!*
Crowd: *Bart's the boy of the hour.*
He's got the power.
So raise your voice and don't be shy,
Tes-ti...tes-ti...
Bart and Crowd: *Tes-ti-fy!*
Crowd: *Testify, testify, come on up and testify!*

****

Milhouse: *Thank you, Bart, for fixing my vision.*
Now I see with total precision.
Bart: *Song's over, Milhouse, but you're welcome.*

(From BABF06, "Faith Off")

Captain Bart and the Tequila Mockingbirds, Commercial Jingles:
(to the tune of "Escape [The Piña Colada Song]")

Bart: *If you like refund adjustments*
And the music I play,
Send a check to my friend, Ralph,
And he'll mail you a tape...

(to the tune of "Day-O [The Banana Boat Song]")
Bart: *Daylight come and you want-a my tape.*
Ralph: *Tape! He say tape-o.*
Bart: *Post Office Box 3-0-4-5-2...*

(From BABF13, "Bart to the Future")

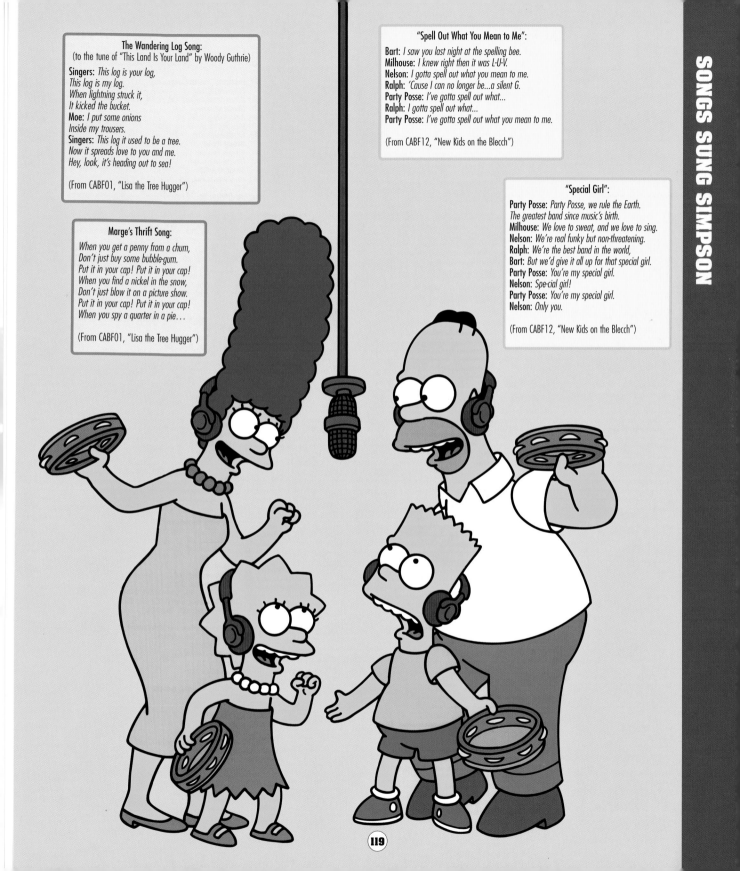

The Wandering Log Song:
(to the tune of "This Land Is Your Land" by Woody Guthrie)

Singers: *This log is your log,*
This log is my log.
When lightning struck it,
It kicked the bucket.
Moe: *I put some onions*
Inside my trousers.
Singers: *This log it used to be a tree.*
Now it spreads love to you and me.
Hey, look, it's heading out to sea!

(From CABF01, "Lisa the Tree Hugger")

Marge's Thrift Song:

When you get a penny from a chum,
Don't just buy some bubble-gum.
Put it in your cap! Put it in your cap!
When you find a nickel in the snow,
Don't just blow it on a picture show.
Put it in your cap! Put it in your cap!
When you spy a quarter in a pie…

(From CABF01, "Lisa the Tree Hugger")

"Spell Out What You Mean to Me":

Bart: *I saw you last night at the spelling bee.*
Milhouse: *I knew right then it was L-U-V.*
Nelson: *I gotta spell out what you mean to me.*
Ralph: *'Cause I can no longer be…a silent G.*
Party Posse: *I've gotta spell out what…*
Ralph: *I gotta spell out what…*
Party Posse: *I've gotta spell out what you mean to me.*

(From CABF12, "New Kids on the Blecch")

"Special Girl":

Party Posse: *Party Posse, we rule the Earth.*
The greatest band since music's birth.
Milhouse: *We love to sweat, and we love to sing.*
Nelson: *We're real funky but non-threatening.*
Ralph: *We're the best band in the world,*
Bart: *But we'd give it all up for that special girl.*
Party Posse: *You're my special girl.*
Nelson: *Spe-cial girl!*
Party Posse: *You're my special girl.*
Nelson: *Only you.*

(From CABF12, "New Kids on the Blecch")

More books from Matt Groening:

Bart Simpson's Guide to Life
The Simpsons Uncensored Family Album
The Simpsons Ultra-Jumbo Rain-or-Shine Fun Book
The Simpsons Handbook
The Simpsons Masterpiece Gallery
Greetings from the Simpsons

Comic Books:
Simpsons Comics Royale
Simpsons Heebie-Jeebie Hullabaloo
Simpsons Spine-Tingling Spooktacular
Simpsons Fun-Filled Frightfest
Simpsons Hoodoo-Voodoo Brouhaha
Simpsons Holiday Humdinger
Futurama Adventures
Futurama: The Time-Bender Trilogy

The Simpsons Library of Wisdom:
The Homer Book
The Bart Book
The Lisa Book
The Krusty Book
The Ralph Wiggum Book
The Comic Book Guy's Book of Pop Culture

The Simpsons Episode Guides:
The Simpsons Complete Guide to Our Favorite Family
The Simpsons Forever!
The Simpsons Beyond Forever!
The Simpsons One Step Beyond Forever!

Life In Hell:
Love is Hell
School is Hell
Work is Hell
Childhood is Hell
Akbar & Jeff's Guide to Life
The Road to Hell
How to Go to Hell
The Big Book of Hell
The Huge Book of Hell
Binky's Guide to Love
Will & Abe's Guide to the Universe

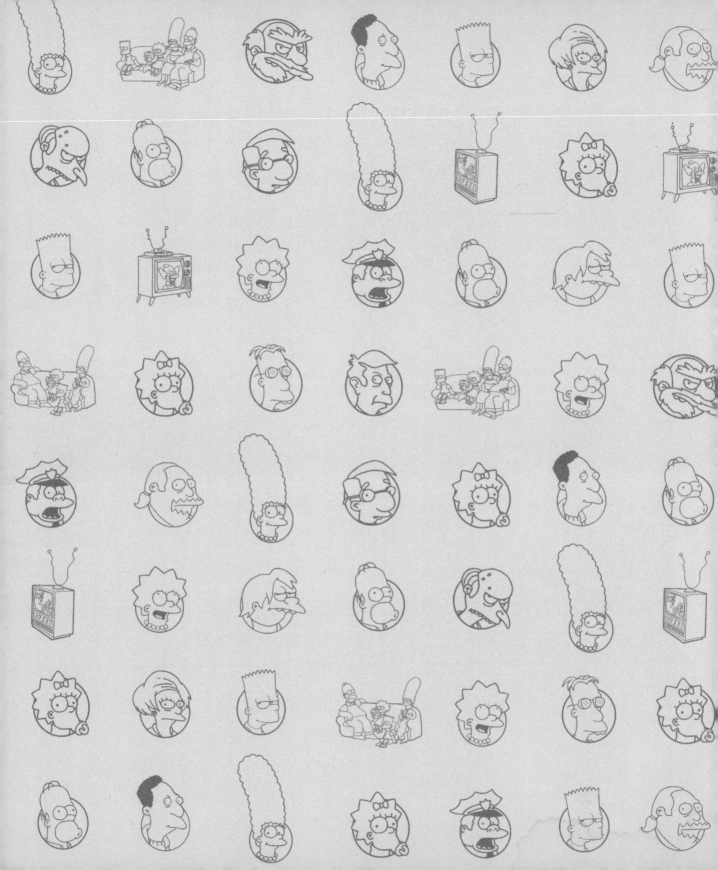

Emmy
the Exaggerating
Elephant

Fenton
the Fearful Frog

Gertie
the Grungy Goat

Herbie
the Happy
Hamster

Ivy
the Impatient
Iguana

Ollie
the Obedient
Ostrich

Perry
the Polite
Porcupine

Queenie
the Quiet Quail

Rupert
the Resourceful
Rhinoceros

Wendy
the Wise
Woodchuck

Xavier
the X-ploring
Xenops

Yori
the Yucky Yak

Ziggy
the Zippy Zebra

NOTE TO PARENTS

<u>Yori and Yetta</u>
A story about tolerance and nature appreciation

In this story, Yori the Yucky Yak introduces his AlphaPet friends to the wonders of the nature around them and, while doing so, helps them learn to accept and understand those with different tastes and ideas.

In addition to enjoying this touching story with your child, you can use it to teach a gentle lesson about the importance of trying to see beauty and merit in all things and people— even if they seem unusual. You might want to discuss how nature has "a place and a purpose" for everything, large and small.

You can also use this story to introduce the letter **Y**. As you read about Yori the Yucky Yak, ask your child to listen for all the **Y** words and point to the objects that begin with **Y**. When you've finished reading the story, your child will enjoy doing the activity at the end of the book.

The AlphaPets™ characters were conceived and created by Ruth Lerner Perle.
Characters interpreted and designed by Deborah Colvin Borgo.
Cover/book design and production by Norton & Company.
Logo design by Deborah Colvin Borgo and Nancy S. Norton.